Methods of
Organizational Research

KARL E. WEICK

LOUIS B. BARNES

TOM BURNS

THORNTON B. ROBY

A product of the 1964 Seminar in the Social Science of Organizations, sponsored by the Graduate School of Business, The University of Pittsburgh, with the support of The Ford Foundation.

Methods of
Organizational Research

EDITED BY VICTOR H. VROOM

UNIVERSITY OF PITTSBURGH PRESS

BRESCIA COLLEGE
LIBRARY
38877

Library of Congress Catalog Number 67-11463

COPYRIGHT © 1967, UNIVERSITY OF PITTSBURGH PRESS

Manufactured in the United States of America

Second Printing 1968

Participants

1964 SEMINAR IN THE SOCIAL SCIENCE OF ORGANIZATION

THE UNIVERSITY OF PITTSBURGH

J. STACY ADAMS, Behavioral Research Service, General Electric Company
LOUIS B. BARNES, Graduate School of Business Administration, Harvard University
BERNARD M. BASS, Graduate School of Business, University of Pittsburgh
SELWYN W. BECKER, Graduate School of Business, University of Chicago
L. VAUGHAN BLANKENSHIP, School of Business Administration, University of California, Berkeley
PETER M. BLAU, Department of Sociology, University of Chicago
TOM BURNS, Department of Sociology, University of Edinburgh
GEOFFREY CLARKSON, Alfred P. Sloan School of Management, Massachusetts Institute of Technology
DEXTER C. DUNPHY, Department of Social Relations, Harvard University
ROBERT HAMBLIN, Department of Sociology, Washington University
L. RICHARD HOFFMAN, Department of Psychology, University of Michigan
ROBERT C. JOYNER, Department of Psychology, University of Toronto
KENNETH E. KNIGHT, Graduate School of Business, Stanford University
EDWARD E. LAWLER, Department of Industrial Administration, Yale University
PRESTON P. LEBRETON, College of Business Administration, University of Washington
FREDERICK MUNSON, Graduate School of Business Administration, University of Michigan
ANTHONY OBERSHALL, Department of Sociology, University of California, Los Angeles
LYMAN PORTER, Department of Psychology, University of California, Berkeley
THORNTON B. ROBY, Department of Psychology, Tufts University
W. RICHARD SCOTT, Department of Sociology, Stanford University
ERIC TRIST, Tavistock Institute of Human Relations, London, England
STANLEY H. UDY, Department of Sociology, Yale University
VICTOR H. VROOM, Graduate School of Industrial Administration, Carnegie Institute of Technology
RICHARD E. WALTON, Krannert School of Business, Purdue University
KARL E. WEICK, Department of Psychology, Purdue University
STANTON WHEELER, Department of Sociology, University of Washington

Preface

This book is an outgrowth of a seminar in methods of organizational research held on the campus of Chatham College from June 8 to June 18, 1964. The Seminar was supported by a grant from the Ford Foundation to the University of Pittsburgh. Twenty-six social scientists attended including ten psychologists, nine sociologists, and seven with their primary training in business administration and allied disciplines. Participants spent approximately two-thirds of their time in small working groups devoted to an intensive examination of one of the following research methods: laboratory experiments, field experiments, comparative field studies, and computer simulation. The remainder of the time was spent in lecture and seminar presentations involving the entire group.

Following the seminar, one member of each of the small groups was given the task of writing a paper on the subject considered by his group. His task was not to summarize the discussions, but rather to present his own perspective on the issues after having had the opportunity to discuss them extensively with others. The four papers contained in this book are the results of that work.

The seminar from which this book is derived is the final one in a series of three sponsored by the Ford Foundation and held during the summers of 1962–1964. Two books emerged from these earlier seminars. *The Social Science of Organizations*, edited by Harold J. Leavitt, was published by Prentice-Hall in 1963, and *Approaches to Organizational Design*, edited by James D. Thompson, was published by the University of Pittsburgh Press in 1966. In the judgement of the committee, the primary objective of these seminars—to stimulate interaction and collaborative efforts among persons from diverse disciplinary backgrounds who share an interest in organizational behavior—has, in large measure, be achieved.

The planning committee for the third seminar wishes to express its appreciation to the Ford Foundation for its financial support, to the Graduate School of Business of the University of Pittsburgh under whose auspices the Seminar was held, and to the participants themselves whose lively and informed interest contributed to its success.

HAROLD J. LEAVITT (Chairman)
BERNARD BASS
PETER BLAU
DANIEL KATZ
VICTOR H. VROOM

Foreword

The last ten years have witnessed a marked increase in the amount of interest shown by behavioral scientists in the systematic study of large-scale formal organizations. One has merely to examine the titles of recently published books to be convinced that first-class scholars and researchers are now directing their energies toward the explanation of organizational phenomena.

A closer examination of the contents of some of the recently edited volumes in this field—such as Haire's *Modern Organization Theory,* Cooper, Leavitt, and Shelly's *New Perspectives in Organization Research,* or March's *Handbook of Organizations*—permits a second inference about the present state of this area of knowledge. One cannot help being struck by the fact that there is substantial disagreement among contributors on such matters as the boundaries of the field of inquiry, the most pressing problems for study, and the relative usefulness of different research methods or theoretical systems. The widespread. use of such terms as "organization theory" and "organizational behavior" conveys to the outsider a misleading image of a collection of social scientists jointly engaged in the construction of a stable edifice of knowledge with general agreement about its final shape and the building materials to be used. But, in fact, it can be argued that different contributors are working from vastly different sets of architectural plans and that many are ignorant of or unsympathetic towards the activities of large segments of other contributors.

If the latter representation is more accurate, it probably stems, at least in part, from the fact that the contributors to the study of organizational behavior are themselves representatives of several different academic disciplines, mainly psychology, sociology, political science, economics, and business administration. While some contributions may be described as truly interdisciplinary, most investigators of organizational behavior have tended to "borrow" their problems, theories, and research methods from their basic disciplines and publish their results where they will be read and recognized by others in the same discipline. In addition to this disciplinary insularity, there is some evidence, particularly in major centers of organizational research, of an institutional insularity. Investigators from the same institution tend to share common perspectives of and approaches to the field and, judging from their citations of the literature, are often unaware of relevant work done in other institutions.

The diversity in approaches to the study of organizations on the part of persons from different disciplines and/or institutions does not in itself constitute a serious problem for the development of the field. The systematic study of organizations has too short a history to warrant universal agreement concerning aims, methods, or theories. The diversity that currently characterizes the field may provide a needed protection against a tendency to "put all eggs in one basket" and may increase the probability that the resources expended will contribute viable knowledge. The unfortunate aspects of disciplinary or institutional insularity stem not from diversity per se but from the fact that investigators all too frequently conduct their research in ignorance of relevant research methods or theory in other disciplines or institutions. The consequence of the many channels of publication and the multitude of methodological and conceptual systems is redundancy in research output and inadequate coordination among the various approaches.

There is pressing need for the articulation of alternative points of view so that readers may see them in juxtaposition, weigh the arguments for themselves, and make their own judgments. In this volume, we seek to accomplish this goal with respect to the problem of methods of organizational research. It contains papers by four social scientists each of whom explores the potentialities of a particular research method for examining organizational processes.

The paper by Karl Weick deals with the increasing adaptation of the laboratory experiment for studying organizational behavior. The possibility of creating in the laboratory, at least in its simplest and most elementary forms, the basic properties of an organization and studying the activities under highly controlled conditions is an attractive one. The laboratory offers the indisputable advantages of precision of observation, and internal validity and replicability. Although the communication net studies of Bavelas and Leavitt date back almost two decades, the potentialities of this research method for illuminating a variety of organizational processes are just being realized.

As Barnes notes in his paper, experimentation is possible not only within the confines of the laboratory but also *in situ*. As behavioral scientists, with increasing frequency, have been called upon to apply their accumulated knowledge to changing organizations or to evaluate the change attempts of others, the opportunities for experiments in naturalistic or field settings have improved markedly. Although sometimes lacking in elegant controls, efforts to study organizations experimentally in ongoing settings provide desirable checks both against causal inferences from non-experimental research and against the applicability of generalizations from the laboratory to the real world.

In most investigations of organizational behavior the researcher has assumed the role, not of an experimenter in the strict sense of that term, but of a relatively passive observer of naturally occurring phenomena. These investigations vary in such respects as the number of systems being observed, the size of the systems being observed (individuals, groups, and organizations), whether the observations are made at single or multiple points in time, and whether the observations are quantitative and systematic or non-quantitative and unsystematic. A relatively recent development is the use of observational field methods to measure the attributes of total organizations. Analyses of the interrelations among organizational attributes provide the basis for inferences concerning the processes that give rise to different organizational forms. This approach, termed the comparative study of organizations, is discussed in detail by Tom Burns. The promise of this approach lies in the possibility of understanding phenomena, such as the impact of the external environment on the organization, which do not become the focus of attention in more microcosmic approaches.

While strictly speaking computer simulation is a method of stating theories rather than a system for collecting empirical observation, it is another potentially valuable addition to the armamentarium with which behavioral scientists approach the systematic study of organization. The invention of the electronic computer less than twenty years ago has major implications for the development of science and technology. One of the sources of the appeal of this innovation to the social sciences stems from the possibility of stating theories about complex behavioral events in the form of computer programs and testing theories by comparing computer output with behavioral observations. To date, the most extensive applications of this mode of theory construction have been on thinking and problem solving by individual human subjects. In his paper, which concludes this book, Thornton Roby concerns himself with the potentiality of computer simulation for formulating and testing theories concerning a wide range of organizational processes. Although this approach, as previously noted, is not a research method in the same sense as are laboratory experiments, field experiments, or comparative field studies, it does have considerable implications for research methodology. Formulation and verification of theories stated in computer languages will undoubtedly require much more extensive observation of the processes intervening between system inputs and outputs than is true of theories stated in verbal and mathematical terms.

One of the factors undoubtedly retarding progress in organization research is the limited power of existing empirical tools in relation to the richness and complexity of the phenomena that they are expected to examine. Few would dispute the fact that the organizational researcher has a difficult task trying to explicate organizational processes with the degree of precision characterizing the work of his colleagues in the physical and biological disciplines or even in some of the social sciences. Accordingly, it is important to recognize both the potential and the limitations of present methods and to be alert to further methodological developments when they occur.

What is the best way to learn about organizations?—by creating them in the laboratory and studying their activities under controlled conditions, by trying to change "ongoing" organizations and measuring the consequences of change attempts, by observing the properties of organizations and correlating these observations with one another, or by constructing computer models of organizational processes? The reader will find not one but four answers to these questions on the following pages. While each author states and develops his own bias, this set of papers sharpens rather than obscures the differences in assumptions underlying the approaches described. The choice among them in any given situation rests with the reader, but, hopefully, the following pages will make it a more informed choice.

VICTOR H. VROOM
Carnegie Institute of Technology

Contents

Figures

Methods of
Organizational Research

1

Organizations
in the Laboratory

KARL E. WEICK

University of Minnesota

Eight people enter an experimental room and sit at separate desks. One of them silently reads through the following passage twice.

MODIFICATION OF SPECIES

One objection to the views of those who, like Mr. Gulick, believe isolation itself to be a cause of modification of species deserves attention, namely, the entire absence of change where, if this were a *vera causa*, we should expect to find it. In Ireland we have an excellent test case, for we know that it has been separated from Britain since the end of the glacial epoch, certainly many thousand years. Yet hardly one of its mammals, reptiles or land molluscs, has undergone the slightest change, even though there is certainly a distinct difference of environment, both inorganic and organic. That changes have not occurred through natural selection is perhaps due to the less severe struggle for existence owing to the smaller number of competing species; but if isolation itself were an efficient cause, acting continuously and cumulatively, it is incredible that a decided change should not have been produced in thousands of years. That no such change has occurred in this and many other cases of isolation seems to prove that it is not itself a cause of modification [Bartlett, 1932, p. 166].

The financial support of the National Science Foundation, Grant number GS–356, is gratefully acknowledged.

1

After reading the excerpt, the subject spends a few minutes performing an unrelated task and then writes the story from memory. Next, his version of the story is given to the second subject who reads it twice, works at another task, and then reproduces it. Each subject responds similarly.

The story written by the last subject reads as follows.

> Mr. Garlick says that isolation is the reason of modification. This has been proved by the fact that snakes and other reptiles were once in Ireland [ibid., p. 167].

Several things have happened to the story. The content has been simplified rather than embellished. Conventional phrases have replaced unusual details. Details have been personalized. Titles have been dropped making it more difficult for persons to place the event. In short, the subjects have tried to "justify whatever impression may have been left by the original" (ibid., p. 176).

The important question here is what relevance, if any, does this experimental exercise have to the study of organizations? Do the eight men constitute an organization? Can we learn about organizations by studying the fate of stories as they are passed from person to person? What can be learned? Questions such as these, phrased in terms of the simple task of serial reproduction, point to several issues involved in learning about organizations through laboratory experiments.

Some persons might contend that experiments on serial reproduction *are* relevant to organizational research. Stogdill (1950) and Vroom (1964) argue that differentiation of positions and a division of labor are defining attributes of an organization. If the eight subjects have different assignments (e.g., one attends to grammar, another attends to plausability) or if they differentiate themselves according to the responsibilities for accurate transmission of the story (e.g., the "first man" must be accurate, the "middle man" must add content because some will be lost), then it is conceivable that the situation of serial reproduction is like an organization. Guetzkow (1961) argues that mediated interaction distinguishes organization from small groups. Since interactions in serial reproduction are seldom face to face, the exercise qualifies as an organization by Guetzkow's standards. A related distinction is suggested by Bass (1964) who maintains that an organization consists of relations among positions, while small groups are relations among persons. It is unclear whether *Ss* perceive each other in positional or personal terms but, again, if positions are salient, serial reproduction has relevance to organizations.

Zelditch and Hopkins (1961) would probably describe the serial reproduction experiment as a "simply structured unit," meaning that it is neither complex nor does it have distinctive organizational properties. However, this type of unit still is relevant to organizations according to Zelditch and Hopkins because (1) it operates like a *subunit* in an organization, and (2) it has certain characteristics of a social system just as an organization does. It might also be argued that a serial reproduction exercise constitutes organizational research because it reproduces a common organizational phenomenon, "uncertainty absorption." March and Simon (1958, p. 165) comment that "uncertainty absorption takes place when inferences are drawn from a body of evidence and the inferences, instead of the evidence itself, are then communicated." This process is much like that observed in serial reproduction.

In each of the preceding instances, the task was potentially an organizational exercise because it resembled a natural organization in some respect or because it tested a proposition of relevance in organizational theory. However, there are other reasons why serial reproduction may not be an organization experiment.

Some of these reasons are definitional. Serial reproduction does not include properties that several investigators regard as crucial to the definition of organization. It does not contain technology (Leavitt, 1964), multiple groups (Simon, 1960), an external environment (Becker, 1964; Krupp, 1961), hierarchy of authority (Schein, 1965), or formality of policies (Zelditch and Hopkins, 1961).

Aside from definitional shortcomings, the task also has the disadvantages of many contrived situations. The interactions between subjects are transitory (Lorge, Fox, Davitz, and Brenner, 1958) and there is little time or reason for group traditions, rituals, and norms to develop. The laboratory group probably is not of the subject's own choosing (Sherif and Sherif, 1964) although neither are many groups in natural organizations. Tasks may appear trivial (Mechanic, 1963), their performance may have few consequences for the subjects (Cook and Selltiz, 1964), and the subjects, if they are students, are probably excessively compliant (Proshansky and Seidenberg, 1965, p. 13).

This brief examination of serial reproduction suggests a few of the issues that arise when attempts are made to study organizations in the laboratory. These issues are especially sharp in the case of serial reproduction because the task is not conceived with organizations in mind. Yet even this task has some relevance, given certain definitions of an organization, and the exercise can be modified to make it more relevant. If eight persons are not enough to constitute an organization, more could be added. Participants could be supplied with selected information about the other communicators (e.g., one is ambitious, a newcomer, skilled, suspicious, trustworthy) and structural or status distinctions could be made explicit. Instead of stories, persons might reproduce communications about controversial issues within the organization. The first person in the chain might observe an event and report his observations rather than read an intact story. Subjects might be given access to earlier messages or spend the time interval prior to reproduction on some activity *related* to the content of the communication.

This introduction suggests three very general conclusions about laboratory studies of organizations.

1. Experimental Organizations are Simplified

The preceding review suggests that any laboratory experiment involving interacting persons contains both features that are typical of natural organizations and features that are not. Thus the same experiment can be seen by some investigators as relevant to the study of organizations, by others, as irrelevant. It all depends on which characteristics of organizations are regarded as crucial.

It is unlikely, however, that any experiment will fully satisfy the investigator who values fidelity between laboratory and natural events. Fidelity typically must be compromised to gain clarity and control. If a person wishes to use experiments, he probably will have to choose among the several characteristics of organizations that he regards as important. To gain control, simple tasks in simple settings are often required. Selectivity need not be detrimental, it may compel the investigator to be more explicit.

2. Tests of Organizational Theory do not Require Organizations

Experiments are often used to test propositions derived from organizational theory. When an experiment is used for this purpose, its content is determined by the theory, not the referent event. This is one of the reasons that a surface resemblance between laboratory organizations and natural organizations often is absent and unnecessary. The relationship between contrived and natural events in hypothesis testing is aptly summarized by Zigler (1963, p. 353).

> What the experimenter is saying is that if such and such holds in the real world because of the principles expounded in the particular theory under investigation, then such and such should hold in the world which the experimenter has created. This translatability is what gives theoretical import to experiments which involve phenomena which, taken in isolation, not only appear picayune but seem to have little relationship with what one observes in nature.

It should not be assumed that Zigler's description affords a blanket justification for all experiments. Instead, it sharpens those things for which an experimenter should be held accountable and those for which he should not. It is clear that the experimenter must be explicit about the "world that he has created." Recent research concerning the social psychology of experiments (Rosenthal, 1963) suggests that it is more difficult to be explicit about the world that one creates than many have expected. Only if an experimenter is explicit can an observer judge if the intended conditions have been created and whether equivalent opportunities exist for "real world" principles to operate. The experimenter's claim is that his design permits these same principles to operate and that the only changes in conditions are minor ones.

While it is probably true that the experimenter can muster a stronger argument for the generality of his findings if the experiment resembles the real world, all this really does is reduce the size of the deductive leap he must make and defend. Assuming that the principles from the real world are explicit, that the experimenter is rigorous in his deductions, and that he has intimate knowledge of the world he has created, he may be less concerned with creating a close replica of the natural event.

3. Organizations can be Created Experimentally in Several Ways

Although this point has some overlap with the first summary statement, it is included to indicate that organizational experiments assume many forms. For example, organizations can be created by appropriate choices of subjects. Any experiment that uses as subjects members of ongoing organizations (e.g., Bass, 1963; French and Snyder, 1959; Maier and Hoffman, 1961) may qualify as an organizational experiment. The subjects do not have to be members of organizations, they could be aspirants as in the case of students of journalism (Lyle, 1961), business (Bass, 1963), or international relations (Guetzkow, 1959). Even further removed from actual membership, but still potentially relevant, are experiments in which subjects either explicitly role play persons in organizations (Rosenberg and Abelson, 1960), engage in activities similar to those of persons in organizations (e.g., Cohen, 1958; Strickland, 1958), identify with one organizational member in a tape recorded interaction (Ring, 1964), or read about the activities of persons in organizations and react to what is read (DiVesta, Meyer, and Mills, 1964).

Organizational experiments also may be constituted by the inclusion of trappings found in actual organizations. Such experiments may range from actual organizations that are created in the laboratory and exist for several days (Wager and Palola, 1964), through partial organizations (Evan and Zelditch, 1961), down to experiments that have a plausible but minimal set of props (Cyert, March and Starbuck, 1961). It could also be argued that any experiment testing a proposition derived from or relevant to organization theory is an organizational experiment (as is one that is multi-person), permits interaction between groups, involves coalitions (Thibaut, 1964, p. 88), or exists for an extended period of time. Clearly, these criteria include most social psychological experiments.

In one sense, arguments over whether an experiment is organizational or not are unnecessary. This judgment depends on the extent to which the specific research promotes understanding of organizational processes. Our reason for illustrating various definitions of these experiments is to suggest some ways in which organizations can be studied in the laboratory and, indirectly, to suggest the flexibility of the laboratory.

SUMMARY

At the outset, it is important to realize experimental organizations seldom resemble natural organizations. Experiments permit persons to look more closely at some problems, but not at others. However, it is the experimenter's theoretical preferences, his preconceptions about experiments and his ingenuity that define the range of problems that are susceptible to experimental inquiry. It is the purpose of this chapter to detail how laboratory studies are created, and what they can and cannot accomplish.

The chapter will contain the following sections. First, characteristics of experiments will be described in terms of the fictions and nonfictions that have emerged about laboratory experiments. Next, various means to construct organizational settings in the laboratory will be examined. The exercises to be discussed range from complex simulations that are property-rich to minimal tasks involving virtually no organizational trappings. Then a comparison between field and laboratory studies of a common problem will introduce an extended discussion of the strengths and problems associated with conducting experiments. Primary emphasis will be placed on problems.

THE NATURE OF ORGANIZATIONAL EXPERIMENTS

Formally, it is possible to define experimentation as "experience carefully planned in advance" (R. A. Fisher, quoted in Kaplan, 1964, p. 147) or as "a process of observation, to be carried out in a situation especially brought about for that purpose" (Kaplan, 1964, p. 154). While these definitions do imply that experiments are intentionally structured "so that the effects of the independent variables can be evaluated unambiguously" (Underwood, 1957, p. 86), they do not hint at some of the controversial issues associated with experimentation. These issues are best portrayed by selections from the folklore about experiments:

> The social science laboratory with its sense of innovation, its mission of experimental proof and its direct, personal confrontation between subject and experimenter, is the highly charged home of chance, accident, hope, fear and danger [Mills, 1962, p. 24].
>
> What can be observed reliably is socially meaningless and what is socially meaningful cannot be observed reliably [Lewin, 1951, p. 155].
>
> No one believes an hypothesis except its originator but everyone believes an experiment except the experimenter [Beveridge, 1950, p. 47].
>
> Some social scientists will do any mad thing rather than study men at firsthand in their natural settings [Homans, 1962, p. 259].
>
> Man is evidently more efficient in his everyday life than in experimental rooms. . . . It is needless to point out how difficult it is for us to make threshold judgments, to not be tricked by an optical illusion, to remember nonsense syllables, and for a rat deprived of cues for proper discrimination to behave properly in a maze. Man and rat are both incredibly stupid in an experimental room. On the other hand, psychology has paid little attention to the things they do in their normal habitats; man drives a car, plays complicated games, designs computers, and organizes society, and the rat is troublesomely cunning in the kitchen [Toda, 1962, p. 165].

While this folklore is rich, colorful, varied, at times polar, and often accurate, it also serves to perpetuate certain fictions about experiments. Generally these fictions suggest that experiments are more fallible, less conclusive, and apply to a more limited range of problems than need be true. Certain myths in the folklore about experiments are sufficiently compelling that, once persons are familiar with them, they shun experiments and thereby forego any opportunities to disconfirm these myths. Therefore, it seems relevant to look briefly at some beliefs about experiments that might otherwise deter the organizational theorist from working in the laboratory.

FICTIONS ABOUT EXPERIMENTS

The four points that follow are not entirely fictions. Occasionally, they are problems in conducting experiments and in generalizing to the real world. However, their potency and disruptiveness is often overrated, hence they are not the deterrents to experimentation that persons believe they are.

1. Experiments Demonstrate the Obvious

A common belief is that laboratory experiments serve mainly "to demonstrate what you are already pretty sure of" (Homans 1962, p. 264).

While there is some support for this belief, it also represents a limited view of what can be accomplished in an experiment.

The impression that experiments amplify obvious phenomena arises from several sources. Experimental tasks often are sufficiently simple that the results appear straightforward and expected. Sometimes experiments are designed to produce a single phenomenon, no additional phenomena can occur in the same setting, therefore, the outcome seems obvious. Furthermore, when only a single variable is manipulated, observers often argue that an outcome is obvious because all the other crucial variables were controlled. It is also probable that the amount of work that precedes an experiment fosters the impression of obviousness. So much information is required to identify the variables, refine the predictions, and create the experimental situation, that it often seems that there is little more to be learned by actually executing the experiment. The important thinking about the problem has already occurred. The claim that obviousness pervades experiments also appears in conjunction with the argument that experiments test theory, but seldom generate hypotheses. As will be shown later, this view is too narrow.

There are several features of experimentation which suggest that obviousness is not as pervasive as many have imagined. And where experiments are obvious, this is often a strength rather than a weakness. Experiments furnish more occasions for hypothesis generation than is often realized. Seldom do the outcomes of an experiment unequivocally confirm a hypothesis. There are usually some measures or deviant cases that are inconsistent and require explanation. Attempts to account for these discrepant data often generate new hypotheses. But experiments can often generate hypotheses in a much more direct manner.

Discovery of hypotheses can be planned and it is in this sense that controls, hypotheses, contrived situations, and simple tasks—all prominent features of the laboratory—can facilitate the discovery of new relationships. It is likely that many potentially important hypotheses go unnoticed in field studies because there are too many distractions. These distractions are reduced in the laboratory and, even though there may be fewer occasions for novel relationships to occur, those that do occur are more likely to be noticed. Thus controls may aid rather than hinder hypothesis generation, and the laboratory may be a more appropriate setting for this activity than the field.

Several examples of planned hypothesis generation can be cited. Each of these is a very general hypothesis that can be explored directly in the laboratory. March and Simon (1958, p. 169) propose that "the basic features of organization structure and function derive from the characteristics of human problem-solving processes and rational human choice."

But, whether structure actually is constrained by human cognitive abilities is an empirical question. One way to explore this question is to vary systematically the composition of a group along some cognitive dimension (e.g., abstract-concrete) and observe differences in the structure and process of problem solving that emerge (Tuckman, 1964). If the problem is one of discovering the processes that perpetuate and disrupt group traditions when membership changes, a more explicit answer is likely to be found in the laboratory than in the field (Jacobs and Campbell, 1961; Kuethe, 1962). Frequently, the laboratory permits one to ask questions in an uncommon fashion and create conditions to arrive at the answers. In order to study what produces change, one could ask, "What does it take to keep an organization from changing?" The experimenter could allow experimental groups to have planning sessions (Shure, Rogers, Larsen and Tassone, 1962), could assign organizational structures that are intolerable and compel change (Bass, 1963, p. 152) or instruct participants to change their work structure every twenty minutes, and then determine what was required to *terminate* the changes that were instigated by these three procedures. A mechanism that terminates changes is apt to be a mechanism that also affects the adoption of change. Or, to study the relationship between organizational structure and motivational phenomena, such as inequity (Adams, 1963), the experimenter could vary organizational structure by creating different communication networks and determine in which kinds of networks participants experience greater and lesser inequity when payment differs from expectancy.

An additional sense in which experimentation aids discovery is implicit in the phrase, *experiment as metaphor*. By metaphor is meant "an implied comparison between things essentially unlike one another. . . . One image is superimposed upon another in order to provide a perspective or better understanding of the subject at hand" (Bruyn, 1964, pp. 101–102). Experiments often provide a means to visualize a complex event. Instead of trying to imagine the effects of different antecedents in the natural event, the experimenter visualizes what would happen if some feature of the experiment were changed. While in a sense such usage of experiments may be nothing more than the manipulation of a verbal model, it does have one important difference. If the experimenter's thinking does generate a potentially valuable observation concerning the real world, it is possible to verify this impression in the very situation where it was generated, the experiment. Errors in translation from one level of abstraction to another are thereby avoided.

Aside from the fact that experiments generate hypotheses, there are other reasons why obviousness is a fictitious shortcoming of experiments.

Whether or not an outcome is obvious is a relative judgment. Findings that are obvious in terms of one set of beliefs are often unexpected in terms of another set. It is one of the truisms of experimentation that unequivocal support for one proposition seriously endangers other propositions. However, many of these disconfirmations are unseen because premises are not made explicit. Intuition is a notoriously misleading basis for prediction, and criticism of obviousness often masks a failure to make intuitions explicit.

In short, the claim that experiments demonstrate the obvious may represent a confusion of explicitness with significance. As experimental operations are made more explicit, experimental outcomes often seem less surprising. This is desirable because it probably means that the findings are less ambiguous to interpret. Unfortunately lack of ambiguity is sometimes mistaken for lack of importance or significance. This is one of the reasons that experiments may appear to add little information.

Aside from the issue of mistaken interpretations of explicitness, there is the fact that experiments are not merely a means to demonstrate phenomena; they also aid hypothesis generation. Hypotheses may be suggested either indirectly by analysis of unexpected findings or directly by exploratory experimentation. The use of experiments for exploration has often been neglected, but this usage seems especially important given the continuing development of organization theory.

Whether or not one can make discoveries seems to depend less on where he looks than on how he looks. It is possible that during a given period of time less may happen in the laboratory than in the field. To some this means that laboratory events are less significant, to others it means that there are fewer distractions from observing the event.

2. Experiments are Artificial

One of the most pervasive fictions about experiments is that they are artificial. This view often is held because novelty is confused with artificiality. Laboratory tasks and settings may be unfamiliar to the subject, but this has nothing to do with the significance of his responses. The laboratory situation is still real, the subject must make some adjustment to it, and there is no reason to believe that his responses will differ from those in other unfamiliar situations. As Kaplan (1964, p. 169) observes, "the experimental situation is not to be contrasted with 'real life' but at most only with everyday life."

It is also true that the novelty of experimental exercises is sometimes exaggerated. There are many organizational processes that have high "ecological validity" in the laboratory setting. Milgram (1964, p. 850), for example, stated that the laboratory "is one social context in which compliance occurs regularly" and, therefore, is an apt site in which to study obedience. Thus, whether the laboratory setting contains events that are novel or events that are expected, the settings coerce behavior and in this sense are not fictitious.

Artificiality, however, may become more of an issue when one considers the goals of people who participate in experiments. Subjects often are concerned with more than just the task assigned by the experimenter. It is this spread of concern to issues such as deciphering the purposes of the experiment and predicting what is a "healthy" or "safe" response, that many persons equate with artificiality.

Once again, however, artificiality is not the problem. The problem is one of control. The subject's motives are in no sense feigned, they simply encompass a larger portion of the experiment than the experimenter intended. The subject's plight is essentially that he knows he is being watched and evaluated while he does not know what is being observed. It is these doubts that lead to "evaluation apprehension" (Rosenberg, 1965) or the "deutero-problem" (Riecken, 1962). While the fact of being observed and evaluated in terms of unstated criteria is not uncommon in organizations, it does cause problems in the interpretation of experimental outcomes. It is sometimes difficult to disentangle the effects of trying to gain clarity from the effects of the experimenter's intended manipulations.

Apprehension, however, is not an unsolvable problem. One way to reduce its effects is to conceal the fact that data are being collected (e.g., Sherif and Sherif, 1964). Another way is to promise the subject *in advance* that information about the experiment, his responses, and those of others, will be provided at the conclusion of the exercise, and then to provide this information. Experiments are an unusually good chance for subjects to learn about themselves, about other people, and about research methods, and these learnings are typically regarded as a fair exchange for participation. Much of the difficulty in experiments occurs because the experimenter faults on his portion of the exchange.

A further characteristic of experiments that is often mistaken for artificiality is the population that is studied. It often appears as if college students are not people. A typical objection to the subject population found in experiments is voiced by Dill (1964, p. 52): "What college sophomores do, alas, may not be much more relevant than the behavior of monkeys for predicting how executives, nurses, or research scientists will perform."

Although college students differ from executives in many ways, they also have many similarities. Thus the question of appropriate subjects resolves to one of "are the ways in which he [the college student] differs from other people correlated with the effects investigated" (Zelditch and Evan, 1962, p. 59). In some studies college students do differ in relevant dimensions. Jensen and Terebinski (1963, p. 87), for example, report that in their simulation of a railroad system, "a PhD with system experience lost interest after four or five sessions in which he learned the . . . appropriate strategies. College sophomores used different heuristics and never seemed to understand the system in the same way as the others; they remained interested much longer." Thus, when system experience is a potential determinant of an effect, sophomores may be inappropriate *unless* the experimenter wishes to hold this variable at a value of zero. Also it is possible that the railroad simulation made demands unlike those of most "systems" which sophomores encounter. It is certainly true that sophomores have some "system experience." If they did not, they would be unlikely to survive in college.

It is unlikely that one could ever find a subject population that is equivalent to a typical organizational member. The reason is simply that there is no such thing as a typical member. Members vary just as subjects do. Observing executives to learn about foremen would be just as suspect as observing college students to learn the same information. Unless the experimenter is explicit about personal variables that moderate his phenomenon, and unless these variables assume quite different values in his subject population and his referent population, the use of a college student is not a serious limitation.

It is possible that most objections to the use of sophomores are really objection to recruitment procedures rather than to the abilities of this particular population. Conditions under which subjects participate in experiments often affect their behavior. Rosenthal (1963) and Hood (1964) detail the ways in which volunteer subjects respond differently than non-volunteers. Gustav (1962) describes the resentment that occurs among subjects when they are required to participate in experiments. The form in which this resentment may be shown is interesting. Subjects often regard the requirement to serve in experiments as "one more harassment imposed by the university." To the extent that they equate experiments with waiting in line for meals and with restrictions on hours and automobiles, they probably exhibit a common response—rebellion and indifference. Thus, students may be less appropriate as subjects for experiments, *not* because of their skills and experiences or lack of them, but rather because the conditions under which they participate influence their reactions to laboratory events.

It can be concluded that even though there are many reasons why laboratory findings may not generalize to other settings, artificiality is not among these reasons. Furthermore, artificiality is a dangerous label to attach to experiments because it focuses attention on pseudo issues and suggests self-defeating solutions. If a situation seems artificial, the only thing to do is make it more real or natural. And this usually means that more "props" are added so that the setting *looks* more natural. But, as more props are added, controls founder and it becomes more difficult to observe what happens. The behavior that is evoked is made no more real by these additions and, in fact, the experimenter has probably made his propositions less accessible.

3. Laboratory Contexts are Oversimplified

Since natural events have multiple determinants, it may not seem helpful to study laboratory events that fail to retain this complex context. If a social system is the unit of analysis, then events "isolated" for study in the laboratory lack crucial properties. Dalton (1964, p. 56), in describing his preference for field methods, comments that "where the problem was inextricably inter-twined with others, I felt that too much injustice would be done to the whole to wrench it out for the sake of sampling and scaling theory. In such cases one might objectively relate the mutilated part to a subjectively established criterion and in doing so inflate the part out of all proportion to the interlinked parts discarded because of quantitative inadequacy."

Although few people would deny that behavior has multiple determinants or that it is embedded in a system, many would disagree about how to act once this fact is acknowledged. That an event has multiple determinants still remains a hypothesis, and whether "wrenching it out" will drastically alter its properties is at least a question that can be tested. It is not necessarily true that factors in close proximity to a natural event affect its course. Human perception is sufficiently affected by considerations of economy (Heider, 1944) that causal attributions made under field conditions may differ from those made in the laboratory.

Aside from the issue of how many determinants there are of natural events, and whether these judgments are susceptible to perceptual bias, it should be noted that laboratory exercises "create a context of their own which is not incompatible with what is being modeled" (Meier, 1961, p. 241). Assuming that laboratory events have some resemblance to natural events, it is not uncommon to find that subjects enrich the laboratory event and invest it with some of the meaning associated with the natural event. While this creates problems for the experimenter, it also indicates that context is not insufficient or unrepresentative.

Laboratory events often look simple because the experimenter has used simplifying assumptions in testing a theory or because a simple replica is an obvious place to launch an investigation. Blalock (1963, p. 402) notes that, even though a formulation or experiment may initially be unrealistic, "by beginning with grossly oversimplified models a cumulative process can be set in motion in which one successively modifies the model or theory until it becomes more and more complex and provides a better fit to reality." There is no implication that the experimenter will retain his simplification indefinitely. He may tarry in complicating the model and demand clear evidence that more variables are needed, but he can add them. And he has the further advantage that it is easier for him to observe the effects of these additions.

Simply because natural events exist in a system and have multiple determinants, they are not thereby disqualified as objects for laboratory experimentation. Laboratory events often generate their own systemic properties and, even when they do not, the experimenter can add them to his model and experimental operations *when he is ready to observe their effects.*

4. Hypotheses Induce Myopia

One reason experiments are avoided is that they all involve hypotheses. It is sometimes assumed that hypotheses retard rather than hasten understanding for they force selective attention toward events. In the quest for hypothesis confirmation, important relationships may be overlooked. Dalton (1964, p. 54) presents an especially colorful picture of this possibility: "A prematurely publicized hypothesis may bind both one's conscience and vanity. . . . A hypothetical statement is also one's attempt to be original. Having once made such a statement, one more easily overlooks negative findings or, on having them pointed out, one's emotional freight often limits creativity to ingenious counterarguments."

Hypotheses serve several functions, one of them being to structure observation. It is inconceivable that an observer can give undivided attention to everything that occurs. Selectivity intrudes in one form or other. And a hypothesis derived from a theory is one means to order observation. The order imposed by a hypothesis extends further than many persons realize. In many experiments incidental phenomena take on added meaning because, if the hypothesis is true, these secondary events should assume a particular form. Hypotheses, in other words, frequently direct attention to new areas rather than force a neglect of them.

The question of how an investigator responds when a hypothesis is not supported is important, but this question must be separated from the issue of whether or not hypotheses are helpful. Even if a hypothesis is retained longer than some observers think it should be, this is no reason for hypotheses to be avoided. Furthermore, it is much more difficult to judge when a hypothesis has outlived its usefulness than Dalton implies. There are numerous occasions when hypotheses have been dropped prematurely more for reasons of taste than of error or disconfirmation (Abelson, 1964; Boring, 1964; Weick, 1965). And experimental results that do not support a hypothesis can occur for many reasons other than an error in the hypothesis. Incorrect independent variables may be chosen, manipulations may be unsuccessful, measurements may be insensitive, effects may be too weak to be observed, or the wrong outcomes may be observed. Even if a hypothesis receives continued negative evidence, it still may be useful to an investigator as a way to think about problems. However, one should not forget that seldom do good investigators propose just one hypothesis in a lifetime. Investments in any given idea tend to be less intense than Dalton suggests. And investigators also are mindful of "the cardinal principle of experimentation . . . that we must accept the outcome whether or not it is to our liking" (Kaplan, 1964, p. 145).

A conclusion about the value of hypotheses is advanced by Blau, a field worker who has used them: "It is all too easy to obtain impressionistic evidence for our broad theoretical speculations. Such evidence, therefore, helps us little in discriminating between diverse or even conflicting theoretical principles. My endeavor to stipulate hypotheses . . . and to collect at least some quantitative data served the purpose of furnishing a screening device for insight. Those ideas that survived this screening test, while still only hypotheses . . . were more apt to be correct than the original speculations" (Blau, 1964, p. 20). Hypotheses, in other words, may uncover problems as often as they obscure them.

Conclusion

Laboratory events are different from everyday events in many ways. But these differences do not always imply that the laboratory event is any less real or any less significant as a means to learn about people. Relationships among variables are suggested in the laboratory just as they are in the field. Laboratory controls do not restrict the richness of data; they frequently make it easier to detect the unexpected when it occurs. There are considerable problems in conducting laboratory studies. But the problems of incomplete knowledge of variables, artificiality, simplicity of events, and focused observation are not among the major drawbacks even though they are often represented as such.

NON-FICTIONS ABOUT EXPERIMENTS

Once the investigator separates crucial from non-crucial issues in experimentation, he can concentrate on ways to cope with these more enduring features of experiments. The following discussion samples the "styles" of thinking associated with the use of the laboratory, styles often taken for granted by experimenters. When these stylistic features are made explicit, they provide a more complete view of demands imposed by experimentation and assumptions made by those who use the laboratory.

1. External Influences on Laboratory Events

Experimenters sometimes overestimate the amount of control they have over the conditions of the experiment. Lewin, for example, propounded the view that the laboratory is an island. "Experimentation in the laboratory occurs, socially speaking, on an island quite isolated from the life of society. Although it cannot violate society's basic rules, it is largely free from those pressures which experimentation with 'life groups' has to face daily" (Lewin, 1951, p. 166). Experimenters currently are giving added attention to the fact that experiments are not as isolated as they would like. Experiments do exist in environments. The ways in which subjects act in experiments are frequently determined by the meaning of the experiment in the larger system. This can be an especially important issue in organizational experiments.

For example, an increasing number of organizational experiments are conducted at human relations training laboratories (e.g., Bass and Leavitt, 1963). Several rather explicit norms emerge in these laboratories and they undoubtedly affect the behavior of trainees when they participate in experiments. Egalitarian norms prevail, shared leadership is valued, status distinctions are discounted, previous experiences are irrelevant, and momentary feelings are expressed. In addition to being exposed to new and possibly unfamiliar norms, the trainees typically become more adept at working in groups.

Given these characteristics, it is not surprising that organization experiments conducted in training settings show that less highly structured organizations are superior to those with high structure. But the influence of the external system is not even this simple. Norms do not develop immediately; their clarification and acceptance take time. Thus it is probable that a person who has been in training for only a short time would feel more comfortable with a structured group since it closely resembles other groups with which he is familiar. As the training progresses, structured conditions probably create increased ambivalence, resentment, and frustration among participants because these conditions are contrary to those valued in the training sessions. Thus it is not surprising that experiments with the "link-pin organization" show superior results when they are conducted during the latter stages of training sessions. The important point is that this superiority may be the result, not of structural characteristics, but of uncertainty in the structured group concerning how they should act.

A further environmental influence in training laboratories is that most group exercises have a moral, and a task that "makes a point" is probably biased toward a particular outcome. If the results of the training exercise are then treated as experimental data, their significance should not be overestimated. It is probably safe to conclude that data collected during the early stages of a training laboratory are more representative of the population at large than are data collected later.

Experiments conducted at training laboratories are not the only ones susceptible to influence from the social system. Some effects of university settings have already been detailed. The point is that the experimenters must not ignore the setting in which experiments occur. The extent of this influence is suggested by Mills (1962, p. 22): "By examining the experiment's place within the institutional settings, its significance for the lives of the subjects, its operations as they represent interaction between observer and observed, by formulating the structure of role relationships and by interpreting the significance of events for this inclusive system, sociological analysis can . . . [help distinguish] that component in our raw data which should be charged to what experimenter and subject are doing to and for one another and that component which should be charged to the experimental group itself as an object of investigation."

2. Psychological Representation of Variables

The same feeling, belief, or perception can be created in several ways. For example, a person may experience uncertainty because he follows a bizarre and confusing route to arrive at the laboratory (Sherif and Harvey, 1952), is misinformed about physical symptoms that he experiences (Schachter and Singer, 1962), or meets persons who mistake his identity (Garfinkel, 1963). Experimenters typically exploit the fact that the same condition can be created in several ways and, as a result, they often expose subjects to contingencies that appear unusual and artificial. Experimenters assume that the critical problem in an experiment is to create the desired state in the subject. It is far less important what the manipulations that create this state look like.

Observers often believe that an event will be represented psychologically only if it unfolds in a manner familiar to the subject. In other words it is assumed that a physical resemblance between the laboratory and the real world is necessary if the input is to make a difference to the subject, i.e., to be represented psychologically. While it is a hypothetical question whether psychological representation can be created by unfamiliar stimuli, most experimenters assume that it can. This simplifying assumption is an important one.

Occasionally experimenters find that subjects become suspicious or at least more attentive when uncommon events are used to create common experiences. But the very uncommoness of these laboratory events prevents accurate labeling of their purpose, with the consequence that the suspicion tends to be "free-floating." As long as suspicion takes this form it is less likely to exert a *systematic* effect on the results.

The implication of these remarks is that any experimental manipulation is a theory. Manipulations represent an experimenter's hunch about the conditions necessary to create psychologically the phenomenon of interest. The manipulation also implies what the experimenter regards as the most important properties of the phenomenon. In the example involving uncertainty, each of the manipulations exploits a slightly different component of uncertainty. One exploits the desire for clear external frames of reference; another, the desire for consistent impressions of self; and the other, the desire for knowledge of the rules that guide the behavior of others. But always the criterion for choosing a manipulation is whether it makes a difference to the subject, not whether it is familiar to him. Lewin's concept of life space is a valuable caution to the person who believes that simulating the visible, physical components of a natural event is sufficient to induce psychological representation. "I do not consider as part of the psychological field at a given time those sections of the physical or social world which do not affect the life space of the person at that time. The food that lies behind doors at the end of a maze so that neither smell or sight can reach it is not a part of the life space of the animal" (Lewin, 1951, pp. 57–58). Unless the object makes a difference to the subject, it is not a part of the life space. And simply creating a physical likeness is not sufficient to insure that an object is included in the life space.

3. Parsimonious Explanations

Experimenters prefer simple explanations and they adopt more complex propositions only when the simple ones prove inadequate. This does not mean that experimenters refuse to study complex propositions. Demands for parsimony have nothing to do with hypothesis testing. As Marx (1963, p. 21) has stated, "the doctrine of parsimony is relevant only to the acceptance of propositions—not to their testing or development. As a matter of fact, it should serve as a spur to scientific advance, since it puts the burden of proof on those who prefer the more complex alternatives; let them find some evidence which *requires* it." Most experiments, therefore, attempt to study "fundamental processes which presumably underlie the behavior of humans in a broad range of organizational [and other] settings" (McGrath, 1964, p. 538).

A somewhat different (and less charitable) view of the experimenter's preference for simple explanations is expressed by Mills (1962, p. 23). He argues that experimenters are disenchanted because their experiments do not tell them more about groups and that, to defend against this disenchantment, they adopt simple models. The rationale for adoption is this: "the less there is to a group, the more we know about it. The more machine-like groups are, the more we can control them." Whether motivated by the strengths or the weaknesses of experiments, pressures toward parsimony are evident in the laboratory.

Among the basic organizational processes studied in the laboratory are delegation, decisions to participate, decisions to produce, and interdependence. Experimenters argue that if these processes are understood a great deal is known about organizations. Delegation is a good example. It is an important property of natural organizations (Selznick, 1948), it assumes several forms (Roby, 1962), and it can be studied in the laboratory (Solem, 1958).

Knowledge about the factors that led a person to join a firm is knowledge that helps predict what to expect from him. The decision to participate is a basic process in organizations, and the bases on which this decision is made can sometimes lead the person to exhibit high productivity (Weick, 1964) or low productivity (Adams and Rosenbaum, 1962). In a sense, any experiment can provide information about determinants of organizational productivity as long as the basis for participation is made explicit. Experiments involve the acceptance, performance and assessment of tasks just as do organizations. Conceivably a portion of the subject's performance is influenced by the conditions under which he accepted the task. At least this possibility can be examined if the bases of participation are known.

Interdependence (Miller and Hamblin, 1963) is also a basic fact of organizational life. Its effects are found everywhere. Events ramify widely, compensatory as well as retaliatory changes take place (Leavitt, 1964) and unanticipated consequences occur in unexpected places. Interdependence is a process that is especially well suited to exploration in the laboratory (e.g., Kelley, Condry, Dahlke, and Hill, 1965; Kelley, Thibaut, Radloff, and Mundy, 1962), and it can be created simply by putting each person's outcomes under at least the partial control of another person (e.g., Raven and Eachus, 1963; Weick and Penner, 1966).

One drawback in studies of basic processes is that they promote patchwork conceptions of organizations. The organization appears to be a set of independent processes or a set of dimensions. These properties are studied individually, and occasionally other dimensions serve as dependent variables. Although such an approach does not yield direct data on the interdependence of dimensions, this shortcoming is not serious at this stage of inquiry. The proposition that processes are complex is also subject to considerations of parsimony. It is probable that processes have multiple determinants; it is also probable that not all these determinants carry equal weight.

4. Experimenter as Artisan

The creation of conditions that establish, control, measure, and disentangle variables requires resourcefulness and imagination. It is difficult to prescribe ways to attack these problems. Precedent is less important in experimental design than in many scientific activities. Although the experimenter examines earlier experiments to learn about factors that may confound the results, he typically must devise new procedures to deal with these sources of error.

Examples of procedural twists that aid measurement and control are plentiful. To combat problems of scoring open-ended remarks, the experimenter can have subjects select their remarks from a prepared list of comments (Pilisuk, 1962; Thibaut and Riecken, 1955). To insure that vacillation in making judgments is recorded, the experimenter can have subjects write their answers with pencils that have no erasers (Krugman, 1960). To help subjects see all the alternatives open to them in a coalition task, an accomplice of the experimenter can suggest different alternatives by his actions (Hoffman, Festinger, and Lawrence, 1954). To control impressions of mutual liking among group members, the experimenter can have subjects rate each other, can scan and then discard these ratings in a wastebasket, and finally retrieve a "planted" set of ratings which are returned to the subjects (Dittes and Kelley, 1956). Perhaps the most important skill of the experimenter-artisan is his ability to embed crucial manipulations and measures in an expected or plausible sequence of events. If embedding is successful, fewer suspicions are aroused and the manipulations may be more potent (Schachter, 1951). Surprises or irrelevant instructions may induce caution or indifference. Festinger (1953, p. 155) states that, unless experimental instructions "are plausible in the sense of being integrally related to the experimental activity in which the subjects are to engage," their impact will be slight. Potential implausibility occurs when "the subjects could have done everything the experimenter required of them without these instructions ever having been given" (ibid., p. 159). It may make little difference to subjects whether they are matched on intelligence, testing a new product, starting a new organization, generating normative data, or competing with other groups, if they can perform the experimental task without knowing this.

A good example of the importance of embedding is found in the methods used to obtain measurements of attitudes before and after attempted persuasion. Attempts to embed the post-persuasion measurement have included interpreting the pre-measure as a "warmup" (Aronson, Turner, and Carlsmith, 1963), obtaining post-measures in a different experiment (Rosenberg, 1965), obtaining post-measure for an unrelated purpose (Festinger and Carlsmith, 1959), or presenting attitudinal items in different questionnaire formats (Hovland and Weiss, 1952). The crucial requirement is that the measurement not attract undue attention. Subjects must regard the event as a legitimate demand, i.e., they must see a rationale for its inclusion.

The consistency with which experimental events unfold affects subject behavior. Attention to subtle procedural details is necessary to maintain consistency. There are several examples in laboratory experiments where theoretically important contingencies were created, but aroused suspicion among subjects because of their implausibility. Ring (1964) varied status (high or low) and compliance (complies or fails to comply) and found that subjects were made uncomfortable by the high-status person who complied and the low-status person who did not comply. These contingencies were unexpected and, in *both* instances, the stimulus persons were regarded unfavorably. The compliant-high-status person was seen as timid and weak, the low-status-noncompliant person as brash and tactless. French and Snyder (1959) report that subjects in a work group found it difficult to comprehend why their supervisor in another room first sent them messages to slow down their work pace and, shortly thereafter, sent messages urging a speedup. Much of the suspicion may have occurred because the notes gave little explanation for the change in policy (e.g., "It's going fine. Forget about mistakes and try for speed"). The point is that tests of some propositions may impose considerable strains on plausibility. It should be noted that this argument does not contradict the earlier discussion of a confusion between novelty and artificiality. The earlier discussion dealt with unfamiliar events, whereas the present concern is more with incongruous events. It has been reasonably well demonstrated (e.g., Carlsmith and Aronson, 1963; Harvey, 1963) that mildly incongruous events are experienced as pleasurable but that marked incongruity evokes negative evaluations.

Demands for consistency and plausibility do not mean that the experimenter must forgo important controls or measurements; but these demands do require ingenuity and revision of earlier procedures. It should be noted that requirements of consistency, plausibility, and embedding can be met in contrived situations. There is no implication that these ends are accomplished only in highly realistic experiments. It does not take an elaborate simulation to achieve satisfactory embedding. What is required is that subjects be given a rationale for the experimenter's demands and that this rationale be acceptable to them. The necessity for being an artisan arises from trying to provide subjects with legitimacy for experimental operations while retaining maximum control over what occurs.

Conclusion

Experiments are responsive to external influences. Experimenters acknowledge this fact when they try to integrate experimental demands with demands of the larger social system and when they legitimate experimental operations for subjects. If external influences are ignored, important sources of error are not controlled. Experimentalists, however, are concerned with problems other than confounding external sources. They are concerned with choosing experimental conditions that make a difference to the subject. These choices are not influenced by considerations of realism and artificiality. Concepts and propositions are continually reexamined for excessive simplicity or complexity. Frequently the act of translating a concept into experimental operations aids this conceptual refinement. Even though the experimenter may seem to dwell on simple methods to study simple explanations, in reality he examines continually the adequacy of these explanations and his methods to insure that they do not generate misleading data. These then represent some of the non-fictitious features of experiments.

THE STRUCTURE OF LABORATORY ORGANIZATIONS

An organization may assume many forms when it is constructed in the laboratory. The purpose of this section is to describe some of the variations that are possible. Several tasks, arranged crudely along a dimension of the number and explicitness of organizational properties contained, will be described. The tasks range from those with virtually no explicit organizational content (minimum content) to those that involve the creation of an actual, ongoing organization (maximum content).

The use of the dimension of minimum-maximum content is to impose some order on the discussion. In actuality no one dimension is involved because, as one moves from task to task, *several* features vary.

Abstract experimental tasks tend to be concerned with a single, basic process. Explicit organization content is at a minimum. Neither the setting nor the task suggest organizational analogies to the subject. The process observed is presumably prominent in organizations, but is stripped of its usual accompaniments. The more concrete laboratory replica includes such salient organizational properties as structure, technology (e.g., telephones), and work activities (e.g., problem solving and conferences). The most concrete replicas involve simulated organizations with several participants, long time spans, tangible products, and hired subjects. A summary listing of tasks that represent these gradations is found in Figure 1.

The remainder of this discussion includes brief descriptions of each of

FIGURE 1

Organizational Replicas in Laboratory Exercises

Abstract Replicas

Group reaction time (Zajonc, 1965)

Common target game (Leavitt, 1960)

Anagrams (Ammons and Ammons, 1959a)

Detective story (Burns, 1964)

Group discussion (Hoffman, Harburg, and Maier, 1962)

Card sorting (French and Snyder, 1959)

Railroad game (Jensen, 1961)

Community exercise (Schein and King, 1964)

Aircraft maintenance (Enke, 1958)

Proofreading (Adams and Jacobsen, 1964)

Concrete Replicas

the benchmark tasks listed in Figure 1. Additional information about laboratory tasks to study organizations is found in Weick (1965).

GROUP REACTION TIME (ZAJONC, 1965)

Undoubtedly one of the most versatile group tasks yet devised is the group reaction timer designed by Zajonc. The subject's task is exceedingly simple. When a colored light goes on, the subject is to depress a key as quickly as possible. If his reaction takes longer than a preset interval, a failure light goes on. If the reaction is quick enough, the failure light remains off. A group task is formed by connecting several individual timers to a central timer. When this is done, numerous contingencies can be created. For example, in a seven man group, the clocks can be set so that each person must exceed an absolute time or all will fail; or each person must exceed his own average or all fail; or at least four of the seven persons must achieve a particular speed for all to succeed. Feedback of group results, division of labor, role structure, and cooperation-competition can all be manipulated with this apparatus.

Even though the reaction time task explicitly resembles few, if any, organizational activities, it has one decided advantage over most other tasks. It involves "individual behavior that is reasonably well understood, behavior extensively examined in individual psychology, behavior whose antecedents are reasonably well known" (Zajonc, 1965, p. 73).

Most tasks, especially those in complex simulations, can be performed adequately only with a rather complex mix of ability and effort. This makes it more difficult to interpret experimental outcomes. Fewer problems of this kind occur with abstract tasks. The principal benefits of the timer task are that it enables the experimenter to create a host of theoretically important contingencies and also incorporate a sensitive measure. It replicates the important organizational property of interdependence. Other tasks especially suitable because they increase the visibility of interdependence are minimal social situation (Kelley, Thibaut, Radloff, and Mundy, 1962), spirit leveling (Raven and Eachus, 1963), target identification (Miller and Hamblin, 1963), and word formation (Cottrell, 1963).

COMMON TARGET GAME (LEAVITT, 1960)

The properties of structure and differentiation, important variables in organizational theory, can be added to the property of interdependence in a strikingly simple exercise, the common target game. Three persons who cannot see each other, hold up fingers when the experimenter calls out a number between one and thirty. The object is for the fingers to sum to exactly the number that the experimenter has announced. If the subjects fail to hit the number, they try until they are successful. The necessity for differentiation occurs with numbers that are not divisible by three. If the experimenter calls the number 11, this number could be achieved by 3–3–5, 4–4–3, or 10–1–0. It is the group's task to arrive at a structure that will solve each problem on the first try.

Variations of this basic exercise have been used to study several organizational problems. Bass and Leavitt (1963) studied differences in productivity when plans were imposed or generated by the group. Zand and Costello (1963) used the situation to study group learning, Joyner (1965) to study concept formation, and Leavitt (1960) to study the effects of problem-solving history on the emergence of structure. The exercise seems appropriate to understand how subsystems in organizations function. Once a group is able to contribute numbers consistently so that a target is achieved on the first try, they may be regarded as having a stable, efficient, asymmetrical, shared decision plan. The relevance to organizations occurs both because of the product and because of the way in which the members achieve it. Joyner (1965, p. 4) characterizes the exercise this way: "Persons have worked together to acquire a structure for coordinating a set of diverse functions and have carried out these functions frequently enough that they constitute a stable set of problem-solving or decision-making procedures."

ANAGRAMS (AMMONS AND AMMONS, 1959a)

Somewhat more task content and complexity of assignment occurs when persons are presented with a set of letters and are instructed to form as many words as possible from these letters. The basic property of the task is that the sets of letters are problems, norms for the number of words derived can be established, and there is no single correct solution. Variations of the basic anagram exercise have been used in several organizational experiments (e.g., Bass and Vaughan, 1962; Kennedy, 1963), partly because the exercise lends itself well to delegation and a division of labor.

Ammons and Ammons (1959b, p. 719) have detailed the similarities that subjects see between the anagram task and real life problem solving. The following list summarizes some of these similarities:

1. Rearrangement of elements into new combinations is called for
2. Many solutions are possible, and differences among them are easily distinguishable
3. Problems vary in difficulty as perceived by Ss
4. Solutions are perceived by Ss as being more or less satisfactory
5. Informed ("literate") Ss can find some solutions, but never all; solutions are not seen as simple

6. Greater flexibility of attack on a problem leads to more solutions

7. Solutions vary in originality

Thus, it appears that some properties of problem solving are retained in this task, and appropriate structural features, such as are present in the next task, can be added easily. These additions would then provide conditions for studying organizational problem solving.

DETECTIVE STORIES (BURNS, 1964)

Seven persons are arranged in a three-level hierarchical structure. The only way they can communicate is by telephone. An intact detective story is divided into forty pieces, the pieces are scrambled and then distributed among the seven members. The task is to assemble the complete story as quickly as possible. Each person can talk to only one person at a time and lateral communications are prohibited. If equal power is desired, then conference calls can be permitted.

There are several reasons why this exercise has more organizational content than the anagram task. At a superficial level, it involves telephones which are a common item for transacting organizational business; but, more importantly, the telephone permits the person to clarify his remarks immediately if they are misunderstood. Unlike note-writing, which is the preferred means of communication in many organizational studies (e.g., Kelley, 1951), phones do not encourage cryptic communiqués. Furthermore, phone conversations enable one to detect, from verbal cues, how a message is received. The phone study also involves a larger group than is commonly found in networks (maximum of five persons). Since a participant can talk to only one person at a time, he must contend with the possibility that workers will devise other problem-solving procedures that involve less dependence on him. In the telephone task, persons in central positions have to do more work to get crucial items of information. In the network, they can set their own pace because they receive notes simultaneously from several persons and can respond when they are ready. In the telephone task, time may be taken from problem solving to try to contact a worker who is already talking to someone else.

Because of the several alternatives that it unfolds and the contingencies involved, this task has several properties found in natural organizations.

GROUP DISCUSSION (HOFFMAN, HARBURG, AND MAIER, 1962)

A considerable portion of organizational activity involves talking. Dubin (1962, pp. 13–14) reports the following two observations: "In the sheer volume of all activities demanded of him verbal interaction is the No. 1 form of contact, consuming upward of 80 percent of all the executive's time. . . . Only 12 times in 35 days of observation was this chief executive able to work undisturbed alone in his office during intervals of 23 minutes or longer." Although the telephone task captures some of this verbal interaction, a more direct means is to have several persons discuss face to face a problem of relevance to organizations as if they were members of the organization. Hoffman et al (1962, p. 206) studied the Change of Work Procedure problem which is a "role playing situation involving a conflict between a foreman and his subordinate workers about the relative merits of two work methods."

The use of group discussion is relevant to organizational theory, not because the group is regarded as a model of an organization, but because it replicates a common occurrence in organizations. Variables that affect the content and form of group discussions are apt to be variables of considerable importance in organizational theory. Assuming that persons implement group decisions, knowledge of the antecedents of these conditions assumes considerable importance. In addition, a group discussion task is equivalent to an all-to-all communication network, so it can be analyzed for its structural implications. Central structures can be allowed to emerge (Hutte, 1965) or they can be imposed by the experimenter (Delbecq, 1965). The meetings need not consist of role playing; they can be used for members to report on the progress of their work.

CARD SORTING (FRENCH AND SNYDER, 1959)

With the possible exception of the anagram task, none of the tasks sampled so far have content that explicitly models a production situation. The card sorting task involves a tangible product, supervisor-subordinate relations, a work-group, group outputs, and mediated interaction. Three workers are given the task of hand sorting a large pile of IBM cards into one of five trays depending on how many punches they contain. Each card has from 21 to 25 punches. This range was chosen purposely to prevent subjects from sorting each card simply on the basis of a quick glance; instead, the workers have to count the holes on each card. Yet the time to sort each card is short enough that partially completed units will have little effect on the productivity measure. Since all three workers sort cards into a common tray, individual contributions are obscured and it is not possible for members to compete with each other for favor with the supervisor who is in another room.

Because of the simplicity of the exercise, individual differences in learning and ability have little effect on the results. Measures of quality (number of cards sorted incorrectly) and quantity are readily available. Finally there is the extremely important property that there is room for an increase or decrease in productivity to occur. The authors state that they wanted the task to be "as routine and uninteresting as possible so that the restraining forces of satiation would prevent maximum performance even during the short time of the experiment" (French and Snyder, 1959, p. 131). It is important to build in satiation so that differences in productivity can occur. A common problem in many experiments is that all subjects work up to full capacity throughout the exercise with the result that dependent variables are insensitive to the manipulations.

Although the subjects still are clearly in an experiment, they experience several contingencies that are quite similar to those in natural organizations. This task represents a transition from the abstract laboratory task of remote relevance to organizations, to studies that are property-rich in organizational features.

RAILROAD GAME (JENSEN, 1961)

Two persons are given the task of running a simulated railroad system for six days (three actual hours). Their task is considerably more comprehensive than that of persons who were sorting cards in the French and Snyder task. The railroad system has ten stations connected by six railroad routes and trains run between all stations every day. The task itself is a scheduling problem and is described to subjects in this way. "You are on the night shift. During the shift you will receive orders to send a certain number of carloads of merchandise between various points. It is your job to determine how this merchandise is to be sent, i.e., in what kinds of cars and over what routes" (Jensen, 1961, p. 61). Subjects are paid a fee for each shipment depending on the car used and the route taken. The object of the exercise is to earn as much money as possible.

Unlike any of the exercises up to this point, subjects must contend with unpredictable events in the environment. Agents at stations follow erratic schedules in sending requests for cars, and changes in the weather affect both the roadbed of the railroad and the date when crops are ready for shipment. Since the decisions made by the subjects actually affect the state of the game, they must cope with their own ineptness and misscheduling later in the game. The exercise has the appearance of a natural organization, it is labeled an organization, and the instructions legitimate this impression.

However, as complexity and realism have increased, so have the problems of knowing what determines the subject's decision. The initial instructions to the subject do not specify the tasks, positions, or functions required to perform the task. Subjects, therefore, are forced to handle organizational problems as well as scheduling problems. While these multiple demands are life-like, it becomes more difficult for the experimenter to know whether the results are due to the ways in which subjects handle the problem of organizing themselves, the ways they handle the scheduling problem, or both.

An additional characteristic of simulations such as the railroad game is that they involve hypothesis generation rather than hypothesis testing. Usually the simulation is started and observers wait to "see what happens." Although hypotheses sometimes emerge from these studies, they are often imprecise, oversimplified, and provide few leads to be followed up under more controlled conditions. This evaluation is not so much an indictment of simulations as it is a caution to investigators who believe that the simulation of an organization is equivalent to understanding it. Simulations often invite tampering, but they seldom invite rigor.

COMMUNITY EXERCISE (SCHEIN AND KING, 1964)

Somewhat more elaborate, but still ideally suited to laboratory administration over a finite period of time, is the two-part community exercise. During the first part (2½ hours) subjects design and build houses from tape and 3×5 cards in competition with other firms. Frequent profit reports, bonuses for novel design, declining prices when the market is glutted, short production periods, pre-exercise planning, strict rules concerning acceptability of construction, group election of the manager, and the manager's appointment of his assistant lend both credibility and interest to the exercise. The second part of the exercise requires each group to plan and draw on a large piece of wrapping paper, a model residential community complete with parks, trees, and the houses built during the first part of the exercise. When the community has been designed, the manager must make a five-minute sales presentation "emphasizing the valuable features of the community design." The proposals of competing groups are judged on functionality, attractiveness, and the presentation.

Execution of the community task is complicated by a major change which is made between periods one and two. The managers and assistant managers of the winning and losing groups assume new positions. The manager of the winning group is transferred and now manages the losing group; the manager of the losing group is demoted to assistant manager of that group; the assistant manager in the losing group is transferred to the winning group as assistant manager "to gain experience" and the assistant manager in the winning group is promoted to manager. These changes pyramid the problems of the losing group. Not only do they have the stigma of losing and a greater desire to win, but they also "desire to defend their general manager who has been 'demoted,' [and] desire to show up their new general manager from the winning group" (King, 1964, p. 2)

One of the advantages this and similar exercises (e.g., Bass, 1963; Bass and Vaughn, 1963; Kennedy, 1963) have is that a tangible product is involved. Errors in production are more apparent, progress is evident, differences in tasks are clear, time is occupied, and management and production distinctions are more obvious. Despite the fact that the exercise covers a relatively short time, the problem is scaled down sufficiently that participants still deal with several organizational activities—finance, engineering design and layout, production, sales—without being overwhelmed by their magnitude. Basically, the exercise is simple, and it becomes complicated only as participants try a greater number and variety of strategies. The community exercise also involves considerable visible activity. The planning discussions, construction activities, evaluations of profit and other activities, permit the experimenter to observe what occurs. This is not always possible when a very small number of persons are involved or when the task requires considerable silent calculation. Because of the simplicity of the exercise, manipulations do not "get lost" in the proliferation of activities, controls can be made explicit, and measurements are less ambiguous. However, the cautions voiced earlier are still relevant. Simulations often induce method-centering rather than problem-centering. It is interesting to note that there is possibly less temptation to stand and gaze at a simple simulation than at a complex one. Manipulations are more plausible and should have more impact on a simple system than on a complex one. Or at least the effects of the manipulation will be easier to trace.

AIRCRAFT MAINTENANCE (ENKE, 1958)

In order to determine the feasibility of three new logistics policies at Air Force bases, Enke constructed two sets of air defense interceptor squadrons that were similar in every way except for the policies. The simulations were extensive. Not only were air bases, overhaul depots, parts repair departments, storage sites, and headquarters offices created, but also factory, transportation, and storage facilities where problems of delay and increased costs could occur. Each hour of laboratory time was the equivalent of one day of flight activities. The experiment lasted the equivalent of five years of the expected life of the aircraft. Each squadron "had the same aircraft, with the same parts, which malfunctioned on the same numbered flight" (Enke, 1958, p. 287). The major dependent variables were costs and number of aircraft in commission and combat-ready under each logistics system.

Such an elaborate simulation is a close approximation to a real organization, the major differences being the reductions in time and number of persons operating each facility. These losses are compensated for by the lengthy run of the system and the multiple contingencies that participants have to handle. It is especially important to have long runs when policy innovations are being tested. Enke (1958, p. 291) reports that it took some time for the managers to become familiar with the new policies and accept them. These problems of learning and acceptance, incidentally, are valuable clues to what may occur if the procedures become adopted throughout the Air Force. For example, one of the new policies required that each base transfer its inventory and record-keeping activities to a data processing center that was several hundred miles away. Reorders were made by the computer, not by the men at the base where the stock was housed. This policy represented a rather drastic change in job control and content for base personnel. When attempts are made to study the effects of new policies by using short-term laboratory studies (e.g., Bass, 1963), participants may be forced to use these new policies before they understand how they work. This means that the success of failure of the new policy may be difficult to interpret.

Enke's work is valuable because it illustrates the use of an elaborate simulation to test explicit hypotheses. He discovered that even though the new policies were responsible for considerable savings, they left the system vulnerable when a "war" occurred unexpectedly. Although fewer parts were destroyed under the new system because the inventory was dispersed, a policy of deferred purchasing led to an inadequate number of parts being stocked. The war occurred before the deferred purchase had been made.

Enke (1958) also hints at a subtle problem in managing a simulation of this magnitude that may affect the generality of the results. Because time and personnel were reduced, some additional procedures and forms were needed to permit the simulation to run. The missing people were replaced by forms. Enke reports that these forms and procedures "would not have been practical in actual Air Force organizations" (p. 292). Therefore, to the degree that the success of the newer policies was due to these procedural shortcuts rather than to the superiority of the policy itself, different outcomes might be anticipated. Fortunately, there is every possibility that the adequacy with which the other features were replicated simply "washed out" any major effect of these shortcuts. Just as it may be harder to generate a manipulation that has a strong impact on a complex simulation, so it may be harder for a single error or change to alter it.

PROOFREADING (ADAMS AND JACOBSEN, 1964)

One way for an organization to be created in the laboratory is for the experimenter to build it. Another way is for the *subject* to build it. This is essentially what occurs when a subject is hired "through normal channels" to work in what appears to be an actual, ongoing organization. If the hiring procedures are plausible and authentic, few additional organizational props are needed. The subject will "fill-in" the appropriate superstructure from the supervisor's "orientation" lecture and from his own experiences with other organizations. The replica is concrete *to the subject*, it only looks artificial and incomplete to the outsider. Psychological representation assumes considerable importance under these conditions.

Several persons have used hiring procedures to manipulate organizational content (e.g., Adams and Jacobsen, 1964; Evan and Zelditch, 1961; Wager and Palola, 1964). Adams and Jacobsen hired persons for part-time employment to proofread a manuscript on human relations. As part of the orientation procedure, the subject completed an application form and took a bogus test of proofreading ability. Undoubtedly the subjects saw the organization to be quite small since they were not exposed to any other members. This is in contrast to the situation created by Evan and Zelditch (1961) where "workers" actually saw other persons who presumably worked at other jobs within the organization. However, even these exposures were minimal because the subjects' contacts were mainly with one person, a supervisor, and these contacts were made by telephone. Extensive and extended contact with fellow workers and various levels of the organization is most apparent in the attempt by Wager and Palola (1964) to actually start and maintain an organization in the laboratory.

Although studies in which subjects were hired seldom explore the degree to which the subject felt he was in an organization, it appears that the channels through which the job was announced, as well as the orientation activities, should not have aroused suspicions. Undoubtedly a student who works part-time for a company during the summer or a university holiday is less concerned with job security, job content, and hours, than is a person for whom the job is a more significant portion of his life space. As yet, there are few data concerning how important this difference in setting is. However, given the experimenter's concern with activating organizational concerns in the laboratory, hiring manipulations seem to be especially potent.

CONCLUSION

To learn about organizations, an experimenter can create relevant processes with varying degrees of attention to the context in which they occur. The process can be established with virtually no explicit tie to organizational properties and in a form different from that in which it naturally occurs. Or both the form and context of the process can assume increasingly natural forms. Since many experiments are tests of theory, resemblance is less important than observability. However, when organizational properties can affect the hypothesized relationship, they may be added to the design if they do not render the measurements meaningless. The principal differences among the preceding tasks are summarized by McGrath (1964, p. 537). He notes that laboratory experiments (abstract tasks in the present discussion) contain discrete trials; the situations are unaffected by the responses of subjects, and generic structures and processes are not closely modeled after everyday life. Simulations (concrete tasks) have continuous stimulus situations that are modeled after real life in which the subject's responses determine the nature of subsequent stimuli.

GAINS AND LOSSES IN THE LABORATORY

While laboratory experimentation as a method of investigation solves some problems, it creates others. The purpose of this section is to detail several problems that may plague the organizational researcher when he turns to the laboratory. These problems are not unsolvable, but they must be identified before anything can be done about them. The advantages of laboratory methods have been well documented elsewhere (e.g., Campbell and Stanley, 1963; Festinger, 1953; Weick, 1965; Zigler, 1963). We will be content in this discussion to suggest some of these gains by means of an example comparing a laboratory and field experiment of the same organizational process. Although the example suggests some gains in the laboratory, it does so more by pointing to faults of the field than by pointing to strengths of the laboratory. After the two experiments have been compared, several problems will be described.

EMOTIONAL DISRUPTION IN THE FIELD AND LABORATORY

Many investigators have puzzled over the question, "Why do changes in organizational procedure often disrupt activities for extended periods of time?" To learn more about changeovers, Schachter, Willerman, Festinger, and Hyman (1961) studied the effects of emotional arousal on the performance of manual tasks before and after the task had been changed. It was hypothesized that harassments would have little effect on habituated or stereotyped activities such as assembly-line work because these activities are executed with little concentration. Even if the harassment disturbs thinking processes, there should be no visible effects. However, when a change in activity occurs, the new task would require close attention until it is learned. A history of prior harassment would be likely to hinder the learning and performance of the new task. The purpose of the field experiment was to test these predictions.

Actually a relatively simple situation is required. "It was the intent of the manipulations to make one set of groups disturbed and upset and the other set as happy as possible" (Schachter et al., 1961, p. 203). The basic experiment was replicated three times using matched assembly lines. The "disfavored" groups received almost daily annoyances for periods ranging from two-to-four weeks before the changeover. Because of considerations of appropriateness, the content of the harassments differed markedly although they apparently had in common continual criticisms of the quality of work performance. Criticisms seldom involved problems unrelated to work. Favored groups were fussed over and sheltered from irritations during this period.

In the execution of the studies, problems were legion. As the authors modestly note, "the problems of attempting to keep tight control of the experimental situation in the hubbub of a major industrial operation forced us to abandon many of these [methodological] niceties if we were to have any experiment at all" (ibid. p. 205). To minimize plant-wide disruptions during the changeovers, rigid schedules were made and could not be changed. When a snowstorm occurred on the day of the planned changeover in one study, only a very few of the experimental subjects could get to work. Replacement operators filled in for the workers who were absent and thereby destroyed the harassment manipulation. Additional groups were lost because workers had instituted an informal job rotation system and, therefore, were not "habituated" prior to the changeover. To conceal the fact that an experiment was being conducted, workers were not interviewed, meaning that valuable data were lost. Favored and disfavored groups occasionally worked different shifts. It was impossible to control discussions among workers off the job. Although no information is given about how the changeover was explained to the workers, it is possible that the results were due to a subtle difference introduced here, and not to the previous harassments. For example, in one of the replications, the change involved "dropping one of the seven assembly workers from the line. Her job was redistributed among the remaining assemblers" (ibid. p. 206). Since all experimental groups had supposedly been together at least six months, it is conceivable that the choice of the person who was removed could have affected the reaction to the changeover. By chance, an informal leader might have been removed in the "disfavored" group, but not in the "favored" group.

Despite such problems, data were collected and the hypotheses seemingly were confirmed although no statistical tests were performed. The complications in this study make it more difficult to know what mechanism mediates these results, or even if there is a stable result that needs to be explained. Although the three studies were described as replications, the situations, tasks, and measures were sufficiently different to raise questions of comparability.

An attempt was made by Latane and Arrowood (1963) to test the identical hypothesis under laboratory conditions. Subjects were presented with a display containing three switches and three lights. Their initial task was to anticipate which light would turn on next by pressing the appropriate switch. The lights followed a simple repetitive sequence that was easily learned and that was paced by the subject. After the task changeover, subjects were to press the switch of the same *color* as the light which was to come on. Previously, they had responded to position.

Harassment occurred after twelve minutes on the first task and arrived in the form of complaining, hostile female (subjects were male) who soundly criticized the subject for the way in which he had filled out a questionnaire at the start of the experiment. The non-harassment condition involved the same instigator, although now she mildly approved the subjects. After the unfriendly female left, the subjects continued the task for three minutes and then changed to the new task which they performed for eight minutes.

The results indicate that the female's harangue left the subjects significantly more tense, but not any more anxious, irritated, content, or happy than the control group. The differences in productivity following the changeover confirmed the predictions. The harassed group did significantly more poorly than the non-harassed group, although the effect was short-lived. Furthermore, the harassment did not affect performance before the changeover. Both groups performed equally well after the encounter but before the change to the new task.

These results are interesting, partly because they demonstrate similar findings in a field experiment and in a contrived laboratory situation. But even more striking is the fact that these similarities occur even though there are marked differences in time span. "While Schachter et al. prolonged their emotional manipulation over 2–4 weeks, we used 2 minutes, while their subjects had become stereotyped on the same job for untold months, ours had to learn a task in 12 minutes. It is not inconsistent, then, that the emotion-produced decrement on nonstereotyped production which they observed lasted from 1 to 3 weeks after changeover, while we obtained effects for only 3 minutes" (Latané and Arrowood, 1963, p. 326). The experiment was not without its shortcomings. The performance curves for the first task were still increasing when the changeover occurred, thereby rendering more questionable the argument that stereotypy had developed. The lesser impact of the emotional disruption may have been due to a weaker manipulation, but it may also reflect stoicism among the male subjects. It will be recalled that the study by Schachter et al. involved mainly females.

It is worthwhile to speculate on how the laboratory findings would be regarded if the related field experiment did not exist. The outcomes are similar and the procedures in the laboratory experiment provide fewer bases for alternative explanations. Schachter et al. have some indication that the effect holds across industrial situations, across tasks, and with subjects who are probably older and more experienced than those in the laboratory. Juxtaposition of the two studies increases the plausibility of the hypothesis. It also indicates the distinct differences in time and financial costs between the laboratory and the field. Perhaps the most apparent fact from this comparison is that controls such as randomization and replication (Blalock, 1963, p. 401) are important and that they can be attained with more certainty when the experimenter can create the situation to his liking than when he is concerned about disrupting factory production.

It is also valuable to compare the question of motivation in the two populations of subjects. McGrath (1964, p. 537) contends that "one important feature of data obtained from a 'real-life' situation is that the humans in that situation are operating under natural (not necessarily stronger) motivational forces, since the phenomena being studied are a part of their actual lives." Our earlier discussion of similarities between the laboratory and the field would suggest that both situations create "natural motivational forces" that are "part of actual lives." It is possible that the harassments were more meaningful in the field because they occurred in a familiar context and because they had implications for the amount of money the worker would earn. It is not clear, however, that there was any less suspicion in the field than in the laboratory. A sudden upswing in harassments is just as apt to be unnatural in the field as in the sudden arrival of a bellowing female in the laboratory. The harassment may be dealt with in different ways. For example, subjects in the laboratory had to solve the problem themselves whereas the workers in the field study could talk with their fellow workers. To argue, however, that the subject's concern in the field is any more real or relevant is to deny that subjects ever get involved in laboratory exercises. And evidence suggests that they do and that experimenters can heighten this involvement.

PROBLEMS OF INTERNAL VALIDITY

Having suggested some of the reasons why persons might wish to use the laboratory, we will describe some additional reasons why they might not. The problems to be discussed are some that are particularly bothersome in conducting organizational experiments. Using Campbell's (1957) classification, the errors will be divided crudely into those that affect internal validity and those that affect external validity. Internal validity is the basic minimum that any experiment must possess. The criterion by which it is evaluated is, "Did in fact the experimental stimulus make some significant difference in this specific intance?" (Campbell, 1957, p. 297). It is not infrequent for some variables other than the ones manipulated to influence systematically the results. If the experimenter fails to realize this, the findings he reports are incorrect in the sense that they are not a function of the manipulated antecedent. Internal validity is concerned with constructing experiments so that it is clear precisely what is controlling changes in the dependent variable. The problem of internal validity, in short, is to establish that the experimenter has actually found what he thinks he found.

Campbell (1957) discusses several quite general hindrances to internal validity. The present listing differs in that it is representative rather then comprehensive, specific rather than general, and, therefore, may apply only to certain kinds of experiments. The errors discussed below are intended to suggest the kinds of procedural subtleties in an organizational experiment that could render the results equivocal. It is anticipated that, with these few examples in mind, the reader will be alerted to a general kind of problem and will be able to locate many additional instances of such errors.

1. Esteem and Degradation

When a subject agrees to be looked at, he naturally wants to know what people see. If they withhold this information, require unpleasant activities, treat him as an object, or violate other social contracts, then it is likely that the subject will become concerned about his esteem as well as the experimenter's instructions. Subsequent behavior may be affected by either or both of these sources. An internally valid experiment exists only if instrumental behaviors are disentangled from those that are expressive.

Expressive behaviors are more likely, for example, when manipulations unintentionally threaten the status of subjects. Pepitone (1964) argues that experiments on aggression, consistency, and conformity often pose dilemmas for the subject in which he feels uncertain, incompetent, or belittled. The existence of these feelings constitutes an alternative explanation for the obtained results. For example, the requirements that subjects write strong arguments opposed to their private beliefs may generate something other than cognitive dissonance. "Inconsistent behavior increases the probability of social rejection. Since rational, intelligent behavior is highly valued by other people, the individual tries to reduce or at least conceal his irrationality for fear of losing status and power or even love and security" (Pepitone, 1964, p. 46). While this explanation seems more applicable to responses that are made in the presence of peers than those made in private, it does imply that persons worry about social censure and ridicule.

Concerns about esteem often undercut attempts to have subjects actually criticize each other or report to the experimenter that they dislike another person. Jones and DeCharms (1957) reported an unwillingness among subjects to dislike a person who obstructed progress. Jones (1964) found that subjects rate a disapproving interviewer quite favorably. Sampson and Insko (1964) used most of a two hour experimental session to get a subject angry. Mills (1962) suggested that the experimenter may have little difficulty creating dislike, but he may have considerable trouble directing it. He suggested that the well known experiment by Schachter (1951) on deviation can be interpreted as displacement onto a stooge of hostility actually felt toward the experimenter. The stooge became a scapegoat because the experimenter failed to fulfill his promises to the subjects concerning the agenda of their meetings.

While one implication of these remarks is that it is difficult to create dislike in the laboratory, the more important point is that the experimenter may get some indication that dislike is present but, overriding its effects, may be actions directed toward maintaining esteem.

Esteem also affects confederacy. Paid accomplices are often used to establish experimental conditions. If subjects are unwilling to be hostile or to deviate, the experimenter can hire someone to act this way in a group. Confederates, even when adequately trained (Efran, 1961), often find their antics costly and present a less explicit and compelling performance than the experimenter requires to test his predictions. Much of the discomfort felt by accomplices occurs because they forget that the attacks which their behavior elicits are directed at *the role*, not at them personally. Professional actors (Milgram, 1963) may be successful at making this distinction, but most amateurs are not. The stooge's discomfort may be increased even more if he has some doubts about his ability to play the role. Suppose he has been trained to be a belligerent manager in a simulation and, when he acts this way, his subordinates express strong resentment. If the stooge feels that he did not play the role well and yet provoked negative reactions in the other subjects, he may convince himself that he did a good job of role playing after all, *or* he may wind up believing that he really is an unattractive person. It is not the objective adequacy of the role playing so much as the stooge's feeling of adequacy that controls this process. It is difficult to institution-alize psychopathy. To insure reliability and intensity in stooge behavior, it is necessary to realize the costs of confederacy and to provide appropriate supports in the form of adequate pre-training, props and scripts during the presentation, and decompression aimed at maintaining a separation of the role from the person.

Threats to esteem are often threats to internal validity. As long as these threats are randomized across treatments they are not a major problem. However, these threats can easily operate *differentially* within the same experiment because they are sensitive to slight differences in manipulations. When these differential effects occur, manipulated variables become clouded. Legitimation of instructions, the promise of an informative decompression, and foreknowledge of the general aims and value of experimentation may enable the subject to postpone concerns about esteem.

2. Detachment in Dyads

Field researchers report that when they become friendly with their informant, they are tempted to see the world solely from his point of view. If this occurs, the field man finds less and less that requires explanation. A related problem exists in the supposedly minimal and "programmed" contact between an experimenter and a subject. That this contact is not standardized has been suggested by several persons (Back, Hood, and Brehm, 1964; Criswell, 1958; Friedman, 1964). The problem of interest here is the way in which the number of subjects that an experimenter confronts at one time produces subtle differences in his behavior.

Schachter (1959) has discussed this problem. He noted that when subjects faced imminent electric shock, they were more anxious when this threat was made to groups of five to eight than when it was made to a single subject, even though the instructions were identical. The following is proposed as an explanation.

> Despite the experimenter's deliberate attempt to behave identically in both experiments, inevitably a more personal relationship resulted in the two-person experiment. In this two-person study, the subjects felt free to ask questions and make comments and frequently did so, resulting in a relationship more informal than in the group setting, where almost no subject seemed to feel uninhibited enough to comment freely [p. 23].

Thus as the size or intimacy of the group changes, subjects may feel more or less comfort in seeking clarification of instructions, expressing dissatisfaction, or approving the experimenter. The experimenter also may act differently in small groups. He may express more interest, be more responsive, and provide more cues about the desired response. If he has any reservations about the reasonableness of demands made upon the subject, these doubts are apt to be sharpened in a dyad and the experimenter may feel greater pressure to weaken the demands.

Obviously several of these problems decrease if all comparisons involve groups of similar size. However, many organizational experiments, especially large-scale simulations, require the experimenter to give different instructions and feedback to small subgroups. When subgroups are instructed, this increases the chances that the experimental outcomes are due not so much to the manipulated variable, as to the fact that selected portions of the instructions were better understood, that distasteful requirements were made less painful, or that some of the hypotheses were more apparent. These influences may be partly countered in simulations simply because subjects have so much factual material to remember. Furthermore, in contrast to Schachter's study, the demands on the experimenter in a simulation are more complex and, therefore, individual requests are not as likely to receive undivided attention.

Aside from the simulations, organization theorists are interested in small groups. Frequently, groups of many differing sizes are lumped into this category, and comparisons are made among experiments in which size varies. The present argument is that size may be a subtle threat to internal validity because it mediates the ease with which the experimenter can remain detached from subjects. As intimacy increases, the number of alternative explanations for a finding also increases.

3. Task Substitution

Subjects frequently work on several problems in addition to the one they have been assigned; this problem has been discussed elsewhere as the problem of redefinition (Weick, 1965). The present discussion focuses on a different aspect of the problem. It is concerned with this phenomenon solely as a problem of internal validity and seeks to avoid the implication that the subject accepts the experimenter's definition before he alters it. Sometimes the subject's task is totally different from the one assigned by the experimenter. Hence, the label "task substitution" is used. While task substitution takes many forms, some are more relevant to organizational research than others. For example, there are several reasons why the internal validity of studies of novel structures might be suspect. Persons who perform novel tasks in unfamiliar structures often feel uncomfortable. Unfortunately, they often interpret this discomfort as a sign of inefficiency, and they proceed to alter the task and/or the structure "to make it more efficient." "Players will equate uncomfortable or strange relations with ineffective relations and fail to give innovative schemes a fair trial. Their behavior is quite rational. They want to win, and the game will last a short time. All the pressure is to convert the new scheme into the old, tried-and-true way of doing things." (Bass, 1964, p. 4). Alterations to increase efficiency do not have to be drastic. They may even go unnoticed. Nevertheless, if alterations are present, the intended structure is not and the experimental outcomes have different antecedents.

There are occasions when just the opposite problem occurs, when persons retain intact a task they are supposed to change. Persons may be given a task but not enough information to complete it (Evan and Zelditch, 1961), they may be placed in a structure that contains contradictory requirements, they may be placed with a partner who is ill suited for a job. The reason for these assignments is that the experimenter wants to force the subjects to make some changes. It is assumed that if persons are bothered by these circumstances, they will try to make them more acceptable. The experimenter wants to find out what is more acceptable and how it is adopted. Unfortunately, persons tend to invest their environment—whatever its content—with meaning, and typically they are reluctant to make changes. They may presume that the experimenter would not have assigned them a structure unless he thought it to be worthwhile. Guetzkow and Bowes (1957) suggest that subjects rarely revise imposed requirements because they are uncertain which revisions are within the rules of the game and which are not. This uncertainty is especially pronounced when lengthy instructions precede task performance.

In short, subjects often make sense out of experimental conditions when they are not supposed to. If subjects "rationalize nonrational requirements" internal validity is lessened. When a novel structure affects behavior, the effect may be due to the reasonableness of the structure instead of its novelty.

Task substitution may also originate in triviality. Many experimental tasks require little concentration and permit the subject to think about other things while he is working. These distractions often become more interesting than the task at hand and the outcomes of the experiment reflect a preoccupation with the substitute task. Rather than working on two tasks simultaneously, the subject may simply change the trivial task to make it more interesting. Schultz (1964, p. 397) argues that a considerable portion of a subject's behavior in experiments can be viewed as an attempt to vary the pattern of stimulation that reaches him. Thus a subject may alternate his responses in order to introduce a change in the number, nature, and temporal sequence of stimuli in his surroundings. Conditions that are especially prone to produce alternation behavior are

(1) no reinforcement and/or knowledge of correctness of response, (2) great similarity between stimuli, (3) prolonged exercise of one response alternative, and (4) a short intertrial interval.

Thus, a simple cooperative game may be made competitive to increase its interest. Friedell (1964, p. 7) suggests that this is a common occurrence. "In many experimental games cooperation is boring and competition is interesting. Cooperative behavior may be represented by monotonous sameness of choice, while competition may involve variety. A structural reason for this is that effective competition often requires that one's opponent cannot predict one's strategy. In symmetrical games competition presents the attraction of testing oneself against a peer rather than a simple situation. Thus, subjects may actually cooperate by tacitly agreeing to compete."

Substitution because of triviality implies that simulations have an advantage because the subject has no time to make substitutions; too many things are going on. Herein lies one of the dilemmas in an organizational experiment. Presumably a simple task is preferable to a complex one and a simple environment is preferable to one with multiple happenings, because the subject can understand the assignment more quickly, there are fewer sources of distraction and, therefore, the independent variables should be less ambiguous. But, when these conditions exist, the subject also may have time on his hands and dream up variations of the basic task. A complex simulation leaves little time for fabrication, but it generates a different kind of substitution. The more an experimental setting resembles a real-life organization, the more an individual is prone to act as if the organization were real and not contrived. This may aid involvement, but it also means that the subject will impose constraints and definitions where none exist, ignore experimental requirements and definitions not in the actual organization, and redefine his position so that it accords with his position in natural organizations. In short, simulations encourage assimilation, simple settings encourage contrast. In both cases, substitutions make the experiment even less like an organization than it really is.

A substitute task is, by definition, not the task assigned by the experimenter or the one he wanted to study. If the substitution is undetected, the experiment has less internal validity.

4. Counter-Reference Demands

Experimental demands often require subjects to perceive or act in ways that are contrary to those which are valued in their reference groups. These contradictory demands may unintentionally produce ambivalence, uncertainty, or vacillation. When these conditions exist, they provide alternative explanations of experimental outcomes.

It may be argued that reference groups are not salient when a subject participates in experiments. However, it is probable that there are more cues that reinstate reference groups than are realized. For one thing, subjects are typically recruited from a homogeneous population. If they had not been members of a particular group, they would not have been contacted for the experiment. Thus, recruitment makes reference groups salient. Furthermore, the experimental instructions often remind the subject of a reference group. He is told that his responses are of interest because he is a typical college student, an engineer, a sophomore, a male, an adult, a psychology student, or an average human being. Although these instructions are usually intended merely to distract or heighten plausibility, they may lead the subject to act as if he is a member of that group. Relevance of a task or a dilemma to specific groups should also heighten their prominence as determinants of subsequent behavior. Jones and DeCharms (1957) report a study involving naval cadets where norms that were created experimentally clashed strongly with existing cadet norms. Subjects were asked to decide what disciplinanry actions should be administered to a turncoat. In one condition, the subjects were told that the norms for judging whether or not a person was a turncoat were unclear. The cadets, however, simply could not accept this information. Undoubtedly the combination of recruitment of a specific group plus a relevant issue contributed to the weakening of this manipulation. Loyalties to the Navy may well have been pitted against felt obligations to the experimenter. Ambivalence was clearly the product. Demands that are inconsistent with reference groups probably can never be completely ruled out of experiments, especially vivid simulations. If experimental conditions are linked randomly with various reference groups, internal validity is not threatened. The implication is that the experimenter should assess whether a reference effect occurred, should examine manipulations to see if they make particular reference groups salient, and, in general, should look for uncertainty or ambivalence as competing explanations of experimental outcomes.

Summary

An apparent relationship among variables may actually reflect attempted solutions to maintenance problems, differential understanding of instructions and preferred behaviors, performance of unassigned tasks, or tenuous resolutions of contradictory demands. These threats to internal validity are common in organizational experiments, are difficult to randomize, and are sensitive to slight changes in an independent variable. They are also difficult to detect. Changes in realism reduce some problems but create other ones. That the recognition and solution of these problems is mandatory can be seen if one looks at the next source of problems, external validity. External validity is concerned with generalization, and one needs to worry about generalization only when there is something to generalize from, namely a stable and valid relationship.

PROBLEMS OF EXTERNAL VALIDITY

Once an experimenter knows something about his laboratory subjects, he wants to know what he has also learned about other populations. This is the problem of external validity. External validity is concerned with the representativeness or generalizability of experimental findings. The criterion is, "To what populations, settings, and variables can this effect be generalized?" (Campbell, 1957, p. 297). External validity is restricted when conditions in the experiment are hard to find in everyday life. If the features of an experiment are rare, it is reasonable to conclude that the incidence of the demonstrated relationship will also be rare.

The following discussion describes five characteristics of experiments that hinder generalization.

1. Task Prominence

Experimental tasks differ from everyday tasks in several ways, the most obvious being that they command undivided attention from the subject. Even if the task is boring and the subject embellishes or makes substitutions for it, a single task is still involved. This contrasts with everyday life where attention is diffuse, where several tasks compete for attention (Atkinson and Cartwright, 1964), and where the existence of alternative tasks affects present productivity (Feather, 1963). Performance in the laboratory seldom reflects these competing demands on effort. As a result, laboratory findings may not hold up when replicated in the field where competing demands exist.

In addition to being prominent, laboratory tasks are also bounded. The subjects know that laboratory events will last for only a short time. Furthermore, many tasks have discrete trials and this may disrupt continuity, concentration, or the feeling that one is accomplishing a significant piece of work. The laboratory exercise, like assembly-line activity, is repetitious and movements become stereotyped (Schachter et al., 1961). These characteristics of tasks are relevant to external validity because they suggest that laboratory findings may obtain if the subject has circumscribed experiences and small exposure to the independent variable but that, as experiences lengthen and exposure becomes more intense and prolonged, relationships will change.

Laboratory tasks are often chosen for their sensitivity to independent variables (Hovland, 1959) and their openness to observation, not their representativeness. Unfortunately, not enough is known about tasks to be certain whether properties that promote sensitivity are also properties that materially affect a relationship when they are absent. The question of sensitivity is not to be confused with the argument that a highly sensitive task is "rigged" so that it amplifies what is, in reality, a trivial relationship. A sensitive task may magnify an insignificant effect. But that is not our concern here. Instead, assuming that some common elements are necessary for generalization, if features that aid sensitivity are features that also have to be present in the actual event for generalization to occur, then it may be difficult to obtain external validity.

A final task variable that may affect external validity is that of error prominence. When organizational activities are scaled down to fit the laboratory, it is seldom possible also to scale down the impact on the system of human errors. As a consequence, errors that would have only a slight effect on a natural system are a major disruption in a contrived system. Bass (1964, p. 5) describes the possible effects in a laboratory exercise of a minor managerial blunder. "As in real-life, a manager may blurt out the wrong words resulting in a 'wildcat' strike, and production will close momentarily. In real-life, this real effect may reduce industry-wide production by, say, 2 percent. In our game, it may reduce it by 35 percent for a given firm. Or, it might easily bankrupt a company in our game; it seldom does in real life." Errors frequently are handled in natural organizations with little enduring effect on the system. Experimental findings may have limited generality because they obtain only when errors have a marked impact on outcomes.

The preceding examples suggest that experimental tasks differ from everyday tasks along dimensions that may affect external validity. Simplicity itself does not necessarily threaten external validity. It depends on what is simplified, the rarity with which experimental task properties exist in everyday tasks, and the centrality of the property for generalization.

2. Limited Alternatives

Just as it makes a difference in productivity whether a person is constrained to one task or several, so it also makes a difference whether a subject feels that he is a member of one group or several. The presence or absence of alternative tasks or groups often has a marked effect on a person's perception of his situation. Kiesler and Corbin (1965) report that conformity decreases linearly as group attractiveness decreases, *unless* the individual is committed to the group, i.e., has a high probability of continued future membership. When a commitment exists there is considerable discomfort if one learns that the group actually is unattractive. To resolve this discomfort, the subject could either devalue the group or enhance it by trying to conform to and be more like the other members. Since devaluation is not wholly satisfying given the prospect of continued membership, increased conformity should occur and Kiesler and Corbin (1965) found that it did.

The implication of these results is that perceived longevity of group membership and the feeling of volition in becoming a group member have a marked effect on subsequent behavior. Even when duration and commitment are not manipulated, the experimenter should assess the subject's conception of these features of group life since they may influence the results. The easiest solution to a discomforting situation is to disown one's acts, reject the group, or be indifferent. Furthermore, realignment of group ties is a common response in everyday life. When these alternatives are unavailable in the laboratory, relationships between variables may be affected. The implication is that it is important to know the extent to which a subject feels he must account for and resolve experimental occurrences. Less pressure for resolution should exist if the event or group is perceived to be fleeting, if alternatives are available, or if the problems are of minor importance. As pressures for resolution increase, the findings may be less applicable to situations where persons can choose among many alternatives, one of which is escape.

3. Recruitment

Procedures to enlist subjects for an experiment may broaden or narrow the populations to which experimental findings can be generalized. Campbell (1957, p. 308) describes two principles that are relevant to recruitment as a source of bias. "The greater the cooperation required, the more the respondent has to deviate from the normal course of daily events, the greater will be the possibility of nonrepresentative reactions. . . . The longer the experiment is extended in time the more respondents are lost and the less representative are the groups of the original universe." Whenever impositions are considerable and subjects can refuse to participate, experimental results may apply only to a highly select population. By the time the experimenter has assembled a group of persons who are able to meet procedural requirements of the experiment (e.g., be free for three hours every day for a week); he may have constituted a highly select group thereby reducing external validity.

Even within a specific population, recruitment biases may appear. In academic environments, students who decide to fulfill their subject obligations early in the school year differ from those who postpone their participation until the last minute. Some manipulations are sensitive to these differences in motivation, others are not. Monetary incentives in experiments probably are more effective near the end of the month than at the start of the month. Extra credit for course grades is probably a stronger inducement after examinations are returned than before.

It is important to realize that experiments impose unique demands. Not everyone can or is willing to meet these demands. The more effort the experimenter has to exert to obtain subjects, the less representative his subjects will be.

4. First-Day-at-Work Syndrome

It is possible that experiments tell us more about how a person will act on his first day at work than on his 400th day. A person who is in an experiment, like the newcomer on a job, often has low confidence in his judgments, is easily influenced, misunderstands instructions, is uniformed, finds the job novel and interesting, is cautious, and tolerates many demands that would anger him in more familiar settings. Many of these behaviors dissipate as he becomes more accustomed to the assignment. Thus data that are collected before a job becomes routinized and familiar may have limited generality. The implication is clear that subjects should be fully instructed about a task and should perform it long enough so that they are completely familiar with it. If it is not possible to produce this much familiarity, then the experimenter should assess the role that novelty and uncertainty play in the findings. If it appears that variations in uncertainty would not change the results, or that familiarity is unrelated to the outcomes, then external validity is not jeopardized.

5. Multi-determinants

Perhaps the most general problem of external validity concerns the fact that field events are affected by more variables than are present when laboratory events occur. These additional variables could increase the magnitude of a laboratory effect, or they could wash it out. The problem is essentially one of how to handle these additional variables in the laboratory so that both control and external validity are retained. For example, if an experimenter regards five dimensions to be important for characterizing an organization and he manipulates one of these five, what should be done with the other four? Should they be ignored for the moment and treated as potential variables that might affect a relationship? Should each of the four variables be set at a value greater than zero so that they are at least present when the relationship is studied?

Undoubtedly when a person becomes highly concerned with these problems he will go to the field rather than remain in the laboratory. However, it should be remembered that the many circumstances surrounding natural events are potential rather than actual influences. If a basic process is being studied, then the question of modifications from additional variables will change the appearance of the process but not its structure.

Summary

Organizational experiments are vulnerable to several threats to external validity. An organization experiment may be unrepresentative because experimental demands impose a high attrition rate on subjects, because tasks are excessively prominent or are performed when novelty and uncertainty are at their height, or because experimental settings provide few alternatives and only a limited number of influences. Simulations are not the complete solution to problems of external validity because they also have difficulties with recruitment, task familiarity, and task prominence. Since both organizational theory and research are in their early stages, it is reasonable to expect that more attention in the immediate future will be focused on internal validity rather than external validity.

CONCLUSION

Despite the recent interest in organizational behavior on the part of behavioral scientists and the large amount of empirical data that has been collected on this problem, there are surprisingly few well-supported causal propositions about the determinants of organizationl behavior. The data and methods have often been unsuited to stating propositions of this kind. Most of the investigators who have studied organizations have been concerned chiefly with problems of external validity. The point of the present chapter is that we are unlikely to learn much about organizations unless we give just as much attention to questions of internal validity.

Laboratories often seem insignificant as a means to learn about organizations because they are judged against criteria established for the more common field investigation. Laboratory experiments often are structured quite differently from natural organizations and, for this reason, questions of generalization can be sizeable, as has been noted throughout. But there are ways in which the investigator can cope with the problem of external validity and can, therefore, benefit from the strength of the laboratory to show unambiguous causal linkages between events.

External *and* internal validity can be achieved if the experimenter moves back and forth between the laboratory and field as in the example of emotional disruption, if he moves between abstract and simulated organizations in the laboratory, or if he structures a field study so that it contains more of the controls found in the laboratory. Instead of changing his setting, the investigator may change his activities. He may establish a stable relationship in a tightly controlled situation and then lessen these constraints to see what variables condition the relationship, or he may find an interesting phenomenon and then tighten the contraints to see why it occurred. *Either* strategy is pointed toward the same eventual conclusion.

Laboratory experiments also seem useful because they press investigators to be explicit. The most common objection to the laboratory is that it does not contain several "obviously" important features of organization, e.g., a complex environment. This objection is well founded. But, when the investigator thinks in terms of building an organization in the laboratory, he has to explicate these variables, and he usually has to state why these variables must be included. It often happens that he finds that a variable really makes no difference to his problem whether it is included or not.

A final problem in laboratory experiments is that it is difficult to tell what the referent reality is for an organizational study. It is unclear what dimensions of a natural organization should be modeled in the laboratory or even what the dimensions are. It is clear that laboratories and natural organizations differ, but it is unclear which of the differences may be crucial because they condition a causal relationship. Non-obvious differences may turn out to be crucial. The point is that, until these crucial differences become clearer, considerable trial and error approximation between the two settings must occur.

Experiments have numerous shortcomings but they are also somewhat more versatile than existing folklore would suggest. As more and more of the shortcomings of the laboratory are pinpointed, it should be possible to strengthen their role in organizational research. Furthermore, an increasing number of phenomena can now be created in the laboratory and it seems clear that imaginative investigators will be able to increase the phenomena that can be brought under laboratory control. Although there is little history of organizations in the laboratory, the promise seems considerable.

REFERENCES

ABBREVIATIONS

ASR   American Sociological Review
HR   Human Relations
JAP   Journal of Applied Psychology
JASP   Journal of Abnormal and Social Psychology
MS   Management Science
SSR   Sociology and Social Research

Abelson, P. "Bigotry in Science." Science, 1964, 144, 371.
Adams, J. S. "Toward an Understanding of Inequity." JASP, 1963, 67, 422–436.
Adams, J. S. and Jacobsen, P. R. "Effects of Wage Inequities on Work Quality." JASP, 1964, 69, 19–25.
Adams, J. S. and Rosenbaum, W. B. "The Relationship of Worker Productivity to Cognitive Dissonance About Wage Inequities." JAP, 1962, 46, 161–164.
Ammons, R. B. and Ammons, C. H. "A Standard Anagram Task." Psychological Reports, 1959a, 5, 654–656.
————. "Rational Evaluation of the 'Standard Anagram Task' as a Laboratory Analogue of 'Real-Life' Problem Solving." Psychological Reports, 1959b, 5, 718–720.
Aronson, E., Turner, J. A., and Carlsmith, J. M. "Communicator Credibility and Communication Discrepancy as Determinants of Attitude Change." JASP, 1963, 67, 31–36.
Atkinson, J. W. and Cartwright, D. "Some Neglected Variables in Contemporary Conceptions of Decision and Performance." Psychological Reports, 1964, 14, 575–590.
Back, K. W., Hood, T. C., and Brehm, Mary L. "The Subject Role in Small Group Experiments." Social Forces, 1964, 43, 181–187.
Bartlett, F. C. Remembering. Cambridge: Cambridge U. Press, 1932.
Bass, B. M. "Experimenting With Simulated Manufacturing Organizations." In S. B. Sells, ed., Stimulus Determinants of Behavior. New York: Ronald, 1963, 117–196.
————. "Some Methodological Issues in Experimenting with Human Simulations of Business Firms." Paper prepared for 3rd Seminar in Social Science of Organizations, U. of Pittsburgh, 1964.
Bass, B. M. and Leavitt, H. S. "Some Experiments in Planning and Operating." MS, 1963, 9, 574–585.
Bass, B. M. and Vaughan, J. A. "Experimenting With the Man-in-the-Middle." Paper presented at 1st Seminar in Social Science of Organizations, U. of Pittsburgh, 1962.
————. "Production Organization Exercise IV." Pittsburgh: U. of Pittsburgh, Graduate School of Business, 1963.
Becker, S. W. "Organizations in the Laboratory." Paper prepared for 3rd Seminar in Social Science of Organizations, U. of Pittsburgh, 1964.

Beveridge, W. I. B. *The Art of Scientific Investigation.* New York: Norton, 1950.

Blalock, H. M. "Some Important Methodological Problems for Sociology." *SSR,* 1963, *47,* 398–407.

Blau, P. M. "The Research Process in the Study of *The Dynamics of Bureaucracy.*" In P. E. Hammond, ed., *Sociologists at Work.* New York: Basic Books, 1964, 16–49.

Boring, E. G. "Cognitive Dissonance: Its Use in Science." *Science,* 1964, *145,* 680–685.

Bruyn, S. "Rhetorical Devices in Sociological Analysis." *Sociological Qtly.,* 1964, *5,* 101–112.

Burns, T. "The Communication Exercise." Paper presented at 3rd Seminar in Social Science of Organizations, U. of Pittsburgh (Pa.), 1964.

Campbell, D. T. "Factors Relevant to the Validity of Experiments in Social Settings." *Psychological Bull.,* 1957, *54,* 297–312.

Campbell, D. T. and Stanley, J. C. "Experimental and Quasi-Experimental Designs for Research on Teaching." In N. L. Gage, ed., *Handbook of Research on Teaching.* Chicago: Rand McNally, 1963, 171–246.

Carlsmith, J. M. and Aronson, E. "Some Hedonic Consequences of the Confirmation and Disconfirmation of Expectancies." *JASP,* 1963, *66,* 151–156.

Cohen, A. R. "Upward Communication in Experimentally Created Hierarchies." *HR,* 1958, *11,* 41–53.

Cook, S. W. and Selltiz, C. "A Multiple-Indicator Approach to Attitude Measurement." *Psychological Bull.,* 1964, *62,* 36–55.

Cottrell, N. B. "Means-Interdependency, Prior Acquaintance, and Subsequent Competition." *HR,* 1963, *16,* 249–262.

Criswell, J. H. "The Psychologist as Perceiver." In R. Taguiri and L. Petrullo, eds., *Person Perception and Interpersonal Behavior.* Stanford: Stanford U. Press, 1958, 95–109.

Cyert, R. M., March, J. G., and Starbuck, W. H. "Two Experiments on Bias and Conflict in Organizational Estimation." *MS,* 1961, *7,* 254–264.

Dalton, M. "Preconceptions and Methods in *Men Who Manage.*" In P. E. Hammond, ed., *Sociologists at Work.* New York: Basic Books, 1964, 50–95.

Delbecq, A. "Managerial Leadership Styles in Problem Solving Conferences, II." *J. Academy of Management,* 1965, 8, 32–43.

Dill, W. R. "Desegregation or Integration?: Comments About Contemporary Research on Organizations." In W. W. Cooper, H. J. Leavitt, and M. W. Shelly, eds., *New Perspectives in Organization Research.* New York: Wiley, 1964, 39–52.

Dittes, J. E. and Kelley, H. H. "Effects of Different Conditions of Acceptance Upon Conformity to Group Norms." *JASP,* 1956, *53,* 100–107.

DiVesta, F. J., Meyer, D. L., and Mills, J. "Confidence in an Expert as a Function of His Judgments." *HR,* 1964, *17,* 235–242.

Dubin, R. "Business Behavior Behaviorally Viewed." In C. Argyris et al., *Social Science Approaches to Business Behavior.* Homewood, Ill.: Dorsey, 1962, 11–55.

Efran, J. S. "Descriptive Account of Training Procedures." In P. Pepinsky, ed., *Studies of the Effects of Sponsorship and Strategy Upon the Actor's*

Independence and Upon the Social Assessment of His Productivity. Columbus, Ohio: Ohio State U. Research Foundation, 1961, C37–C46.

Enke, S. "On the Economic Management of Large Organizations: A Laboratory Study." *J. Business,* 1958, *31,* 280–292.

Evan, W. M. and Zelditch, M. "A Laboratory Experiment on Bureaucratic Authority." *ASR,* 1961, *26,* 883–893.

Feather, N. T. "Persistence at a Difficult Task With Alternative Task of Intermediate Difficulty." *JASP,* 1963, *66,* 231–238.

Festinger, L. "Laboratory Experiments." In L. Festinger and D. Katz, eds., *Research Methods in the Behavioral Sciences.* New York: Holt, Rinehart & Winston, 1953, 136–172.

Festinger, L. and Carlsmith, J. M. "Cognitive Consequences of Forced Compliance." *JASP,* 1959, *58,* 203–210.

Fiedler, F. E. "A Contingency Model of Leadership Effectiveness." In L. Berkowitz, ed., *Advances in Experimental Social Psychology,* New York: Academic, 1964, I, 149–190.

French, J. R. P., Jr. and Snyder, R. "Leadership and Interpersonal Power." In D. Cartwright, ed., *Studies in Social Power.* Ann Arbor: U. of Michigan Press, 1959, 118–149.

Friedell, M. F. "The Experimental Game as an Instrument for the Study of Social Behavior." Paper presented at Midwestern Psychological Assn., 1964.

Friedman, N. "The Psychological Experiment as a Social Interaction." Unpublished Doctoral Dissertation, Harvard U., 1964.

Garfinkel, E. "A Conception of, and Experiments With 'Trust' as a Condition of Stable Concerted Actions." In O. J. Harvey, ed., *Motivation and Social Interaction.* New York: Ronald, 1963, 187–238.

Guetzkow, H. "A Use of Simulation in the Study of Inter-Nation Relations." *Behavioral Science,* 1959, *4,* 183–191.

Guetzkow, H. "Organizational Leadership in Task-Oriented Groups." In L. Petrullo and B. M. Bass, eds., *Leadership and Interpersonal Behavior.* New York: Holt, Rinehart & Winston, 1961, 187–200.

Guetzkow, H. and Bowes, A. E. "The Development of Organizations in a Laboratory." *MS,* 1957, *3,* 380–402.

Gustav, A. "Students' Attitude Toward Compulsory Participation in Experiments. *J. Psychology,* 1962, *53,* 119–125.

Harvey, O. J., ed. *Motivation and Social Interaction.* New York: Ronald, 1963.

Heider, F. "Social Perception and Phenomenal Causality. *Psychological Rev.,* 1944, *51,* 358–374.

Hoffman, L. R., Harburg, E., and Maier, N. R. F. "Differences and Disagreement as Factors in Creative Group Problem Solving." *JASP,* 1962, *64,* 206–214.

Hoffman, P. J., Festinger, L., and Lawrence, D. H. "Tendencies Toward Group Comparability in Competitive Bargaining." *HR,* 1954, *7,* 141–159.

Homans, G. C. "The Strategy of Industrial Sociology." In G. C. Homans, ed., *Sentiments and Activities.* New York: Free Press, 1962, 257–268.

Hood, T. "The Decision to Participate in Small Group Experiments: Patterns of Self Disclosure and the Volunteer." Technical Report 14, Durham, N.C.: Duke University, Dept. of Psychology, 1964.

Hovland, C. I. "Reconciling Conflicting Results Derived From Experimental and Survey Studies of Attitude Change." *American Psychologist*, 1959, *14*, 8–17.

Hovland, C. I. and Weiss, W. "The Influence of Source Credibility on Communication." *Public Opinion Qtly.*, 1952, *15*, 635–650.

Hutte, H. "Decision-Taking in a Management Game." *HR*, 1965, *18*, 5–20.

Jacobs, R. C. and Campbell, D. T. "The Perpetuation of an Arbitrary Tradition Through Several Generations of a Laboratory Microculture." *JASP*, 1961, *62*, 649–658.

Jensen, B. T. "Instructions for 'The Railroad Game.'" Technical Memorandum 608, Santa Monica, Calif.: System Development Corp., 1961.

Jensen, B. T. and Terebinski, S. J. " 'The Railroad Game:' a Tool for Research in Social Sciences. *J. Social Psychology*, 1963, *60*, 85–87.

Jones, E. E. *Ingratiation*. New York: Appleton-Century, 1964.

Jones, E. E. and DeCharms, R. "Changes in Social Perception as a Function of the Personal Relevance of Behavior." *Sociometry*, 1957, *20*, 75–85.

Joyner, R. C. "SIN–Simulation of Interaction in Communication Networks, II: Experiments With the Common Target Game." Unpublished *MS*, Carnegie Institute of Technology, 1965.

Kaplan, A. *The Conduct of Inquiry*. San Francisco: Chandler, 1964.

Kelley, H. H. "Communication in Experimentally Created Hierarchies." *HR*, 1951, *4*, 39–56.

Kelley, H. H., Condry, J. C., Jr., Dahlke, A. E., and Hill, A. H. "Collective Behavior in a Simulated Panic Situation." *J. Experimental Social Psychology*, 1965, *1*, 20–54.

Kelley, H. H., Thibaut, J. W., Radloff, R., and Mundy, D. "The Development of Cooperation in the 'Minimal Social Situation.'" *Psychological Monographs*, 1962, *76*, (19, Whole No. 538).

Kennedy, J. L. "Experimenters Manual: Research and Development Game." Unpublished MS, Princeton University, 1963.

Kiesler, C. A. and Corbin, L. H. "Commitment, Attraction, and Conformity." *J. Personality and Social Psychology*, 1965, *2*, 890–895.

King, D. C. "Summary of Intergroup Exercise I." Unpublished MS, Purdue University, 1964.

Krugman, H. E. "The 'Draw a Supermarket' Technique." *Public Opinion Qtly*, 1960, *24*, 148–149.

Krupp, S. "Pattern in Organization Analysis." New York: Holt, Rinehart & Winston, 1961.

Kuethe, J. L. "Social Schemas." *JASP*, 1962, *64*, 31–38.

Latané, B. and Arrowood, A. J. "Emotional Arousal and Task Performance." *JAP*, 1963, *47*, 324–327.

Leavitt, H. J. "Task Ordering and Organizational Development in the Common Target Game." *Behavioral Science*, 1960, *5*, 233–239.

————. "Applied Organization Change in Industry: Structural, Technical, and Human Approaches." In W. W. Cooper, H. J. Leavitt, and M. W. Shelly, eds., *New Perspectives in Organization Research*. New York: Wiley, 1964, II, 55–71.

Lewin, K. *Field Theory in Social Science*. New York: Harper, 1951.

Lorge, I., Fox, D., Davitz, J., and Brenner, M. "A Survey of Studies Contrasting the Quality of Group Performance and Individual Performance." *Psychological Bull.*, 1958, *55*, 337–370.

Lyle, J. "Communication, Group Atmosphere, Productivity, and Morale in Small Task Groups." *HR*, 1961, *14*, 369–379.

Maier, N. R. F. and Hoffman, L. R. "Organization and Creative Problem Solving." *JAP*, 1961, *45*, 277–280.

March, J. G. and Simon, H. A. *Organizations*. New York: Wiley, 1958.

Marx, M. H. "The General Nature of Theory Construction." In M. H. Marx, ed., *Theories in Contemporary Psychology*. New York: Macmillan, 1963, 4–46.

McGrath, J. E. "Toward a 'Theory of Method' for Research on Organizations." In W. W. Cooper, H. J. Leavitt, and M. W. Shelley, eds., *New Perspectives in Organization Research*. New York: Wiley, 1964, 533–556.

Mechanic, D. "Some Considerations in the Methodology of Organizational Studies." In H. Leavitt, ed., *The Social Science of Organizations*. Englewood Cliffs: Prentice-Hall, 1963, 139–182.

Meier, R. C. "Explorations in the Realm of Organization Theory IV: The Simulation of Social Organization. *Behavioral Science*, 1961, *6*, 232–248.

Milgram, S. "Behavioral Study of Obedience." *JASP*, 1963, *67*, 371–378.

Milgram, S. "Issues in the Study of Obedience: a Reply to Baumrind." *American Psychologist*, 1964, *19*, 848–852.

Miller, L. K. and Hamblin, R. L. "Interdependence, Differential Rewarding, and Productivity. *ASR*, 1963, *28*, 768–778.

Mills, T. M. A Sleeper Variable in Small Groups Research: The Experimenter. *Pacific Sociological Rev.*, 1962, 5 (1), 21–28.

Orne, M. T. "On the Social Psychology of the Psychological Experiment: With Particular Reference to Demand Characteristics and Their Implications." *American Psychologist*, 1962, *17*, 776–783.

Pepitone, A. *Attraction and Hostility*. New York: Atherton, 1964.

Pilisuk, M. "Cognitive Balance and Self-Relevant Attitudes." *JASP*, 1962, *65*, 95–103.

Proshansky, H. and Seidenberg, B., eds., *Basic Studies in Social Psychology*. New York: Holt, Rinehart & Winston, 1965.

Raven, B. H. and Eachus, H. T. "Cooperation and Competition in Means-Interdependent Triads." *JASP*, 1963, *67*, 307–316.

Riecken, H. W. "A Program for Research on Experiments in Social Psychology." In N. F. Washburne, ed., *Decisions, Values, and Groups*. New York: Macmillan, 1962, II, 25–41.

Ring, K. "Some Determinants of Interpersonal Attraction in Hierarchical Relationships: A Motivational Analysis. *J. Personality*, 1964, *32*, 651–665.

Roby, T. B. "Subtask Phasing in Small Groups." In J. H. Criswell, H. Solomon, and P. Suppes, eds., *Mathematical Methods in Small Group Processes*. Stanford: Stanford U. Press, 1962, 263–281.

Roby, T. B. and Lanzetta, J. T. "Considerations in the Analysis of Group Tasks. *Psychological Bull.*, 1958, *55*, 88–101.

Rosenberg, M. J. "When Dissonance Fails: On Eliminating Evaluation Apprehension from Attitude Measurement." *J. Personality and Social Psychology*, 1965, *1*, 28–42.

Rosenberg, M. J. and Abelson, R. P. "An Analysis of Cognitive Balancing." In M. J. Rosenberg et al., *Attitude Organization and Change*. New Haven: Yale U. Press, 1960, 112–163.

Rosenthal, R. "On the Social Psychology of the Psychological Experiment: The Experimenter's Hypothesis as Unintended Determinant of Experimental Results. *American Scientist,* 1963, *51,* 268–283.

Sampson, E. E. and Insko, C. A. "Cognitive Consistency and Performance in the Autokinetic Situation." *JASP,* 1964, *68,* 184–192.

Schachter, S. "Deviation, Rejection, and Communication." *JASP,* 1951, *46,* 190–207.

――――. *The Psychology of Affiliation.* Stanford: Stanford U. Press, 1959.

Schachter, S. and Singer, J. E. "Cognitive, Social, and Physiological Determinants of Emotional State." *Psychological Rev.,* 1962, *69,* 379–399.

Schachter, S., Willerman, B., Festinger, L., and Hyman, R. "Emotional Disruption and Industrial Productivity." *JAP,* 1961, *45,* 201–213.

Schein, E. H. *Organizational Psychology.* Englewood Cliffs: Prentice-Hall, 1965.

Schein E. H. and King, D. C. "The House Building and Community Planning Intergroup Exercise." Unpublished MS, Massachusetts Institute of Technology, 1964.

Schultz, D. P. "Spontaneous Alternation Behavior in Humans: Implications for Psychological Research. *Psychological Bull.,* 1964, *62,* 394–400.

Selznick, P. "Foundations of the Theory of Organization." *ASR,* 1948, *13,* 25–35.

Sherif, M. and Harvey, O. J. "A Study in Ego Functioning: Elimination of Stable Anchorages in Individual and Group Situations. *Sociometry,* 1952, *15,* 272–305.

Sherif, M. and Sherif, C. W. *Reference Groups.* New York: Harper, 1964.

Shure, G. H., Rogers, M. S., Larsen, I. M., and Tassone, J. "Group Planning and Task Effectiveness." *Sociometry,* 1962, *25,* 263–282.

Simon, H. A. "Comments on the Theory of Organizations." In A. H. Rubenstein and C. J. Haberstroh, eds., *Some Theories of Organization.* Homewood, Ill.: Dorsey, 1960, 157–167.

Solem, A. R. "An Evaluation of Two Attitudinal Approaches to Delegation." *JAP,* 1958, *42,* 36–39.

Stogdill, R. "Leadership, Membership, and Organization." *Psychological Bull.,* 1950, *47,* 1–14.

Strickland, L. H. "Surveillance and Trust." *J. Personality,* 1958, *26,* 200–215.

Thibaut, J. "The Motivational Effects of Social Dependence on a Powerful Agency of Control." In W. W. Cooper, H. J. Leavitt, and M. W. Shelly, eds., *New Perspectives in Organization Research.* New York: Wiley, 1964, 87–96.

Thibaut, J. and Riecken, H. W. "Some Determinants and Consequences of the Perception of Social Causality." *J. Personality,* 1955, *24,* 113–134.

Toda, M. "The Design of a Fungus-Eater: A Model of Human Behavior in an Unsophisticated Environment." *Behavioral Science,* 1962, *7,* 164–183.

Tuckman, B. W. "Personality Structure, Group Composition, and Group Function." *Sociometry,* 1964, *27,* 469–487.

Underwood, B. J. *Psychological Research.* New York: Appleton-Century, 1957.

Vroom, V. H. "A Working Paper on Laboratory Experiments on Organization." Paper prepared for 3rd Seminar in the Social Science of Organizations, U. of Pittsburgh, 1964.

Wager, L. W. and Palola, E. G. "The Miniature Replica Model and Its Use in Laboratory Experiments of Complex Organizations." *Social Forces,* 1964, *42,* 418–429.

Weick, K. E. "Reduction of Cognitive Dissonance Through Task Enhancement and Effort Expenditure." *JASP,* 1964, *68,* 533–539.

——. "Laboratory Experimentation with Organizations." In J. G. March, ed., *Handbook of Organizations.* Chicago: Rand McNally, 1965a.

——. "When Prophecy Pales: The Fate of Dissonance Theory." *Psychological Reports,* 1965b, *16,* 1261–1275.

Weick, K. E. and Penner, D. D. "Triads: a Laboratory Analogue." *Organizational Behavior and Human Performance,* 1966, *1* (2).

Zajonc, R. B. "The Requirements and Design of a Standard Group Task." *J. Experimental Social Psychology,* 1965, *1,* 71–78.

Zand, D. E. and Costello, T. W. "Effect of Problem Variation on Group Problem Solving Efficiency Under Constrained Communication." *Psychological Reports,* 1963, *13,* 219–224.

Zelditch, M. "Some Methodological Problems of Field Studies." *American J. Sociology,* 1962, *67,* 566–576.

Zelditch, M. and Evan, W. M. "Simulated Bureaucracies: A Methodological Analysis." In H. Guetzkow, ed., *Simulation in Social Science: Readings.* Englewood Cliffs: Prentice-Hall, 1962, 48–60.

Zelditch, M. and Hopkins, T. K. "Laboratory Experiments with Organizations." In A. Etzioni, ed., *Complex Organizations.* New York: Holt, Rinehart & Winston, 1961, 464–478.

Zigler, E. "Metatheoretical Issues in Developmental Psychology." In M. Marx, ed., *Theories in Contemporary Psychology.* New York: Macmillan, 1963, 341–369.

2

Organizational Change and Field Experiment Methods

LOUIS B. BARNES

Harvard University

One group attending the 1964 Pittsburgh conference was asked to relate field experiment methodology to the issue of organizational change. In some ways the task seemed too ambitious. Each area encompassed vast amounts of thought and confusion. Each area also contained elements which became highly complicated when related to the other area. Any major organizational change involves complex approaches, relationships, and processes that have been only roughly identified and described in the literature on change. These complex variables also create problems for the designer of experiments. In conventional experimental designs, a *single* variable (approach, phase, or relationship) is usually manipulated so as to study its effects on other variables. In complex organizational changes, too many changes occur too fast to permit this isolation of strategic variables.

Organizational change and field experimentation is not an impossible subject for a group to discuss, but it is most certainly a difficult one. It involves identifying, categorizing, and relating multiple variables. It

Particular appreciation for comments on an earlier draft is given to Drs. Douglas R. Bunker, Dexter Dunphy, Larry E. Greiner, Edward Lawler, Preston LeBreton, D. Paul Leitch, Victor H. Vroom, Richard E. Walton. I also wish to thank Miss Margaret Hennig for help with the bibliography. Support for writing this chapter was furnished by the Division of Research, Harvard Graduate School of Business Administration.

means relating criteria and more complex experimental designs to "better" defined change efforts. Finally, it assumes that the field experiment is a truly useful way to study organizational change, an assumption not yet well supported by evidence.

These were some of the problems facing the group discussing Organizational Change and Field Experiment Methods during a two-week summer period in 1964. This chapter expands upon those discussions and is divided into two major parts. The first part describes organizational change in terms of its (a) approaches, (b) relationships, and (c) processes. With these change dimensions in mind, the second part examines issues surrounding social science experimentation in general and organizational field experiments in particular. We hope to show that the field experiment is one of the most promising, but inadequately-used methods now available for the study and measurement of organization change.

ORGANIZATIONAL CHANGE

APPROACHES TO ORGANIZATIONAL CHANGE

Industrial managers are fond of noting that change is the only thing that remains constant in their work. They live from one upset to the next. They encounter a steady stream of new machines, processes, procedures, structures, and management faces. As education and technical knowledge have increased, so has the pressure within even conventional organizations for the introduction of new people, practices, and procedures.

Yet despite the common occurrence of organizational change, its dynamics and underlying processes are understood in only rough, ill-defined ways. Managers and social scientists who create and study change situations find that organizational changes involve multiple sets of complex variables whose identity, interaction, and impact vary from situation to situation. Those involved in the serious study of organizational change face an even greater problem in describing change with a static language system when the very concept involves the shifting of dynamic variables in relation to each other. The situation can be illustrated by an example.

Before the orbiting of Russia's Sputnik I, most American aircraft manufacturers were in the airframe business. They designed, sold, and produced propeller or jet aircraft for military and commercial customers. Their interests were largely defined by the traditions of manned flight at subsonic speeds. The heroes of the industry were the men who designed and flew jets using knowledge of aerodynamics and engine performance. The great names of the industry were names that dominated it during and after World War II—Douglas, Martin, Lockheed, Grumman, Boeing, North American, Republic.

Since the advent of the Sputniks, the picture in and around these companies has changed considerably. Most of the airframe companies were subjected to severe internal shakeups and stresses as they tried to decide whether they were in the airframe, spacecraft, electronic systems, engine, or missile business. As technology and market possibilities expanded, so did the drain on financial resources and the entrance of new firms into the field.

As a project became not an aircraft but an entire space exploration system, new forms of coordination and cooperation developed. The single decision-maker found himself surrounded by a new breed of technical experts, hardware, problems, and problem-solving processes. He ignored these at his peril. Yet more than one aircraft company almost disappeared in an attempt to adapt to space technology requirements.

This rough sketch describes a series of changes that drastically affected one industry. The changes involved more than technology, fuels, engines, and electronic systems. Along with the changing technology came changes in manpower, training, production facilities, personnel, scheduling, organizational structure, performance criteria, marketing strategies. In some cases, a new management was needed to introduce the new technologies. In other cases, an old management was able to adjust itself and alter an existing organization. Most important, the airframe–space age example shows that organizational change involves variable causes and effects not easily isolated from each other. A change in technology may result in management changes which may lead to new procedures and policies which may again result in new technologies, and so on. Under the circumstances, oversimplification becomes desirable and almost inevitable. An analyst almost *has* to choose a limited number of variables which are recognized as dynamically interdependent and then try to work from there toward a more accurate understanding of reality.

In an effort to do this, Leavitt (1965) selected four interacting variables which he called Task, People, Technology, and Structure. Task refers to the organization's production of goods and services and, while these sometimes change independently, according to Leavitt, they change more often in response to People, Technology and/or Structural approaches which influence the Task variable and each other.

Leavitt also notes that the People, Technology, and Structural approaches represent potential strategies for organizational change. Each attracts specialists who develop expertise in changing the strategic variable and then use this change strategy as their lever for improving organizational Task performance. The People specialists tend to focus on personnel placement, management development programs, job counseling, and human relationships within organizations. Technology specialists approach change as production engineers, computer experts, or systems designers. Structural specialists work on organization planning, work flow procedures, and staff–line configurations, among other things.

Needless to say, each of the professional specialists may find himself overlapping into another's area from time to time. Despite these overlaps, each tends to develop strong biases for one variable being more "strategic" than another. The preferences probably reflect the skills and talents of the proponents more than they do any single "best" approach to change. Thus Chapple and Sayles (1961) argue for work flow and structural changes while attacking those People approaches that attempt to train and "convert." Golembiewski (1964) chooses Structure as the strategic approach whose dimensions either permit or frustrate human relationships. By contrast, industrial engineers introduce new work systems and Technology variables through the use of machine replacement, operations research, or simulation techniques. People strategists use training programs, placement procedures, and testing as their major tools.

All of these efforts have led to many large scale organizational changes but few systematic studies. In order to correct this shortage, social scientists have recently become heavily involved in the study of organizational change both as participants and observers. They have even begun to design, plan, and implement changes that seemed exclusively within the manager's realm a generation ago. Behavioral scientists can be said to work with the same four variables mentioned above: Task, People, Technology, and Structure. However, their major contributions are in the area of People approaches to organization change. These approaches have involved what Leavitt (1965) calls "power equalization" and what some behavioral scientists like to call "planned change." As Bennis (1966, p. 82) describes the planned change approach, it involves "a *change agent* who is typically a behavioral scientist brought in to help a *client system* which refers to the target of change. The change agent, *in collaboration* with the client system attempts to apply *valid knowledge* to the client's problem."

The "planned change" approach may or may not apply more "valid" knowledge to the Task-People-Technology-Structure variables. It does, however, specify an outside change agent *collaborating* with a client system. But collaboration obviously is only one way of distributing power in a People approach to change. There are other ways which involve shifting attention from *what* is being changed (the variables) to *how* the changes are being introduced and implemented.

In this second vein, Bennis (1966) constructs a typology of seven other change styles in addition to "planned change." The eight approaches differ according to power distribution, goal setting, and change implementation. Briefly, the other seven approaches can be described as:

1. *Indoctrination Change.* Mutual and deliberate goal setting but under unilateral power.

2. *Coercive Change.* Unilateral goal setting with deliberate intentions using unilateral power. Coercive change would be exemplified by Chinese "brainwashing" and thought control practices.

3. *Technocratic Change.* Unilateral goal setting but shared power. One party defines the goal; the other party helps to reach that goal without question as to the goal's value.

4. *Interactional Change.* Shared power under conditions where goals are not deliberately sought.

5. *Socialization Change.* Unilateral power but collaborative goal implementation; e.g., small children develop under the influence of parents who unilaterally define the goals.

6. *Emulative Change.* Unilateral power without deliberate goals. This is found in formal organizations where subordinates "emulate" their superiors.

7. *Natural Change.* A residual category. Shared power with non-deliberate goal setting; i.e., changes are due to accidents, unintended events, etc.

Bennis' typology, according to its author, is only a crude and overlapping approximation of approaches to change. But it does go one step beyond a consideration of the four change variables (Task, People, Technology, and Structure). It suggests that change can be initiated by using various power distributions which may be as important or more important than the variable itself in determining the outcomes.

In another study Greiner (1965) searched the literature on organizational change and identified the most commonly used approaches as:

1. *The Decree Approach.* A "one-way" announcement originating with a person with high formal authority and passed on to those in lower positions (e.g., Taylor, 1911; Gouldner, 1954).

2. *The Replacement Approach.* Individuals in one or more key organ-

izational positions are replaced by other individuals. The basic assumption is that organizational changes are a function of personnel changes (e.g., Gouldner, 1954; Guest, 1962).

3. *The Structural Approach.* Instead of decreeing or injecting new blood into work relationships, management changes the required relationships of subordinates working in the situation. By changing the structure of organizational relationships, organizational behavior is also presumably affected (e.g., Burns and Stalker, 1962; Chapple and Sayles, 1961; Woodward, 1958; Dalton, Barnes, and Zaleznik [in press]).

4. *The Group Decision Approach.* Participation by group members in implementing alternatives specified by others. This approach involves neither problem identification nor problem solving, but emphasizes the obtaining of group agreement on a predetermined course (e.g., Coch and French, 1948; Lewin, 1958).

5. *The Data Discussion Approach.* Presentation and feedback of relevant data to the client system by either a change catalyst or by change agents within the company. Organizational members are encouraged to develop their own analyses of the data which has been given to them in the form of case materials, survey findings or data reports (e.g., Mann, 1957; Andrews, 1953).

6. *The Group Problem Solving Approach.* Problem identification and problem solving through group discussion with the help of an outsider. This would be one type of "planned change" (e.g., Sofer, 1961).

7. *The T–Group Approach.* Training in sensitivity to the processes of individual and group behavior. Changes in work patterns and relationships are assumed to follow from changes in interpersonal relationships. T–Group approaches focus upon the interpersonal relationships first, then hope for, or work toward, improvements in work performance (e.g., Argyris, 1962; Foundation for Research on Human Behavior, 1960).

Not surprisingly, Greiner's seven approaches, like Bennis', tend to emphasize the power distribution style in each case. The approaches described above move in a roughly descending order from unilateral power to mutually-shared power; i.e., the Decree approach represents unilateral initiation by formal authority while the T-Group approach represents a highly collaborative attempt at shared influence. (At the same time, Greiner's Replacement and Structural approaches can be more generally classified as People and Structure approaches which can be implemented by any one of the other five power styles described by Greiner.) Without question, the Decree approach is more prevalent in industry than the other approaches. However, a survey of the literature shows increasing emphasis on Greiner's last four approaches and their greater uses of shared power. According to McGregor (1960) and Likert (1961) Problem Solving and T–Group approaches with most shared power) are even supplanting the earlier (and more manipulative) Group Decision approaches.

Leavitt (1965) attributes the increase in shared control to the fact that power distribution is more directly confronted in organizations than it once was. Whereas power historically accompanied formal status positions, it no longer does to the same extent. In a modern industrial society, power conflicts can arise when formal status differs from status depending upon knowledge, informal social control, or professional reputation. Formal status no longer overshadows other sources of power to the extent that it once did. When other sources of power became more evident, says Leavitt (1965, p. 1153): "It was to be expected then that the next moves . . . would be toward working out the power variable. And it was obvious too that the direction would be toward power equalization rather than toward power differentiation. The theoretical underpinnings, the prevalent values, and the initial research results all pointed that way."

The importance of Leavitt's observation is shown in some further work by Greiner (1965) who sought to identify the conditions that differentiated "successful" from "less successful" large-scale change efforts. Greiner found that *all* of the nine published accounts that qualified for inclusion (on the basis of large-scale change effort and data adequacy) involved attempts at what Leavitt has called "power equalization." In these cases, the change approaches differed but power equalization seemed a common feature.

Our review of organizational change has so far described *what* is being changed and *how* it is being changed. Leavitt's four variables, Task, People, Technology, and Structure emphasize *what* is being varied. The Bennis and Greiner descriptions show that differences in power distribution can affect how the changes will be initiated and implemented; change can be arbitrarily introduced by a single authority source, or the power can be more widely shared by the individuals concerned.

In addition to *what* approaches are used and *how* power is distributed, organizational change also involves the changing of human relationships —*who*. Some individuals assume key positions from which they try to influence others in an organizational change situation.

CHANGING RELATIONSHIPS

The folklore of change thrives on accounts of courageous individuals who unilaterally defied a complacent majority. These courageous (with hindsight) individuals usually advanced an idea they tried to demonstrate to society with little or no initial success. Under these circumstances, a David and Goliath syndrome developed. David, the courageous advocate of righteousness, progress, and a changed social order must slay the giants of resistance and tradition. The timid majority are pictured as unwilling to support the Davids, while those who support the Goliaths do so in order to maintain their vested interests. In the end, however, David slays the giant, Jack slays the beanstalk giant, and the prince slays the dragon. Virtue triumphs, and society (as represented by the next generation) sees the folly of its forebearers. The David's, Sophocles', Pasteur's, and Galileo's are elevated to positions of social reverence and respect. Individualistic courage is praised while conformity and resistance to change are eternally condemned.

Forgotten in these accounts of courage and individualism are the times some silly David clung to an idea that was intellectually and socially worthless. In these cases the forgotten resisters of change performed a service to society, for the initiators of change (again in retrospect) were rightly held in check.

These patterns of initiative and resistance are as familiar in organizations as in other social situations, except that the picture is more complex. Typically, the charisma of the change initiator sparks support among a sympathetic group of change advocates. The advocates challenge the change resisters. Either group may, with hindsight, turn out to have been rational and reasonable while the other was not. In either case, the process of change involved initiation, advocacy, and resistance.

For the moment, we shall ignore the creative initiators of change. They have received much attention in the writings on individualism, conformity, and courage. Their offspring range from the world's great religions and sciences to the fantasies of Don Quixote. They have overshadowed those we wish to focus upon briefly: their followers who advocate change and their adversaries who resist it.

Figure 1 describes a typology in which *either* advocacy or resistance may be accompanied by reasoned or emotional behavior. Rational Advocates may (and usually do) have to cope with change Radicals as well as with the resisters of change. Rational Resisters must cope with their own Traditionalists (who resist for the sake of resistance), as well as with the advocates of change. Both advocacy and resistance can be rational and realistic. Likewise, neither one may be. There is no guarantee that "change for its own sake" is any more rationally based than is "resistance to change."

Within organizational change situations, all four types probably operate, even though they are hard to isolate and identify at the time.

Nevertheless, some patterns and symptoms seem to characterize each type. In Figure 1, we describe the four types as Rational Advocates, Radicals, Rational Resisters, and Traditionalists.

FIGURE 1

Relationships of Persons
Within Organizational Change
Situations

	Advocates	Resisters
Rational Objective	Rational Advocates	Rational Resisters
Emotional Subjective	Radicals	Traditionalists

Rational Advocates

The Rational Advocates (R.A.'s) tend to create data-based pressures for change within the organization and respond favorably to pressures for change from outside. Though not the initiators of change, they are early to recognize change proposals and to support change initiators. The more the R.A.'s represent upper management, the easier it is for a change initiator to gain sponsorship. Once they personally test and observe the merit of new proposals, the R.A.'s begin to work changes into their own areas of responsibility. Because their understanding and advocacy of change is based upon data, their chances of success are also fairly strong. The importance of an R.A. group is indicated in a study of major organizational change by Barnes and Greiner (Blake and Mouton; Barnes and Greiner, 1964) in which the R.A.'s demonstrated a proposed change approach successfully to themselves first on a limited organizational scale, then began to move the approach systematically into other areas of the company.

Radicals

The Radicals become change advocates mostly in response to emotional influence and nonrational appeals. They continue change advocacy in this same vein. They may simply identify themselves with the change-for-its-own-sake initiators, or they may seek to identify themselves with prestigeous movements. Their advocacy of change, in any case, depends more upon subjective identification than upon objective analysis. This means that Radicals tend to support change movements almost regardless of a proposal's real merits. Such forms of influence and advocacy are described by Frank (1963) in a book called *Persuasion and Healing* describing various movements of psychotherapy, religious healing, and Communist brainwashing. Frank also describes studies in which an inert medicine hastened a healing process. The real "medicine" was the patient's psychological response to the inert placebo. The same placebo-type effects were found among psychiatric patients who improved simply because they *believed* (with no basis for this belief) that they would be helped. As Frank (1963, p. 24) notes: "Comparison of the effects of psychotherapy and placebos . . . suggests that certain symptoms may be relieved equally well by both . . . and raises the possibility that one of the features accounting for some of the success of all forms of psychotherapy is their ability to arouse the patient's expectation of help."

For the Radical who wants help, the placebo of an emotionally-based change proposal may be enough to draw his support. Not surprisingly, Frank reports that placebo successes occurred most often with patients who tended to be dependent, emotionally reactive, conventional, and more trusting than other patients.

Most likely, both types of change advocates (Rational Advocates and Radicals) respond partly to objective and partly to emotional appeals. Like any typology, the split is an oversimplification. Yet, it does serve to point out that change advocacy has its placebo enthusiasts as well as those who base their advocacy on realism. The same is true to those who resist change. For example:

Rational Resisters

The Rational Resisters represent reality-based resistance. They represent those who would lose status, prestige, or influence because of proposed changes. Rational Resisters are often found resisting political coups, company faceliftings, and threatening improvement programs. Their resistance can be useful unless their defensiveness becomes more habitual than their data-based appraisal of a situation. By constantly defending the status quo, they may also hasten the chances of their own defeat. The Rational Resister (R.R.) category suggests that resistance to change is as mature a response under some conditions as is change advocacy. Because of their rational tendencies, the R.R.'s may be valuable organizational members. They nevertheless pose a problem for change advocates who may feel obligated to repair or replace R.R. losses after a successful change introduction.

Traditionalists

The Traditionalists, like the R.R.'s, resist changes, but for less objective reasons. Their type of conservatism tends to respond negatively to almost any change other than changes "back" to the old ways. Just as the Radicals sponsor change for its own sake, the Traditionalists cling to conventional practice as an end in itself. They may suffer no actual deprivation as a result of proposed changes, but still take "prophet of doom" positions. When the doom prophesied fails to materialize or convince others, the Traditionalists tend to react with anger and envy toward the change advocates. Because they rely for defense upon emotional traditionalism, they tend to become isolated from reality as changes continue to develop. Furthermore, change advocates attempt to seal off the Traditionalists from change influences so as to accelerate change in the organization. They also tend to seek the removal of Traditionalists from the scene altogether.

Again, the four types, like categories in any typology, are less distinct in reality than on paper. Under the pressures of emotional strain, R.A.'s and R.R.'s may move toward less realistic positions. Nevertheless, the typology helps to define some of the change relationships found among organizational members. It also will help us to discuss the *processes* of change which lend a dynamic to change approaches and human relationships. This is done in the next section. After that, we shall examine field experiments as a methodology for studying these change phenomena.

CHANGE PROCESSES

Up to this point, our review of organizational change takes account of change variables, change approaches, and change relationships. The map is a simple one, but it helps to separate *what* is being changed (variables) and *how* it is being changed (approaches) from *who* the crucial parties are (relationships) in the change process.

At the same time, the organizational change process typically involves a passage of time. Starting with one complex of dynamic equilibria, the organization shifts to others during and after changes. This transition from one set of equilibria to another suggests that there may also be some identifiable phases of change which make up the whole process.

The most familiar of these change phase concepts was first suggested by Lewin in 1947 (Lewin, 1958). Three phases are involved: the unfreezing of an old pattern, the changing to a new one, and the refreezing of the new pattern. Lewin's model assumed that opposing forces create varying amounts of pressure on a situation. When the opposing pressures are equal, the situation does not change. However, when pressure is added to one force or subtracted from another, change begins to occur and the equilibria move to another level. This force-counterforce struggle keeps changing the equilibria while new pressures and the shifting weights of old pressures are constantly at work.

The Lewinian model furnishes a rough picture of the change process. However, it remains unclear on the subprocesses of change that occur within the three major phases. Our understanding of the subprocesses is rudimentary at best. Schein (1961) describes them as well as anyone in his paper on attitude changes. Referring to the "unfreeze" process, he notes:

> Some of the elements which all unfreezing situations have in common are the following: (1) the physical removal of the influence target from his accustomed routines, sources of information, and social relationships; (2) the undermining and destruction of all social supports; (3) demeaning and humiliating experiences to help the target see his old self as unworthy and thus to become motivated to change; (4) the consistent linking of reward with willingness to change and of punishment with unwillingness to change [p. 8].

With regard to the "change" process, Schein describes two components which may or may not be sequentially phased:

> The actual influence is most likely to occur by one of two processes. The target finds one or more models in his social environment and learns new attitudes by identifying with them and trying to become like them; or the target confronts new situations with an experimental attitude and develops for himself attitudes which are appropriate to the situation and which remove whatever problem he faces. These two processes—identification and internalization—probably tend to occur together in most concrete situations, but it is worthwhile, for analytical purposes, to keep them separate [p. 8].

Finally, Schein has a few comments on the subprocesses of "refreezing." He states:

> If the new attitude has been internalized while being learned, this has automatically facilitated refreezing because it has been fitted naturally into the individual's personality. If it has been learned through identification [with a role model] it will persist only so long as the target's relationship with the original influence model persists unless new surrogate models are found or social support and reinforcement is obtained for expressions of the new attitude [p. 10].

Although these comments by Schein help to clarify the workings of Lewin's concepts, they still leave the subprocesses largely unspecified. We need further clarification of the specific steps and subphases.

Greiner (1965) tried to do this in an effort to learn more about major organizational change efforts. He examined nine large scale studies. Four of these studies he labeled "successful" change efforts (Jaques, 1952; Rice, 1958; Guest, 1962; Seashore and Bowers, 1963). Organizational change in these situations seemed to be "growing in intensity, spreading throughout the organization, having a marked effect on actual behavior, and resulting in improved organization performance" (Greiner, 1965, p. 24). Several other studies appeared to report successful major change efforts but contained insufficient published data (e.g., Whyte, 1951; Mann, 1957; Lawrence, 1958; Dalton, Barnes, and Zaleznik, in press). A third set of reports and cases were labeled "less successful" by Greiner. This set of studies showed changes which "seemed to be fading, showing confinement to small parts of the organization, revealing little in the way of actual behavior change, and pointing to few signs of improved organization performance" (ibid., p. 24). In this set of studies were contributions by Gouldner (1954), Strauss (1954), Argyris (1962), and cases in Whyte (1955), and Lawrence et al. (1961).

In comparing the findings, Greiner reported ten conditions that seemed to differentiate the successful from the less successful. The "successful" major change efforts followed a sequence where:

1) The organization is under great pressures for improvement both from within and outside the organizational unit. These pressures precede the change attempts.

2) The organization and its management experience great difficulty in coping with the pressures.

3) A newcomer with experience and a reputation for improving organizations enters the picture.

4) The newcomer enters the organization at or near the top and begins to work with top-level managers.

5) An initial act of the newcomer is to clarify the working relationship he wishes to have with the organization.

6) The head man of the organization assumes a direct and highly involved role in implementing the changes.

7) The newcomer engages many parts of the organization in a collaborative, fact-finding, problem-solving diagnosis of organizational problems.

8) The newcomer provides new methods and recommendations for solving problems and taking action.

9) The newcomer's proposals are tested on a small scale and found useful for problem-solving before they are introduced to the rest of the organization.

10) The change effort is spread through a series of success experiences and absorbed into other parts of the organization.

The "less successful" change efforts showed uneven gaps in the above sequence. Some of the conditions seemed to be present while others were not, or else they appeared in highly distorted forms.

Greiner's ten phases shed some light on the subprocesses that occur in major organizational change. With some rephrasing, the ten points can be fitted to the Lewinian change model and to our earlier discussion of change, approaches, and relationships. For example, the "unfreeze" subprocesses become:

a) Pressures for improvement come from both inside (R.A.'s and Radicals) and outside (e.g., technology, economic, etc.) the organization. Management is unable to adequately meet the demands for improvement.

b) A change initiator appears with a record of success behind him. He sets forth the power distribution approach he wants to use in an effort to clarify his relationships with management.

c) The change initiator gains the initial support of the top-level manager (or else he *is* the top level manager) and the support of a few R.A.'s and Radicals as he sets up a diagnostic study of the organization's problems.

The "change" subprocesses are:

d) The change initiator suggests a series of new steps involving the Task, People, Technology, and/or Structure variables. These new steps are suggested in a way consistent with the power approach specified by the change initiator as necessary for his relationships with management.

e) The top-level manager agrees to try out the change initiator's proposals, at least on a limited basis. The proposals are initially tested and found workable by a small number of R.A.'s and Radicals.

f) Resistance begins to form among the R.R.'s and Traditionalists.

The "refreeze" subprocesses become:

g) Resistance strengthens among the R.R.'s and Traditionalists.

h) Change proposals are tested on a wider basis throughout the organization by R.A.'s and Radicals. Successes outnumber failures. Failures are explained by R.A.'s and Radicals as due to faulty approaches by R.R.'s and Traditionalists.

i) Change proposals become part of the organization's way of life. Exaggerated claims of success tend to come from Radicals.

During the transition, individual attitudes tend to change, goals become reshaped, new alliances are formed, and the R.A. and Radical proponents multiply in number so that the change program becomes internalized within the organization. Dalton, Barnes, and Zaleznik (in press) describe this internalization process as follows:

The model which we shall describe contemplates four subprocesses which proceed concurrently as part of the process of socially induced change: a) a movement from sense of negative self worth toward a heightened feeling of positive worth on the part of the individual or individuals who are the objects of influence, b) a move from generalized and global goals toward specific and concrete objectives, c) a movement away from prior social ties toward new relationships, and d) a movement from an external locus of motivation for change toward an internalization of the induced behavior.

Put another way, during the unfreeze, change, and refreeze phases (a) positive self worth increases, (b) goals become more specific and concrete, (c) new alliances and relationships are formed, and (d) motivation comes more from within and less from outside. At the same time, R.A.'s and Radicals use their power (either unilaterally or in some shared fashion to change Task, People, Technology, and/or Structure variables in a manner prescribed by a change initiator. Their efforts are resisted by the R.R.'s and Traditionalists, but with diminishing success as the change effort spreads within the organization.

Figure 2 presents a summary diagram of this organizational change process. An organizational equilibrium is unfrozen by internal and/or external pressures. The internal complaints and pressures are verbalized by those whom we have called R.A.'s and Radicals. They provide the early support for a change initiator who seems to have answers for some of the organization's unsolved problems. The change initiator communicates to management *how* he believes the problems should be solved by specifying a power distribution approach which involves both himself and others in the organization. This approach receives the support of the top-level manager as well as of R.A.'s and Radicals within top management. The change initiator also develops with management a plan for *what* approaches (Task, People, Technology, and/or Structure) should be emphasized. An initial trial change is attempted and found successful. Change efforts are expanded, although by this time .resistance has formed among the R.R.'s and the Traditionalists. As the resistance stiffens, change efforts intensify, successes mount, and the overclaiming of success begins. Under these conditions of refreezing, the organization reaches another equilibrium which remains only until further major change efforts unfreeze the situation again.

The major problem with Figure 2 is that it depicts a change process that occurs often but has been studied little in a systematic way. In addition, though major organizational change does occur often, much of the literature on change in organizations focuses upon the behavioral scientist and upon his interests in "planned change," (e.g., Argyris, 1962;

FIGURE 2

The Change Process in Organizations

UNFREEZE

Pressures for improvement from both the inside (R.A.'s and Radicals) and outside (e.g., technology, economic, etc.) the organization. Management is unable to meet adequately the demands for improvement.

Change initiator appears with a record of success behind him. Sets forth the power distribution approach he wants to use in an effort to clarify his relationships with management.

Change initiator gains the initial support of the top-level manager and of a few R.A.'s and Radicals as he sets up a diagnostic study of the organization's problems.

CHANGE

The change initiator suggests a series of new steps involving the Task, People, Technology, and/or Structure variables. These new steps are suggested in a way that is consistent with the power approach specified by the change initiator as necessary for his relationships with management.

The top-level manager agrees to try out the change initiator's proposals, at least on a limited basis. The proposals are initially tested and found workable by a small number of R.A.'s and Radicals.

Resistance begins to form among R.R.'s and Traditionalists.

REFREEZE

Resistance strengthens among R.R.'s and Traditionalists.

Change proposals are tested on a wider basis throughout the organization by R.A.'s and Radicals. Successes outnumber failures. Failures are explained by R.A.'s and Radicals as due to the power approaches used by R.R.'s and Traditionalists.

Change proposals become part of the organization's way of life. Exaggerated claims of success tend to come from Radicals.

------------> INCREASE IN SENSE OF POSITIVE SELF WORTH ------------>

------------> GROWING SPECIFICITY OF GOALS ------------>

------------> FORMATION OF NEW ALLIANCES AND RELATIONSHIPS ------------>

------------> INTERNALLY RATHER THAN EXTERNALLY GENERATED MOTIVATION ------------>

Coch and French, 1948; Bennis, 1963; Foundation for Research on Human Behavior, 1960). This is unfortunate since behavioral scientists have really done more work with change in group settings than with organizational change. As Bennis (1966, p. 174) admits a bit ruefully toward the end of his paper on planned organizational change: "Up to this point, I have used the phrase organizational change rather loosely. In Argyris' case, for example, organizational change refers to a change in values of eleven top executives, a change which was not necessarily of an enduring kind and which apparently brought about some conflict with other interfaces. In most other cases of planned organizational change, the change induction was limited to a small, elite group."

This failure to either influence or study large-scale changes in organizations prompted Blake and Mouton (1964) to design a set of programmed learning exercises around a theoretical construction called the Managerial Grid. Blake and Mouton set up their laboratory seminars so that managers were the teachers, students, consultants, and researchers. In this way, the educational phase of the program was spread through an entire managerial system with little help from professional educators or change catalysts. As Bennis (1966, p. 174) points out: "Only in the work of Blake is organizational change discussed confidently in a systems way; his program includes the training of the entire management organization and at several locations he has carried this step to include wage earners."

Blake and Mouton claim that their approach has one major strength which relates to our earlier discussion of change "approaches"; they place great emphasis upon the fact that their Managerial Grid programs are based upon a theoretical framework involving five basic styles of management. Some behavioral scientists argue that Grid theory is not a theory but rather a description of power distribution approaches with one "best" approach. Blake and Mouton maintain that Grid theory furnishes not only a set of alternative power distribution approaches, but that it permits managers to compare these approaches with each other so that a manager can better evaluate and predict performance on problem-solving tasks. In addition, though they disclaim the "one best" approach, Blake and Mouton have definitely furnished a model which serves as an impersonal authority figure in an organizational change process. First reports on the Grid approach as it was tried in a large industrial plant and then researched in a field study by Barnes and Greiner (Blake and Mouton; Barnes and Greiner, 1964; Greiner, 1965) are impressive. In addition, the writer knows of three actual and five drawing board field experiments using the Managerial Grid approach and sponsored by the companies involved. All eight experiments involve large-scale change efforts.

With such a promising report of work in progress, it seems hard to understand why there should be any pessimism on the related topics of organizational change and field experiment methods. And yet there is. To begin with, Bennis (1966, p. 172) hedges his enthusiastic report of the behavioral scientists' "planned change" efforts when he notes that: "It is not at all obvious to me that the types of change induced by the change agents are: 1) compatible with 'human nature' or in accord with 'findings from the behavioral sciences' as some change agents assert, or 2) desirable even if they are in tune with man's need structure, or 3) functional." These cautious words partly open up a problem currently important to behavioral scientists themselves. In essence, the question being debated is whether or not their "science" permits active involvement and advocacy of preferred change approaches within organizations or anywhere else. The dispute is also found wherever behavioral scientists have voiced professional opinions or taken action on issues such as foreign policy, nuclear disarmament, civil rights, job retraining, executive development, or political elections.

This problem need not concern us if we are interested only in organizational change, but it becomes crucial as soon as we turn our thoughts to the *study of* change. Some behavioral scientists (e.g., Blake and Mouton, Argyris, Shepard, Bennis, Sofer, Rice, Jaques, Trist, F. Mann) seek and apparently achieve proficiency in both areas. But behavioral scientist critics decry these dual attempts to change organizations and also do research on the changes. The possible bias of social scientist involvement is of major concern in more than one academic setting these days. The dilemma posed by these bias problems cannot be avoided by anyone interested in field experiment methods. By exploring and taking a position on this underlying dilemma now, we can begin to clarify our later position on field experiment methods.

THE UNDERLYING DILEMMA

The underlying dilemma exists for a behavioral scientist when he feels forced to identify himself *either* with the values of scientific inquiry or with the values of change advocacy. Some behavioral scientists feel that the choice is necessary for the good of the profession. For them, the essence of professionalism is the impersonal detachment that goes with medicine, law, and, of course, science. They believe that professional inquiry becomes subjectively distorted as soon as a scientist finds himself emotionally involved in his data. They also point to the social sciences' struggle to gain respect from the "hard" natural sciences which have historically valued objectivity, detachment from personal interests, and the search for truth (Shepard, 1956; Merton, 1957; Barnes, 1960).

In their efforts to demonstrate objectivity and gain respect from the "hard" sciences, social scientists have tended to make a fetish out of detachment while creating an impressive array of research designs and methodological tools. These efforts, however, have not been entirely successful. Professional meetings continue to ring with sharp attacks on subjective analysis in study after study. The attacks are sharpest where the behavioral scientist–observer also tried to influence human behavior toward more "productive," "participative," "creative," "healthy," "reality centered," patterns. However, those attacked for subjective analysis have included not only changers of organizations, but also therapists, experimenters, psychoanalysts, and the architects and implementers of most educational changes within and beyond universities (e.g., Eysenck, 1960).

In essence, the critics of observer "involvement" want a science built upon the observation of human behavior rather than a science which involves attempts to practice as well as observe. Observers, so the reasoning goes, remain detached and relatively objective. Participants become involved and overly subjective; they begin to overvalue and push their own beliefs and "normative" theories.

In some cases, the distinction becomes rather fine. Although "observer" scientists would approve a study designed to compare certain variables (e.g., organizational structure "A" and organizational structure "B"), they would criticize observers who then became advocates and helped management to adopt one structure over another, even though the change efforts were based upon "scientific" evidence gained from the first study. In effect, the normative position of the "observer" scientist is that, since involvement corrupts, behavioral scientists should stick to the external observation of data; they should not be part of the data they wish to study.

Nevertheless, an increasing number of behavioral scientists have begun to work on the application of change knowledge as well as on the understanding of it. They subscribe to Kurt Lewin's statement that: "If you want to really understand how something works, try to change it." Instead of picturing themselves as studying unresponsive systems, they propose the physician-patient relationship where the physician tries to understand the patient's symptoms first, but then works to improve the patient's health as well. The behavioral scientist advocates see no real dichotomy between their own efforts and the "important" values of science (i.e., the overall search for knowledge and truth). They also see no real conflict between dedication to science and interest in practical application. Most would take the position of Kaplan (1964, p. 398–399) who writes that:

Whether the behavioral scientist should concern himself at all with matters of policy, personal or social, is a question on which no concensus has been reached in the scientific community. On the one hand, many behavioral scientists are very much occupied with the problems that arise *in* human behavior (and not only in the attempt to describe or explain behavior), and are also professionally engaged with questions of what is to be done by people in quandries, in contexts ranging from marital to foreign affairs. On the other hand, there are those who regard such concerns as lying quite outside the scientific enterprise itself, and perhaps even as antithetical to that enterprise. Science, as they conceive it, is the search for truth, not usefulness. Whether the truth is useful is of no professional interest to the scientist, but only whether it is indeed true; how it is put to use is no business of his. . . . To engage in inquiry so as to achieve a utilitarian end is nothing other than a prostitution of the scientific intelligence.

This second point strikes me as singularly lacking in perspective, especially on the history of science itself. Even the eighteenth century tradition of science as an occupation for gentlemen of leisure manifested a striking concern with the practical interests of war, commerce, industry, and agriculture, and even the purest of the sciences owe a not inconsiderable debt to such interests. The fact is that the distinction between "pure" and "applied" science, whatever its logical ground, is not of much help in understanding the actual growth of knowledge. . . . The irony is that the behavioral scientist, in his aspiration eventually to achieve the scientific standing of physics, is so often more royalist than the kings; the first two laws of thermodynamics, for example, were formulated long after the scientific data were available, "and they arose because of the social stimulation of steam power engineering," (R. S. Cohen in Frank, 1961). In its resolve to remain "pure," as in so many other respects, behavioral science is imitating physics, not as it is but as particular reconstructions have represented it to be.

This dilemma will not be settled easily. Some "observer" scientists will pursue an artificially pure ideal of science which stumbles against both history and reality. Other "participant" scientists will advocate personal theories without moving beyond their limited biases. However, the dilemma is not hopeless, e.g., different roles can be taken under different conditions. The change advocate in one study may be an observer in another. In the one case, he is observed as a participant in action, trying to change variables which will be studied by another researcher or team of researchers. In the other case, he is the observer of someone else's change efforts. Within the more tolerant traditions of science, he may take the role of the organizational change catalyst during one time or space period, the role of the painstaking observer during another.

Neither is necessarily incompatible with the reknowned "scientific method" which, as Kaplan (1964) has sagely noted, is as difficult to define as the "method" of baseball.

Into the confusion surrounding "observer" versus "participant" science enters the field experimenter. His interests, almost of necessity, encompass organizational practices as well as experimental methodology. His problem is to apply an experimental methodology to "real life" field situations. If he overcomplicates his research procedures, he may lose the cooperation of those who work in the organizations he is studying. If he oversimplifies research procedures, he may lose the respect of his professional peers who pass valued judgement on his work. Consequently, the field experimenter must consider the fine points of both organizational life and experimental design. In the following sections of this chapter, we shall examine the methodology and its possibilities.

FIELD EXPERIMENT METHODS

In theory, the field experiment provides the ideal vehicle for studying organizational change. It offers the possibility of controlled situations and before-after measurements of change. It can help trace causality, something that neither the single case study nor the comparative organizational study can do. It implies that the sophistication of the laboratory experiment can be transferred to the field situation, thus furnishing the field worker with a rigorous methodological approach.

In fact, however, the rigors of experimental design seldom reflect the realities of organizational life. The experimental laboratory must always oversimplify the variables found within a complex organization. Likewise, the complex organization cannot easily provide laboratory conditions. The laboratory involves a temporary system; the organization is a quasi-permanent system that exists beyond the lives of its members. The laboratory sets up temporary human relationships which all too often have a pretend-like quality. Organizations require relationships that are, so the slang expression goes, "for real." The laboratory builds an ambiguous hierarchy in which subjects report to an experimenter most often as volunteer or nonvolunteer enrollees taking his college course. An organization has several complex hierarchical systems which depend upon both formal authority and colleague influence over a period of time. To change and study a single variable in a laboratory may be relatively easy compared with isolating, changing, and studying the variable within an organization.

Organizational research also differs from laboratory experiments with regard to researcher status. The experimenter is typically master within the laboratory. He has defined the operating conditions and can call the tune. The organizational researcher, however, is typically a guest in someone else's establishment. The various organizational parts and persons may all choose to ignore him, or they may all demand attention simultaneously. When they demand attention, it may not be for purposes of cooperating. They may be only suspicious or curious about "what's going on?" At times, the organizational researcher will feel that he has absolutely no control over his "subjects." He can only cross his fingers and hope that natural events and some skill will permit him to carry out his work.

Under these conditions, it is not too surprising that large-scale field experiments have been relatively few and imperfect in design. As recently as 1964, Seashore (1964, p. 165) noted in one of the few papers written on field experimentation:

> A scanning of five recent major works on research design in the behavioral sciences uncovered not a single example of experimental work with formal human organizations, and no reference to the problems of conducting such research in field setting. . . . The total number of research ventures that might be reasonably considered to be field experiments with formal organizations is very small, perhaps from five to ten, depending upon how generous one chooses to be in tolerating deviations from ideal experimental conditions. None of these fulfills the canons of experimental design to the degree ordinarily expected in laboratory or field experiments in small groups. One must view these as rather primitive, pioneering ventures.

Seashore's pessimistic report is influenced somewhat by the stringent requirements he set for including a study as an organizational field experiment. He excluded those experiments conducted with organizational employees which were concerned with small groups rather than formal organizations. In addition, he included only those studies where there were: "a) a definable and measurable change in organization environment, structure, or process, b) some means for qualification of variables, c) the provision for testing of causal hypotheses through the method of difference." These criteria were set, says Seashore, "for no other reason than to narrow attention to the special problems that arise or become accentuated when one attempts field studies of relatively large and complex organizational units with methods that approach those of classical experimental design" (ibid., p. 164).

Another even more extensive paper on field experimentation was written by Seashore's Michigan colleague, John R. P. French, Jr., for a handbook on *Research Methods in the Behavioral Sciences,* edited by Festinger and Katz (1953). French's criteria for inclusion as a field experiment were slightly different from Seashore's in that French was less concerned with the size of the organizational units (i.e., small groups are included) and more concerned that the experimenter be the source of changes. To French (1953, p. 99):

> The essential feature which distinguishes the field experiment from the more common "field study" is the design of the research. The field experiment involves the actual manipulation of conditions *by the experimenter* [author's emphasis] in order to determine causal relations whereas in the field study the researcher uses the selection of subjects and the measurement of existing conditions in the field setting as a method of determining correlations. . . . In the field experiment (as opposed to the natural experiment where the researcher opportunistically capitalizes upon some ongoing changes and studies their effects in an experimental design) the manipulation of the independent variable is not left to nature, but is contrived, at least in part, by the experimenter . . . beforehand.

In the same chapter, French further emphasizes the experimenter's role and the classical experimental design when he presents his working definition of field experiments: "For the purposes of this chapter, then, we shall define a field experiment as a theoretically oriented research project in which the experimenter manipulates an independent variable in some real social setting in order to test some hypotheses" (ibid., p. 101).

Both French and Seashore use the classical experiment as practiced in the laboratory as a model for field experiments. Both writers also stress the importance of the experimenter's role in manipulating and controlling the relevant variables. At the same time, both writers recognize that they are placing an almost impossible demand upon the field researcher. Seashore talks about the problems of "scientific versus ethical and practical considerations" while French notes that there is a conflict between "research objectives and practical objectives." The underlying dilemma referred to earlier (science vs. application) is acknowledged but not resolved by Seashore or French. Both writers imply that the best resolution will come when researchers can do a better job of establishing laboratory conditions in field situations.

The field experimenter is thus left with an ideal (classical design), a prescribed role (manipulator and controller of variables), and little hope of achieving either in an organizational setting. The laboratory experimenters add further discouragement, if that is possible. Leon Festinger (1953, p. 137) writes that:

> It would seem clear that the experiments in industry such as have been described in [French's] chapter should not be called laboratory experiments. There is little or no attempt to set up special conditions. Typically, the situation is accepted as found and some manipulation is

imposed. The manipulation of the independent variable is usually a simultaneous manipulation of a set of factors. The degree of control obtained in these experiments is usually not sufficient to guarantee that the effects obtained are unequivocally related to the independent variable.

At this point, the would-be field experimenter must make a choice. He either must work toward an apparently hopeless ideal of classical design and experimenter influence, or else he must begin to revise his goals and procedures. We shall take the second path, but not until we have explored some of the problems which accompany the concepts of classical experimental design and experimenter influence. Our analysis will tend to suggest that the problems of field experimentation are not all in the field. Several issues plague laboratory experimenters as well. Some of these issues seem serious in the light of recent research findings.

THE PROBLEMS OF CLASSICAL DESIGN AND EXPERIMENTER INFLUENCE

The Classical Design Model

The classical model of experimental design includes what Campbell (1957) calls a "Pretest-Postest Control Group Design." This means that observations are made both before (pretest) and after (postest) a treatment is applied to one or more experimental groups. Similar observations are made in one or more control groups in which no treatment is applied. By using before-after measures and an experimental-control group structure, the researcher hopes to test specific hypotheses concerning the treatment's effects on one or more dependent variables. Such effects are reflected in different degrees or directions of change in experimental groups as compared with control groups.

As Campbell notes, the Pretest–Postest Control Group Design became the ideal of the social sciences in the 1900's because it seemed to overcome problems which tended to accompany simpler study designs. Campbell describes these earlier problems as: (a) History, (b) Maturation, (c) Testing, (d) Instrument Decay, (e) Statistical Regression, (f) Selection, and (g) Experimental Mortality. Each could contaminate or confound the data if not controlled or recognized. The confounding factors can be summarized as follows:

a) *History*. Some changes are due to external incidents which would influence the subjects, just as an experimental variable might. Though these extraneous stimuli may become part of the group's history, they are not intended as change variables.

b) *Maturation*. Changes take place in an experimental group which might be due to the passage of time alone. A control group would presumably show these same maturation tendencies over time. Hence the experimenter would not incorrectly attribute changes to the experimental inputs.

c) *Testing.* The process of testing itself can affect the attitudes and scores that subjects report in an experiment.

d) *Instrument Decay.* Measurements might be affected by the increasing fatigue, boredom, sophistication of those who are doing the observations in an experiment. In addition, different observers may have vastly different perceptions of similar incidents.

e) *Statistical Regression.* Changes can appear due to the fact that an experimental group began the experiment at one extreme or the other as reflected by the measuring instruments. Under these conditions and with "only one way to go," the experimenter could not know whether it was the change variable or just natural shifts toward the mean that accounted for the changes that took place according to his measuring instruments.

f) *Selection.* Members of an experimental group may be quite unrepresentative of the population. Without a strictly matched control group the experimenter can not tell whether it is his sample or the experimental variable which accounts for the changes.

g) *Experimental Mortality.* Changes may occur due to the dropping out of subjects who represent a crucial subset of biases, attitudes, etc.

Stouffer (1950) expressed the hopes of social scientists in general when he spoke of the classical model as an ideal. He pictured the model as a four-celled diagram shown in Figure 3 in which X_1, X_2, etc., refer to observed events.

FIGURE 3

Classical Experiment Design

	Before	After	
Experimental Group	X_1	X_2	Treatment Effect $=$ $(X_2 - X_1) - (X'_2 - X'_1)$
Control Group	X'_1	X'_2	

However, this classical-controlled model did not remain ideal for long. It had already become suspect in 1949 when Solomon (1949) showed that Before measurements tended to sensitize subjects to react to an experimental change differently than if there had been no prior measurement. As French (1953, p. 115) noted: "Solomon has shown that the conventional design with a single control group is inadequate where the pre-experimental measures interact with the experimental treatment and influence its effectiveness." Solomon's work also suggested that the experimental setting itself posed a problem for experimenters. It now appeared not only possible but highly likely that a subject would behave differently under experimental conditions than he might under more natural work conditions. Solomon tried to eliminate the effects of pre-measurement and the experimental setting by designing an elaborate Four Group Design which we shall examine later. But the important lesson his work teaches is that the classical design is but one of a number of imperfect alternatives from which an experimenter, either in the field or in the laboratory, can choose. Furthermore, while field settings create many problems for experimental work, laboratory conditions create their own problems of artificiality and subject self-consciousness.

The Influence of the Experimental Environment

Some of the problems posed by experimental settings are well illustrated in the work of Orne (1962), Orne and Evans (1965) and Milgram (1965). Their work shows that the relationship between subject and experimenter and other aspects of the laboratory setting may be more powerful determinants of subjects' behavior than the experimental manipulation of variables. For example, Orne (1962, p. 777) comments that: "A particularly striking aspect of the typical experimenter-subject relationship is the extent to which the subject will play his role [as a passive responder] and place himself under the control of the experimenter. . . . Just about any request which could conceivably be asked of the subject is legitimized by the quasi-magical phrase, 'This is an experiment,' and the shared assumption that a legitimate purpose will be served by the subject's behavior." Orne and Evans (1965) also provide a good example of how the experimental setting influences subject behavior. They conducted an experiment in which the experimenter tried to persuade hypnotized subjects to perform antisocial actions (e.g., throwing dangerous acid at another person, picking up a poisonous reptile). Ostensibly, the research was to determine whether or not hypnotized persons could be persuaded to perform antisocial acts. The subjects were actually in no danger from either the acid or the poisonous reptile. Some of the subjects, however, only pretended to be hypnotized during the experiment, though the experimenter did not know which subjects were hypnotized and which were not. A third group of "control" subjects were clearly not hypnotized during the experiment. The experimenter attempted to treat all subjects alike in persuading them to throw acid and handle the snake.

Orne and Evans report that the non-hypnotized subjects (both those who simulated hypnosis and those who did not) demonstrated antisocial behavior about as much as the hypnotized subjects did. They explain their findings as due to the fact that: "though they reported feeling rather uncertain about the tasks, and reported strong emotional reactions to the repugnant activities, the [non-hypnotized] subjects reported that they were quite convinced that they would not be harmed *because* the context was an experimental one, presumably being conducted by responsible experimenters" (1965, p. 199).

In another set of experiments, Milgram (1965) discovered that an experimenter obtained slightly greater (65%) obedience from subjects engaged in a sadistically unpleasant task when the setting was a university laboratory rather than an unimpressive office setting. However, even in the second "laboratory," almost half the subjects obeyed the experimenter's instructions. With regard to the authority of the experimental setting, Milgram (1965, p. 71) comments: "It would be valuable to study the subjects' performance in other contexts which go even further . . . in denying institutional support to the experimenter. It is possible that beyond a certain point, obedience disappears completely. But that point had not been reached in the Bridgeport office."

Quite clearly the experimental setting forms an important part of the relevant environment for subjects participating in a study. The Orne, Evans and Milgram studies indicate that this environment also can be a major determinant of subjects' behavior. If this is true, it poses a serious question as to the traditional role of the experimenter as a part of the subjects' environment. Laboratory experimenters in particular stress the importance of the experimenter's and his design's control of subjects and the relevant environment. Cronbach (1957) differentiates an experiment from a correlational study by noting that an experimenter is interested only in variations which he, himself, is responsible for introducing. Argyle (1957, p. 46) defines experiments on social behavior as: "investigations in which the investigator himself manipulates the conditions and makes observations in order to test an hypothesis." Festinger (1953, p. 137) writes that: "A laboratory experiment may be defined as one in which the investigator creates a situation with the exact conditions he wants to have and in which he controls some and manipulates other variables. He is then able to observe and measure the effect of the manipulation of the independent variables on the dependent variables in a situation in which the operation of other relevant factors is held to a minimum."

In these definitions it is the experimenter, not the subjects or environment, who creates, controls, manipulates, observes, tests, measures, and holds other factors to a minimal variation. However, one is tempted to wonder whether these are realistic expectations even under experimental conditions. Although the intended pattern of influence goes from experimenter to subjects and environment, studies cited above suggest that influence moves in other directions as well. It seems likely that not only the subjects and environment exert influence in a variety of unplanned ways, but also that experimenters exert "unintended" influence over the other two. Figure 4 shows these intended and potential influence patterns.

FIGURE 4

Intended Influence Patterns and
Potential Influence Patterns

For the most part, behavioral science experimenters act as though the potential influence patterns either do not or should not exist in the laboratory. Meanwhile, the *intended* forms of experimenter influence are treated as an attainable goal. However, other writings, in addition to those already cited, suggest that subject and environmental influence may be *more* powerful and experimenter influence *less* predictable than once suspected. For example, a study by Brunswik (1956) attacked the assumption that one variable could be experimentally isolated from another when the two were related in the real world environment. Yet most laboratory experiments make at least several such assumptions. Even earlier, Tolman and Brunswik (1935) wrote of the "causal texture of the environment," a concept expanded upon recently by Emory and Trist (1965) in connection with organizational change. All four authors, though dealing with different settings, suggest that environmental influence may determine subject behavior more than the experimental treatment does and yet go disregarded as a major influence. Bronowski (1953, p. 89) makes essentially the same point in discussing the physical as well as the social sciences:

> It was assumed in the classical science of the last century that such a
> phenomenon as radioactivity, or the inheritance of a blood group, or

loss of nerve, or the rise of prices in a time of scarcity, is each the result of many influences, and that step by step these could be taken apart and the phenomenon traced to all its causes. In each case, what was happening could be treated as a laboratory experiment. It could be isolated from these events in the world which had no bearing upon it, and lay as it were beyond the box of the laboratory. And within this box, the causes could be studied one by one, much as we study how the volume of gas changes when the pressure is varied while we keep the temperature the same, and then when the temperature is varied while we keep the pressure the same.

But the picture of the phenomenon in isolation from the rest of the world and from the observer turns out to be false. There comes a time when it will not do any longer even as an approximation. Then it turns out that time and space, which Newton thought absolute, cannot be given physical meaning without the observer. The laboratory cannot exist in a void, and the experimenter cannot be put in a box. And as we refine our measurements, the limitations of the observer look larger and larger.

The Influence of the Experimenter

The "limitations of the observer" are further shown in a series of papers by Riecken (1962), Vikan-Kline (1962), McGuigan (1963), Rosenthal (1963a, 1963b, 1964, 1965) and Rosenthal et al. (1963). Riecken points up the complexity of the experimenter's influence by noting that subjects too can play the game of selective behavior. In describing the social situation formed by an experiment, Riecken (1962, p. 31) notes:

> In the light of these five features of the experiment—its invitational (to the subject) quality, the unspecified nature of the invitation's terms, the attributes of the relationship between the two principal personages (subject and experimenter), the temporal and spatial segregation of the experience, and the one-sidedness of the distribution of information—it is easy to see how the subject is impelled to "put his best foot forward." He attempts to appear in the best possible light within the constraints imposed by the situation, by concealing or exhibiting, exaggerating or belittling those qualities he believes will be positively and negatively evaluated in the particular experiment.

McGuigan (1963) goes on to show how different experimenters come up with different findings from the same experiment. He also attempts to point out that experimenters may influence subjects in ways that are quite different from their intended patterns of influence. In noting that the experimenter is a "neglected stimulus object," McGuigan (1963, p. 421) also observes that:

> While we have traditionally recognized that the [personality] character-istics of an experimenter may indeed influence behavior, it is important

to observe that we have not seriously attempted to study him as an independent variable.

In partial response to McGuigan's plea, Rosenthal et al. (1963) published a series of papers which showed the unintended impact of experimenters' expectations on subjects' behavior. Using both human and animal subjects in different experiments, Rosenthal et al. showed that the experimenter's own biases were partial determinants of the experimental results. In other words, the experimenter's expectations helped to determine subjects' responses even though experimenters did not consciously communicate these expectations before or during the experiment.

Still further evidence of varying experimenter influence is illustrated by Milgram's studies. Milgram (1965) studied the willingness of subjects to disobey the experimenter-authority figure who told them to administer powerful electrical shocks to another person. Subjects' obedience varied according to such things as the physical proximity of the experimenter to the subject and the extent to which colleagues supported subjects' disobedience. Milgram found that the experimenter exercised more control over the subject when (a) the two were in close proximity and when (b) the experimenter and subject worked alone without other subjects there to support disobedience. (See also Asch, 1952.)

The impact from these various studies has only begun to be felt in the social sciences. In a recent review on experimenter influence, Klintz et al. (1965) noted that personality, experience, sex, expectancy, modeling behavior, and early data returns have all been found possible determinants of *unintended* influence by experimenters. Klintz et al. (1965, p. 224) contend that:

> Wherever an experimenter-subject relationship exists, the possibility also exists for E [the experimenter] to complicate his data. . . . It appears that experimental psychology has too long neglected the experimenter as an independent variable. . . . It is hoped that experimental psychologists will no longer accept on faith that the experimenter is necessary but harmless.

An even sharper attack on experimenter "objectivity" and "observer" science experiments was written by Tooley and Pratt (1964) who argue that it is time for the experimenter to recognize himself as more than an objective outsider to the experimental situation. In a letter discussing the implications of Rosenthal's work on experimenter influence, Tooley and Pratt (1964, p. 254–255) comment:

> One popular approach to the problem [of experimenter influence over data] has been systematically to track down, and wherever possible

control (usually meaning "attempt to eradicate"), all sources of experimenter influence. This approach is based largely on the tired epistemology and inoperable value system of a passé "classical" physics paradigm which placed much value on so called "value free" inquiry and sanctioned ill-defined uses of the term "scientific objectivity"—both terms so fraught with surplus and often antithetical meaning as to be virtually meaningless. . . . Every inhuman attempt was made to "include the observer out" of the observed system.

An alternative approach entails a radical reconceptualization of the historic ideal of "scientific objectivity" and a radical revision of the role of investigator who has been structured and stereotyped as a detached, outside-looking-in observer. From our point of view, the investigator is inextricably involved in the system which he studies as a *participant-observer*, and is to be considered as *one* source of variation(s), among others to be accounted for in the experimental system. This can be as a source of within, between, or interaction variance (i.e., emergent or transaction variance). In some experimental systems, depending upon the purposes of the particular investigation, it might be desirable to minimize his participation (influence) in the system by programming his role in a highly structured, constricted, and stabilized manner. In other participant-observer situations (e.g., psychotherapy, education change induction, action research, etc.) the purpose might be to influence the system under investigation as much as possible, but still accounting for (though now exploiting) the variance within the system attributable to the several significant and relevant aspects of the investigator's participant-observation. From this perspective the quixotic attempt to eliminate the effects of participant-observation in the name of misplaced pseudo-objectivity is fruitless, not so much because it is impossible but because it is unproductive. Indeed if science succeeded in being totally "objective" in the erroneous sense of being value free and devoid of experimenter influence—then there could be no science, just a series of unrelated, uninterpreted, meaningless "facts" (which in themselves, as a matter of fact, constitute phenomenological inferences of varying degrees).

These different studies and comments have implications for field researchers in connection with the problem of unintended influence. They suggest that the field researcher may be both better and worse off than he has been accustomed to thinking. For many years, field researchers have lived with the stigma attached to the expression "Hawthorne effect" when laboratory purists discussed the pitfalls of field researcher influence. And the laboratory purists were right. The research in the Hawthorne plant's Relay Assembly Test Room showed that outside researchers and management had indeed created a new kind of environment for the workers (Roethlisberger and Dickson, 1939). Yet, the recent evidence suggests that it was partly *laboratory* conditions themselves that contributed to experimenter influence. The evidence also suggests that these conditions are not easily avoided through the use of more and tighter controls. Consequently, a tentative hypothesis might be that: *The more the experimental setting* (a) *deprives the subject of his customary controls* (*including self-control*) *and* (b) *places the subject under new controls imposed by the experimental design, then the more the subject becomes dependent upon the experimenter for cues on appropriate behavior.*

The experimental subject undoubtedly has some choice as to whether he will accept or reject the cues he receives from the experimenter or other subjects. Milgram's (1965) and Asch's (1952) research suggest that subject resistance to experimental authority will increase when the subject is supported by fellow subjects. But like Riesman's "other-directed man" who becomes more other-directed in times of uncertainty; uncertain subjects seem most sensitive to cues emitted by the experimenter. To the extent that the experimenter represents a non-threatening temporary authority, the subject probably tries to fulfill the experimenter's expectations (Binder, McConnell and Sjoholm, 1957; Spires, 1960). Because the conditions of non-threatening authority are probably more present under the usual laboratory conditions where the subject is a student volunteer, one might also suspect that experimenter influence would be greater here than where adult nonvolunteers are working in organizations (Rosenthal, 1965).

In this respect, the problem of unintended experimenter influence is probably less crucial in field experiments than in laboratory experiments. The field researcher typically poses less of an authority problem. Participants in a field study tend to be older than college student subjects and are already working within an established organizational hierarchy. The same lack of authority which prevents the experimenter from setting up exacting controls in an organization now becomes a mixed blessing. It also makes organizational members less dependent upon him than they might be under most laboratory conditions.

The Influence of the Subjects

At the same time, the field researcher faces the problem of "subject influence" upon him. He can become victimized by his own involvement and identification with people who work in the field situation. The researcher is, as Scott (1965, p. 278) says: "susceptible to the danger of becoming over-socialized with respect to the subject group so that he begins to see the world as his fellow participants see it . . . he finds less and less that requires explanation as he comes to share the premises and values of the group in which he is immersed." Scott proposes two antidotes for this problem of subject influence including (a) going back to early field notes in order to gain a more objective perspective, and

(b) discussions with more detached professional colleagues. Moreover, the problem possibly becomes reduced due to lower involvement when a team of researchers studies multiple organizational units (e.g., a comparative study or field experiment). However, it remains a source of unintended influence in field study observations just as experimenter bias may influence laboratory observations.

What is the proper attitude to take with regard to this wider influence network that varies from intended patterns and yet can contaminate supposedly "pure" experimental conditions? Unfortunately, as Klintz et al. (1965) suggest, many experimenters have tended to ignore or rationalize away the implications of these potential influence patterns, particularly those patterns resulting from their own involvement. There are reasons for this, some of them touched upon earlier: the experimental world is complicated enough without trying to take account of the experimenter's effects; the problem introduces another variable which is irrelevant for purposes of many experiments under study; scientists are supposed to remain detached from their data and be objective about it. Furthermore, by accepting experimenter involvement as a reality, social scientists acknowledge that they are still more social than scientist. For many, this is a bitter pill to swallow. They have struggled long and hard to gain membership within the fraternity of science while building their own foundation of detached objectivity. They fail to note that such foundations have flaws, even in the natural sciences as shown by recent developments in quantum theory. Percy Bridgman, a Nobel Prize winner in physics, wrote (1958, p. 88):

> The point of view of quantum theory has implications for us much wider than the technical details. It forces us to realize that we cannot have information without acquiring that information by some method, and the story is not complete until we have told both what we know and how we know it. In other words we have to remember that we always have an observer. Furthermore, the observer is ourselves, and therefore we cannot get away from him. But getting away from itself is what the human race has been trying to do ever since it started philosophizing or worshipping.

ALTERNATIVES AND ALTERATIONS

The above comments and the findings on environmental influence, experimenter influence and subject influence suggest that field experimenters need to search further for useful design alternatives and alterations. Even though, as Bridgman says, the experimenter cannot get away from himself, he can at least reformulate his role so as to take into account the problem of his own involvement. He must find ways to treat himself as a variable rather than eulogize his role as a detached controller of other variables. He also needs to explore further the possibilities for altering environmental and subject variables beyond the limits of those assumed by classical design requirements. In short, as McGuigan (1963), Tooley and Pratt (1964), and Klintz et al. (1965), suggest, it seems time to review and broaden our notions of experimental design.

We can do this in the final parts of this chapter by examining some procedures for altering experimental designs in terms of (a) environmental alterations, (b) subject involvement, and (c) experimenter involvement. To be sure, these various alternatives complicate the problem of experimental design. However, they also give the experimenter greater freedom of design and deserve more extensive use without accusations of scientific treason. The findings reported in the previous section indicate that experimental design is still in a rough and rudimentary stage of development. Rather than stifling further experimentation through such verbal constraints as "scientific method," "value-free objectivity," and "good experimental practice," it seems better to explore, innovate, reevaluate, and loosen up some of the unrealistically tight traditions of social science. This seems particularly possible now when data processing and computational procedures are themselves springing loose from the era of paper-and-pencil analysis. As Kaplan (1964, p. 162) has noted:

> The mathematics and statistics of the eighteenth and nineteenth centuries could conveniently manage only two changing variables at a time, and the ideal experiment was therefore conceived as an experiment in which all the variables but two were held constant. One, the "independent variable," was then manipulated, while observations were made on the other, the "dependent variable." This was the practical basis of the classical one-factor theory of experiment mentioned in the preceding section. But contemporary mathematics no longer imposes this constraint, and manipulation—whether to hold "everything else" constant, or to introduce changes in the one factor—is correspondingly no longer absolutely essential. Reconstructed logic is still occupied largely in catching up with the developments in statistical theory and technique of the early decades of this century. It has scarcely begun, it seems to me, to take account of the revolutionary changes in the logic-in-use by present-day scientists that have been brought about by the fantastic developments in the capacities of computers and of the whole data processing technology.

Environmental Alterations

A review of environmental alterations shows a series of procedures used by experimenters to help them control and understand what goes on within the experimental situation. Experimenters tend to treat these procedures as devices which help protect the experimental situation from outside interferences. They are referred to most often as experimental "controls" and they usually help to define the boundaries and limits of the experimental environment. French (1953) discusses some of these experimental-environmental controls in his chapter on field experiments in the Festinger and Katz (1953) book. Briefly paraphrased he mentions:

1. *Control Groups.* Matched with experimental groups on all variables which, if they differed, might confound the data. Control groups are usually established in laboratory experiments by placing a randomly drawn selection of subjects in both experimental and control groups. In field experiments, control groups are more often "matched" as closely as possible with the experimental groups.

2. *Measurement Controls.* Achieved through statistical manipulation of the data. For example, two similar but unequal sets of data may be equalized so as to permit direct comparison. In addition, the effects of one variable may be separated from the other variables through the use of multivariate techniques of analysis. Measurement controls and statistical records appear to have increasing promise as data processing methods improve.

3. *Replication.* Involves the repetition of an earlier experiment under as close to identical conditions as possible. French (1953) believes that field experiments should be replicated in the same setting as the first experiment. However, Selltiz et al. (1959) disagree and argue that the true test of replication comes from the repetition of studies under *different* unique conditions. In either case, the intent is to establish boundaries for the generalizations that can be drawn from the first experiment.

4. *Preliminary Experiments.* Designed to pretest procedures, instruments, and hypotheses and, as French says, "work the bugs out of the experimental manipulations."

5. *Standardization.* The uniformity of conditions as well as the uniformity of procedures. An effort is made to keep "all other things equal" for both experimental and control situations by standardizing all but the crucial experimental variable(s). This involves not only matched control group(s) but the standardizing of environmental influences and experimenter behavior.

6. *Insulation.* Eliminating some conditions that might otherwise influence the experimental or control situation. The experimental laboratory itself is one form of insulation, designed to prevent contaminating outside influences.

7. *Safety Factors.* Provide a form of data collecting "insurance" by urging the experimenter to collect enough data to make a good field study out of an unsuccessful field experiment.

8. *Size of Units.* A crucial criterion for organizational field experiments for Seashore (1964). But, as French (1953) points out, the smaller the unit, the greater the possibility of control. Consequently, French leans toward small-group field experiments as scientifically more feasible.

9. *Length-of-time Controls.* Subject to the same logic as the unit-size control mentioned above. The shorter the length of time, the less chance for contaminating variables to creep into the experiment. By shortening the time of the experiment, the experimenter also probably restricts the scope of changes that can be introduced.

The fact that these devices are thought of as "controls" tends to highlight their restrictive qualities and undervalue their potential as substitutes for each other and as design alternatives. Too often a potential experiment founders for lack of one of these devices when another might have taken its place. By altering the environmental structure of the experiment slightly, the same experimental variables might be tested in a different way.

Several such environmental alterations are suggested by Selltiz, Jahoda, Deutsch, and Cook (1959) and French's (1953) list of control devices suggests others. For example:

1. Measurement controls or different types of "control" groups can substitute for the direct manipulation of the experimental variables. Measurement controls can be used by establishing data collection procedures which show that certain events consistently occur prior to certain other events. The risk is that this relationship will demonstrate correlation but not causality. The researcher must then search for and study examples of each set of variables which were unaccompanied by the other set. He may also wish to set up a comparative study (instead of an experimental-control group study) in which he introduces the first set of variables into one group and the second set into the other group.

2. Control groups which cannot be matched well with experimental groups can be turned instead into comparative study units. In reality, most field experiments take the form of comparative studies in that the control groups or organizational units are not deprived of the experimental variable but simply experience a substitute in a different degree or form. A well-known example where potential control groups were intentionally turned into comparative groups would be the Morse and Reimer (1956) "field experiment" involving four clerical divisions of a large organization. Two of the divisions were coached toward more participative decision-making procedures. The other two divisions were coached toward more hierarchical decision making. There were no "control" divisions in the classical design sense. Campbell (1957, p. 306)

touches upon the artificiality of the "control" group concept in social research when he notes that:

> In presenting the above designs, X (symbolizing the exposure of a group to an experimental variable) has been opposed to No-X as is traditional in discussions of experimental design in psychology. But while this may be a legitimate description of a stimulus isolated physical science laboratory, it can only be a convenient shorthand in the social sciences, for any No-X period will not be empty of potentially change inducing material. The experience of the control group might better be categorized as another type of X, a control experience, an X_c instead of No-X.

3. Measurement controls can substitute for other forms of standardization. In many cases, it is possible to equalize data from two situations so as to make them directly comparable. In other cases, where randomized control groups cannot be established, a matched sample of both experimental and control populations can be drawn using certain basic criteria (e.g., age, organizational status, experience, test scores). These matched samples can be compared with each other and with the rest of the population in both experimental and control situations. In still other cases, an analysis of variance will permit the researcher to separate out for himself the variables he wants to compare in two or more groups. Thus the standardizing of situations can be replaced somewhat by a statistical isolation of variables.

The greatest possibilities for environmental alterations seem to come from control group or measurement variations. We noted earlier that the classical design involved one or more experimental groups and one or more control groups measured both before and after experimental treatment. But it is important to consider other experimental-control group configurations just as it is important to consider other measurement strategies.

For example, the reader will recall that Solomon (1949) indicated that "before" measures could influence behavior by sensitizing subjects to behave during the experiment differently than if the measurement of behavior, attitudes or relationships had not been made. As a partial remedy for the problem he posed, Solomon proposed altering both the group structure and the timing of measurements. He added two new groups to the experimental design; one was to be experimental, the other control. Neither group was to be measured before the experimental treatment. Using an extension of Stouffer's (1950) diagram, Solomon's Four Group Design would appear as shown in Figure 5. Campbell (1957) has referred to it as the "new ideal design for social scientists."

In effect, Solomon's (1949) model can be tested both for the effects of

FIGURE 5

Solomon Four-Group Design

	Before	After
Experimental Group 1	X_1	X_2
Control Group 1	X'_1	X'_2
Experimental Group 2		X''_2
Control Group 2		X'''_2

Treatment
Effect $= X''_2 - \dfrac{X_1 + X'_1}{2}$

Measurement
Effect $= (X'_2 - X'_1) - (X'''_2 - \dfrac{X_1 + X'_1}{2})$

experimental treatment and for the effects of "before" measurements on "after" responses. However, the "new" ideal model poses major problems of implementation for field experimenters. It requires at least four matched groups or organizations, a difficult task if done with any precision. In addition, if the experimenter wishes to study the effects of experimental variable No. 2 over and above the effects of variable No. 1, he needs two more experimental groups, one measured before the experiment, the other not measured. If he wants two "after" measures (e.g., short-term and long-term effects of experimental treatment) he needs four more groups. Finally, given the problems of poorly matched organizational units, experimenter influence, and subject involvement, it may be too much to hope that any "before" measure of the X''_2 experimental group would equal the average of X_1 and X'_1, the two groups which were measured before the experimental treatment. However, the researcher is required to make this assumption when using the Solomon design.

Once exposed to the complexities of the Four Group Design, the field experimenter is strongly tempted to look for simpler alternatives. One of these can be called the "One-Group Before-After Design." It is diagrammed in Figure 6. Argyle (1957) refers to this design as the "Simple Successive Conditions" design where the "before" condition is either the first of two or more experimental conditions or a pre-experimental situation. The big advantage of this design is that it requires no matching control groups. In addition, with before and after (or successive experimental conditions) measures, both change and no-change subjects can be studied. Argyle describes a more complicated version of this design and its conditions for success in discussing the Lewin, Lippitt, and White (1939) experiments. These experiments tested different styles of leadership among boys' groups using a counterbalanced treatment of different conditions. Several groups were used. Each received each treatment in a successively counterbalanced order. Argyle (1957, pp. 48–49) writes that: "Lippit (1940) . . . used successive conditions in his experiment . . . and furthermore was able to observe interesting transfer effects at the change-over. The boys were unaware that an experiment was in progress and it may be that the successive conditions design is practicable only when this is the case."

Like Argyle (1957), Selltiz, Jahoda, Deutsch, and Cook (1959) believe the One-Group Before-After Design is most useful when (a) the "before" measure will affect neither subsequent behavior nor responses to the "after" measure, and (b) "other" influences (e.g., history, maturation, etc.) which might affect the experimental treatment are absent. However, they view this design as being adequate only in fields where much experimental work is underway (e.g., learning and sensory preception) and as vulnerable in fields such as organizational behavior. Campbell (1957) takes somewhat the same attitude and refers unenthusiastically to the One-Group Before-After Design as "pre-experimental." Campbell notes that there are too many opportunities for unmeasureable contamination of results. Without control group comparisons, a single group may be influenced by unknown extraneous variables.

The problem with this position is that it places more faith in control groups than they deserve in field situations. Control groups are theoretically identical with experimental groups in every respect but experi-

FIGURE 6

One-Group Before-After Design

	Before	After	
Experimental Group	X_1	X_2	Treatment Effect $= X_2 - X_1$
Control Group			

mental treatment. In most field situations, however, such matched organizational units are difficult to arrange and almost impossible to maintain over any period of time. Under some conditions, the statistical control of a "before" measure would be superior to control group structures. It seems that experimental designers have been more puritanical than practical in their early dismissal of this design. Under conditions where the researcher knows his organization and its available statistics, he may be able to determine the importance of "other" influences to some extent. He may also be able to gather much of his "before" data from these same statistical sources or disguise "before" measures so that they interfere minimally with subjects' later responses and behavior. Minimal interference of "before" measures seems likely when there is a long period of time (e.g., a year or more) between successive measures, and such intervals are often required in organizational change efforts. As we noted earlier, however, long-time intervals also increase the possibility of extraneous influences due to maturation effects.

Still another design alternative is the "After-Only" Design, considered useful when assignments to experimental and control groups can be made according to randomization or matching procedures. Again, however, the problem of achieving randomized or truly matched organizational units limits this design. As a substitute, some field researchers compare individuals rather than organizational units as when randomly picking a sample of salesmen rather than a single district to test-market a new product. In other cases, researchers will fall back upon a design which Campbell (1957) critically labels the "Static-Group" comparison (i.e., the control group has not been equated with the experimental group on a randomized basis before the study). Figure 7 pictures the After-Only Design using both experimental and control groups. Despite its limitations, Argyle (1957) notes that the After-Only Design has been

FIGURE 7

After-Only Design

	Before	After	
Experimental Group		X_2	Treatment Effect $= X_2 - X'_2$
Control Group		X'_2	

preferable in the majority of social experiments because it avoids (a) the problems of unknown changes occurring over time, and (b) the problems of "before" measurements affecting later measurements.

A good example of an After-Only experiment is found in the studies of longwall coal mining done in England by the Tavistock Institute. Trist and Bamforth (1951) describe how a mechanized longwall mining procedure was compared on an After-Only basis with a composite method which contained work practices of both the old hand-got methods and the mechanized longwall methods. By using measurement controls to help equalize the data, the researchers convincingly compare the two work methods in terms of productivity, absenteeism, down time, and satisfaction.

The above environmental alterations can be introduced without altering experimenter-subject relationships. However, there is nothing in environmental alterations that prevents either subject involvement or experimenter involvement from being changed. These two variables often affect each other more than either responds to environmental alterations. Thus, the extent and ways in which an experimenter behaves will affect subjects' involvement and vice versa. Although few subjects are encouraged to be more than subjects, there are a few exceptions. These we shall examine under the heading of Subject Involvement Alterations.

Subject Involvement Alterations

An experimental design *can* be varied so as to encourage different kinds of subject involvement. This is typically the least varied of the three dimensions discussed in this section (i.e., environment, subject, and experimenter), although laboratory experiments tend to treat the subject according to one model while field studies use another. The prevailing laboratory assumption holds that the subject should be kept unaware of the experimenter's intentions so as not to contaminate the data with false reports, adjusted behavior, etc. The same assumption would "ideally" hold in field studies but field conditions usually force compromises in the direction of disclosure. To the extent that each of these practices prevails, they need serious revaluation.

For example, some laboratory experimenters go to great lengths to disguise the true nature of the experiment. Abstract tasks, confederates with false reports, misleading instructions or incorrect data feedback are used, among other devices. At the same time, as Orne (1962) and Orne and Evans (1965) have reported, the typical laboratory experiment is surrounded by enough mystique so that the subject is both second guessing the experimenter and willing to go along with the game. There is further evidence from the reports of McGuigan (1963) and Rosenthal

(1963 a and b, 1964) that subjects do a pretty good job of second guessing the experimenter's hypotheses while Orne and Evans' (1965) work suggests that subjects comply with an experiment's instructions to an extent that they would not consider under more normal conditions.

One of the interesting things about some of Orne and Evans' work, however, was the use of an "aware" control group. As we noted earlier, some of the "hypnotized" subjects pretended to be hypnotized but were actually not. Orne and Evans wanted to learn whether these "aware" subjects would comply with experimenters' instructions as fully as hypnotized subjects did. The aware subjects did follow instructions, but their compliance was apparently due largely to their desire to "go along" with the experiment. By using this "aware" control group, Orne and Evans showed that an "unaware" experimenter can induce compliance among non-hypnotized as well as hypnotized subjects. More important for our purposes right now, they also showed that varying degrees of subject involvement can help to show an experiment's impact upon "unaware" subjects and upon "unaware" experimenters. This experiment-within-an-experiment made some experimenters into subjects and some subjects into experimental assistants. In this case, however, the experimental assistants were not deceiving their own colleagues (e.g., fellow students); they were simply asked to take a role (hypnotized students) and then follow their own dictates.

The problem of subject involvement in field situations is both similar to and different from laboratory settings. It is similar in that organizational members typically "go along with" management and the experimenter without any clear-cut benefits for themselves. It is different in that subjects are less under the control of either the experimenter or the experimental situation. As a result, they can usually demand (and get) a fuller explanation of the study's purposes and design. For example, in an organizational field experiment now underway with eight widely dispersed districts of a large government agency, we found it useful and necessary to take elaborate steps to make sure that the study "made sense" to the 2,800 people participating. Once the study with its eventual feedback of data did make sense to agency personnel, questionnaire responses were quite high. Returns were over 90 percent on a two-hour questionnaire the first time and over 80 percent a year later when the questionnaire was readministered.

Under these conditions, subjects in a field experiment can be *too* aware of the experimental variables. However, as we have already seen, the same is true in almost any experimental situation involving subjects who "know" that a study is underway. The important requirement would seem to be not the withholding of information, but the *equalized distribution of information.* When one field setting receives a certain message, questionnaire, or visit from the experimenters, it is important that the other field settings receive the same treatment. The assumption here is that subjects in field settings should not necessarily be isolated from experimenter involvement, but that the involvement should be made as identical as possible.

These comments suggest that subject isolation and unawareness may be less important than attempting to identify the impact of each variable upon subjects, some of whom may be highly aware of the experimental design. The above comments also suggest that keeping all other things "equal" in experimental situations is more important than keeping all other things "constant." Moreover, input variables *can* be more and more easily identified and equalized through measurement controls and statistical manipulation. Consequently, the day may still come when multiple variables acting upon a field situation may be seen as a useful path for varying subject involvement rather than as a serious block to field experimentation.

Experimenter Involvement Alterations

The most challenging and potentially productive alterations in field experiments will come from alterations the experimenter makes in his own involvement. Although traditional experimental design combines the "observer-scientist" and "detached-controller" roles (Bernard, 1957), this makes little sense in light of the complexity of field experiments and the findings on experimenter involvement-influence.

The complexity of field experiments suggests a dividing of responsibility into experimental treatment and data collection and analysis. The individuals who plan and implement a new organizational approach through Task, Technology, People and/or Structure changes may lack adequate knowledge of field research, statistics, psychometrics, or interviewing procedures. The opposite is also true. Both designer and observer tasks require manpower and talents that increase with knowledge of experimental design and analysis. As in almost any other field, expertise and specialized skills are increasingly useful in such subareas. It is difficult at best for one man or group to work on all facets of a field experiment and keep abreast of methodological developments.

The findings on experimenter involvement and influence suggest that dividing the traditional designer and observer roles may lead to more "objective" studies. The irony is that some experimenters value the traditionally combined roles of detached-manipulator and observer-scientist while they avoid the research which tells them that the detached-manipulator may be what they respect least of all—an involved participant who influences subjects despite his best intentions (Klintz et al., 1965). Laboratory experimenters who defend their science are in the uneasy position of being found to be involved participants. One way of resolving the dilemma is for them to evaluate anew those times and places where a division of the designer and observer roles might prove useful. There is nothing inherent in the rules of "good" experimental design (only in its traditions) that prevents the observer from being a different person or group than the designer of the experiment. In fact, accurate observation, regardless of who does it, should receive a higher priority than the overlapping of designer-observer roles, particularly when the overlapping jeopardizes the truly "scientific" nature of an experiment.

The possibility of splitting as well as combining the roles of designer and observer suggests a series of alternative designs based upon alterations in experimenter involvement. These alternatives appear in Figure 8 which shows how the designer of an experiment may or may not be the same person(s) as the observer. In addition, the diagram suggests that these different roles may be taken by either members of the organizational system or by one or more outside researchers. In Figure 8, two outside research units are shown (Outside Researcher $_1$ and Outside Researcher $_2$).

The diagram suggests that by arranging the designer-observer roles in different ways, a number of experimental alternatives become explicit. The first is the familiar Classical Design Field Experiment. As shown in Figure 8, the same outside researcher designs and observes the experiment. Thus when Outside Researcher $_1$ both designs and observes the study, it is, in a sense, controlled by him from beginning to end. The same would be true if Outside Researcher $_2$ fulfilled both functions.

However, the other four alternatives shown in Figure 8 are less familiar than the classical design model. They include the Internal Experiment, the Natural Experiment, the Split-Role Experiment, and the Operational Experiment.

An *Internal Experiment* uses members from within an organizational system as both designers and observers of experimental efforts. Though probably the least impressive to behavioral scientists, variations of this design are probably the most common within organizational situations. At the same time, accounts of internal experiments rarely get published in behavioral science journals. Most of the time, the accounts are anecdotal in nature or else restricted to After-Only case descriptions of a single organizational unit. The method is further hampered by the fact that many managers are awed by the terminology and research barriers put up by the behavioral scientists themselves. These language and re-

FIGURE 8

Experimental Designs Influenced by
Allocation of Designer-Observer Roles

OBSERVER

	Organizational System Members	Outside Researcher₁	Outside Researcher₂
Organizational System Members	Internal Experiment	Natural Field Experiment	Natural Field Experiment
Outside Researcher₁	Operational Experiment	Classical Design Field Experiment	Split-Role Field Experiment
Outside Researcher₂	Operational Experiment	Split-Role Field Experiment	Classical Design Field Experiment

DESIGNER

search technology barriers hide the fact that ample data often exist in the form of company records, reports, and observations. If these data were collected and ordered by organizational personnel, the chances are that some fairly sophisticated experimental studies could emerge.

An example of an internal experiment was one by Carron (1964) who studied the attitude changes resulting from a Human Relations Training program given to selected managers within his company. As a corporate staff member, Carron set up both an experimental and a matched control group and took attitude measurements before training, after training, and seventeen months later. Using vector geometry to help analyze his data, Carron found significant attitude changes among the experimental group which persisted over time.

The *Natural Field Experiment* was referred to earlier in this chapter as a situation in which the researcher "opportunistically capitalizes upon some ongoing changes" (French, 1953). In a natural field experiment, members of the organizational system initiate and implement changes, while an outside researcher assumes the task of observing, measuring and analyzing the changes.

An example of a natural field experiment is a study of attitude changes done by Lieberman (1956) while a member of the Survey Research Center at Mighigan. Lieberman was engaged in a larger research study in a company and took advantage of promotions and role changes among union members. Some of the union members were promoted to foremen. Others were elected to be union stewards. Still later, some of the foremen and stewards were forced to return to the worker ranks; the foremen because of an economic recession and the stewards because they either resigned or were not reelected.

Lieberman thus had (a) an experimental group of workers who became foremen, (b) another experimental group of workers who became union stewards, and (c) a control group of workers who could be individually matched with members of the two experimental groups. In addition, Lieberman could compare the "demoted" foremen or stewards with those who stayed in the higher-status positions.

The hypothesis being tested was "People who are placed in a role will tend to take on or develop attitudes that are congruent with the expectations associated with that role." Attitude measures were taken before and after the promotions. They were taken once again after the demotions. The results showed that attitude changes tended to follow role changes; new foremen tended to become more pro-management than they had been as workers, while new union stewards become slightly more pro-union. Following demotion, those who had been foremen reverted to their old attitudes; those who had been stewards retained more of their steward attitudes, but these were fairly close to their old attitudes as workers.

Lieberman's study, together with the author's own experience with natural field experiments (Dalton, Barnes, and Zaleznik, in press), suggests that ample opportunities exist for field experimentation if the researcher has already established field relationships and has some awareness of the changes being planned by or imposed upon the organization. One problem is that contacts between behavioral scientists and managers are typically limited to specific consulting activities and/or to the researcher's own specified research projects. However, observation opportunities still exist for researchers who maintain their field contacts over time.

Not surprisingly, the criticism of natural experiments centers largely on the fact that the experimenter loses some control over the design. For this reason, most experimenters would consider the natural experiment a lower form of design than the classical design field experiment. For example, Selltiz, Jahoda, Deutsch, and Cook (1959, p. 93) quote Greenwood in support of their contention that:

> Natural situations are complicated and do not permit the investigator to assume, with any confidence that the groups to be compared differ only by chance. As Greenwood (1945) has stated: ". . . the created situation gives us better control power over our phenomenon. We can determine at our own discretion the circumstances which shall be present, and thus arrive at more conclusive evidence of causality. . . . The ability to produce the necessary changes permits the test of hypotheses otherwise not amenable to vertification."

However, a more positive view of natural experiments is reported by Daniel Katz (1953, p. 78) who writes:

> The best opportunity for the use of hypothesis testing is on the occasion of the "natural experiment." The difficulty with the use of hypotheses in field studies is the inability to determine causal relationships with any definiteness, since most of our measures are not taken with respect to systematic changes in some ascertained independent variable. Now, a natural experiment is a change of major importance engineered by policy-makers and practitioners and not by social scientists. It is experimental from the point of view of the scientist rather than of the social engineer.

An argument can be made that, aside from experimenter control, the natural field experiment has several advantages over the classical design experiment. The natural experiment divides research roles by leaving the design and implementation of the experiment with management and the data collection and analysis with outside researchers. Although both parties might check on the timing of experimental treatments so as to match these best with observation-measurement opportunities, each deliberately avoids influencing the other's work. For some managers, this has the advantage of keeping behavioral scientists out of the day-to-day operations of the organization. Likewise, for some researchers, it has the advantage of leaving the power and the headaches of implementing changes up to management. Furthermore, the loss of experimenter control in natural field experiments seems exaggerated. Almost all the relatively few controls available to an outside researcher are available under natural experiment conditions as well.

A *Split-Role Field Experiment* involves not only the organization, but also two separate researchers or research teams from outside the organization. In this case the experiment is designed and partly implemented by one of the two outside researchers (e.g., Outside Researcher₁). The other researcher (e.g., Outside Researcher 2) serves as the observer and collector of data. The Split-Role design has the advantage of separating the designer and his vested interests or hypotheses from the observer-evaluator function.

An example of the Split-Role field experiment is found in the Seashore and Bowers (1963) study of five departments in an industrial plant. In this experiment, the change advocate (Outside Researcher 1) was a colleague of Seashore's and Bowers' from the Survey Research Center. The changes were implemented by management with considerable coaching from Outside Researcher 1. The observation and evaluation of the changes were handled by Seashore and Bowers in their Outside Researcher 2 roles. Four independent change variables were introduced by Outside Researcher 1. These experimental variables were derived from Likert's (1961) modified theory of management and involved the introducing of purposeful change into three of the five departments. The independent variables were:

1) Increase in emphasis on the work group as a functioning unit of organization.
2) Increase in the amount of supportive behavior on the part of supervisors.
3) Increase in participation by employees in decision-making processes within their area of responsibility
4) Increase in amount of interaction and influence among work group members.

Seashore and Bowers (1963) report that the introduction of these variables by Outside Researcher 1 appeared to be relatively successful in the three experimental departments. Survey results after the changes also showed greater increases in employee satisfaction within the experimental departments. Company records showed somewhat more ambiguous findings in the areas of production, machine efficiency, waste, and absence rates. In their analysis of the results, Seashore and Bowers (1963, p. 101) note that:

> On the face of it, the experiment appears to be a success, and the theoretical propositions embodied in the experiment appear to have considerable support. However, the evidence is not conclusive and there is room for difference of opinion about the significance of these results.

With regard to the Split-Role Design, Seashore (1964, p. 169) comments:

> To accommodate the requirements of both experimental change and practical application ventures, there is likely to arise a new professional group devoted to change agentry, different in important respects from their professional colleagues in the fields of training and management consulting. The researcher himself is not likely to have the qualifications or time to perform this essential research function, and in the interests of objectivity, he probably should not be involved in it. For such practical reasons, the research plans in field experiments should in many cases provide for some kind of division of labor between those who do the theoretical, analytic, and interpretative work, on the one hand, and those who engage in active and personal interventions in the subject organizations.

The *Operational Field Experiment* is the final alternative shown in Figure 8 involving different patterns of experimenter involvement. The Operational Experiment places an outside researcher in the role of designer with members of the organizational system filling the observer-evaluator roles. A similar relationship often exists in many consultant-client relationships. In addition, however, Outside Researcher $_1$ makes an explicit attempt to base the suggested change variables upon previous research and social science hypotheses. Then, as in the case of the Split-Role Design, Outside Researcher $_1$ becomes highly involved in the implementation of the change variables in key areas of the organizational system (e.g., LeBreton, 1965). Meanwhile, the organization sets up (or already has available) controls by which to measure the success of the changes in the experimental units.

Among the field researchers who most strongly advocate Operational Experiments are members of the Tavistock Institute in England. Because they tend to treat organizations as "open systems" responding to environmental influences, the Tavistock representatives (e.g., Trist, Higgin, Murray, and Pollock, 1963) also treat the outside researcher as a source of potential influence. Rather than trying to eliminate his influence, they consider him a change advocate who works closely with members of the organizational system in implementing change in crucial areas of the organization. In this sense, the experimental design becomes a collaborative endeavor during its implementation stages, even though the original design may have been formulated by Outside Researcher [1]. In discussing operational experiments, Trist et al. (1963) have written:

> In all [our] projects described, it is the intention to take them through to the point where the research findings have been built into working models of system change which have been thoroughly tested out (validated) under real life conditions. We usually refer to these as operational experiments. . . . A main responsibility of the research team is to work out general principles on the basis of which working models or operational experiments may be constructed.

In this experimental relationship, organization members served as observers and used both conventional and special measures of efficient performance. In the Operational Experiments reported by Trist et al. (1963) on methods of coal mining, the measures most used were those collected in the daily course of mining operations (e.g., tonnage produced, labor efficiency, output per man shift). The outside researchers did most of their data collecting during the early stages of the research while they were trying to formulate their hypotheses on the important change variables.

One major problem of Operational Experiments is the one it poses for those who conceptually think in terms of more traditional models of experimentation. For them, the Operational Experiment appears to be a gross distortion of experimental method. It intermingles experimenter and subjects, neglects the "control" of environmental variables and typically pays more attention to change than to experimental design. With all these objections, the Operational Experimentalists would probably agree. They would argue back, however, that, in field experiment situations, the experimenter tends to influence his subjects whether he wishes to or not; that the environmental variables will influence the setting regardless of the controls attempted by the experimenter and that the problems of changing an organization are more challenging and realistic than the problems of observing one while using a conventional experimental design. Again, as we saw before, a dilemma confronts the would-be field researcher. Does he identify himself with the values of scientific objectivity or with the values of applied change induction? The Operational Experimentalists would argue that such a forced choice is not necessary. Others would see it as imperative. Our own opinion is that the state of current field experiment design leaves room for all of these alternatives as long as the researcher has thought carefully about the alternative he is choosing and the reasons for his choice.

CONCLUSION

I have attempted to conceptualize and describe organizational change in terms of *approaches, human relationships,* and *change processes.* The *approaches* to change are grossly identified as Task, Technology, People, and Structure. Their design and implementation hinge largely on aspects of power distribution among managers, employees, and outsiders. *Human relationships* during organizational change are viewed as relationships among subgroups of change initiators and organizational members who either advocate or resist the changes in data-based rational or emotional ways. *Change processes* are divided into a sequence of subprocesses moving toward changes in attitude, reshaped goals, new alliances, and internalized motivation.

In the second part of the chapter, field experiment methodologies are analyzed as ways of studying the above components and subcomponents. In general, the discussion group in Pittsburgh felt dissatisfaction with the restrictiveness of classical experiment designs. At first glance, such designs seemed suited for laboratory experiments but constraining on field experimenters; at second glance, classical designs seemed restrictive even in laboratory settings. In an attempt to broaden thinking on an experimenter's range of design possibilities, I have examined experimental designs that could be worked out around *environmental alterations, subject involvement alterations,* and *experimenter involvement alterations.* Taken together with the components of organizational change, these alternative design possibilities suggest a massive amount of work for the behavioral science fraternity. This in itself, of course, is healthy. What did not seem healthy to the discussion group in Pittsburgh was the inclination of some behavioral scientists (ourselves included at times) to prematurely formalize the experimental process in field research. With the "search" taken out of research design, organizational field experimentation has become bogged down in the intricacies of design detail and is left partly paralyzed. Our hope was that through our discussions, some of the excitement of organizational research might henceforth be redirected toward large-scale field experiments in organizational settings.

REFERENCES

ABBREVIATIONS

ASR	*American Sociological Review*
RH	*Human Relations*
JAP	*Journal of Applied Psychology*
JASP	*Journal of Abnormal and Social Psychology*
MS	*Management Science*
SSR	*Sociology and Social Research*

Andrews, K. "Executive Training by the Case Method." In K. Andrews, ed., *Human Relations and Administration; The Case Method of Training*, Cambridge: Harvard U. Press, 1953.

Argyle, M. *The Scientific Study of Social Behavior*. London: Methuen, 1957.

Argyris, C. *Interpersonal Competence and Organizational Effectiveness*. Homewood, Ill.: I–Dorsey, 1962.

Asch, S. E. *Social Psychology*. New York: Prentice-Hall, 1952.

Barnes, L. B. *Organizational Systems and Engineering Groups*. Boston: Harvard Graduate School of Business Administration, Division of Research, 1960.

Bennis, W. G. "A New Role for the Behavioral Sciences: Effecting Organizational Change." *Administrative Science Qtly.*, 1963, 8 (2), 126–165.

————. *Changing Organizations*. New York: McGraw-Hill, 1966.

Bernard, C. *An Introduction to the Study of Experimental Medicine*. Trans. by H. C. Greene. New York: Dover Publications, 1957 (first published in the French edition in 1865).

Binder, A., McConnell, D., and Sjoholm, N. A. "Verbal Conditioning as a Function of Experimenter Characteristics." *JASP*, 1957, 55, 309–314.

Blake, R. R. and Mouton, J. S. *The Managerial Grid*. Houston: Gulf Publishing Co., 1964.

Blake, R. R. and Mouton, J. S.; Barnes, L. B. and Greiner, L. E. "Breakthrough in Organization Development." *Harvard Business Rev.*, November–December 1964, 133–155.

Bridgman, P. W. "Quo Vadis." *Daedalus* 1958, 87 (1), 85–93.

Bronowski, J. *The Common Sense of Science*. Cambridge: Harvard University Press, 1953.

Brunswik, E. *Perception and the Representative Design of Psychological Experiments*. Berkeley: U. of California Press, 1956.

Burns, T. and Stalker, G. M. *The Management of Innovation*, London: Tavistock Publications, 1961.

Campbell, D. T. "Factors Relevant to the Validity of Experiments in Social Settings." *Psychological Bull.*, 1957, 54 (4), 297–312.

Carron, T. J. "Human Relations Training and Attitude Change: A Vector Analysis." *Personnel Psychology*, 1964, 17 (4), 403–424.

Chapple, E. D. and Sayles, L. R. *The Measure of Management*. New York: Macmillan, 1961.

Coch, L. and French, J. R. P., Jr. "Overcoming Resistance to Change." *HR*, 1948, 1, 512–532.

Cronbach, L. J. "The Two Disciplines of Scientific Psychology." *American Psychologist*, 1957, 12, 671–684.

Dalton, G. W., Barnes, L. B. and Zaleznik, A. *The Authority Structure as a Change Variable* (in press).

Emory, F. E. and Trist, E. L. "The Causal Texture of Organizational Environments." *HR*, 1965, *18* (1), 21–32.

Eysenck, H. J. "The Effects of Psychotherapy." In H. J. Eysenck, ed., *Handbook of Abnormal Psychology*. New York: Basic Books, 1960, 697–725.

Festinger, L. "Laboratory Experiments." In L. Festinger and D. Katz, eds., *Research Methods in the Behavioral Sciences*. New York: Dryden Press, 1953, 136–172.

Festinger, L. and Katz, D., eds., *Research Methods in the Behavioral Sciences*. New York: Dryden Press, 1953.

Foundation for Research on Human Behavior. *An Action Research Program for Organizational Improvement (in Esso Standard Oil Co.)*. Ann Arbor, Mich., 1960.

Frank, J. D. *Persuasion and Healing*. New York: Schocken Books, 1963.

French, J. R. P., Jr. "Experiments in Field Settings." In L. Festinger and D. Katz, eds., *Research Methods in the Behavioral Sciences*. New York: Dryden Press, 1953.

Golembiewski, R. "Authority as a Problem in Overlays." *Administrative Science Qtly.*, 9 (1) June 1964, 22–49.

Gouldner, A. *Patterns of Industrial Bureaucracy*. Glencoe, Ill.: Free Press, 1954.

Greenwood, E. *Experimental Sociology; A Study in Method*. New York: King's Crown, 1945.

Greiner, L. E. "Organization Change and Development." Unpublished Ph.D. dissertation, Harvard U., 1965.

Guest, R. *Organizational Change, The Effect of Successful Leadership*. Homewood, Ill.: Dorsey, 1962.

Jaques, E. *The Changing Culture of a Factory*. New York: Dryden Press, 1952.

Kaplan, A. *The Conduct of Inquiry*. San Francisco: Chandler, 1964.

Katz, D. "Field Studies." In L. Festinger and D. Katz, eds., *Research Methods in the Behavioral Sciences*. New York: Dryden Press, 1953, 56–97.

Klintz, B. L., Delprato, D. J., Mettee, D. R., Persons, C. E., and Schappe, R. H. "The Experimenter Effect." *Psychological Bull.*, 1965, 63 (4), 223–232.

Lawrence, P. R. *Changing of Organizational Behavior Patterns: A Case Study of Decentralization*. Boston: Harvard Graduate School of Business Administration, Division of Research, 1958.

Lawrence, P. R., Bailey, J. C., Katz, R. L., Seiler, J. A., Orth, C. D., Clark, J. V., Barnes, L. B., and Turner, A. N. *Organizational Behavior and Administration*. Homewood, Ill.: I. Dorsey, 1961.

Leavitt, H. J. "Applied Organizational Change in Industry: Structural Technological, and Humanistic Approaches." In James G. March, ed., *Handbook of Organizations*. Chicago: Rand McNally, 1965, 1144–1170.

LeBreton, P. *General Administration: Planning and Implementation*. New York: Holt, Rinehart & Winston, 1965.

Lewin, K. "Group Decision and Social Change." In E. E. Maccoby, T. M. Newcomb, and E. L. Hartley, eds., *Readings in Social Psychology*. 3d ed. New York: Holt, 1958, 197–211.

Lewin, K., Lippit, R., and White, R. K. "Patterns of Aggressive Behavior in

Experimentally Created 'Social Climates.' " *J. Social Psychology,* 1939, *10,* 271–299.

Lieberman, S. "The Effects of Changes in Roles on the Attitudes of Role Occupants." *HR,* 1956, *9,* 385–402.

Likert, R. L. *New Patterns of Management.* New York: McGraw-Hill, 1961.

Mann, F. C. "Studying and Creating Change: A Means to Social Organization." In C. M. Arensberg, et al., eds., *Research in Industrial Human Relations.* New York: Harper, 1957.

McGregor, D. *The Human Side of Enterprise.* New York: McGraw-Hill, 1960.

McGuigan, F. J. "The Experimenter: A Neglected Stimulus Object." *Psychological Bull.,* 1963, *60* (4), 421–428.

Merton, R. K. *Social Theory and Social Structure,* Glencoe, Ill.: Free Press, 1957.

Milgram, S. "Some Conditions of Obedience and Disobedience to Authority." *HR,* 1965, *18* (1), 57–76.

Morse, N. C. and Reimer, E. "The Experimental Change of a Major Organizational Variable." *JASP,* 1956, *52,* 120–129.

Orne, M. T. "On the Social Psychology of the Psychological Experiment." *American Psychologist,* 1962, *19,* 776–783.

Orne, M. T. and Evans, F. J. "Social Control in the Psychological Experiment: Anti-Social Behavior and Hypnosis." *J. Personality and Social Psychology.* March 1965, *1* (3), 189–200.

Rice, A. K. *Productivity and Social Organization, The Ahmedabad Experiment.* London: Tavistock Publications, 1958.

Riecken, H. W. "A Program for Research on Experiments in Social Psychology." In N. F. Washburne, ed., *Decisions, Values, and Groups.* New York: Pergamon Press, 1962, II, 25–41.

Riesman, D., Glazer, N., and Denney, R. *The Lonely Crowd.* New Haven: Yale U. Press, 1950.

Roethlisberger, F. J. and Dickson, W. J. *Management and the Worker.* Cambridge: Harvard U. Press, 1939.

Rosenthal, R. "The Volunteer Subject." *HR,* 1965, *18* (4), 389–406.

————. "The Effect of the Experimenter on the Results of Psychological Research." In B. Maher, ed., *Progress in Experimental Personality Research.* New York: Academic Press, 1964.

————. "Experimenter Modeling Effects as Determinants of Subjects' Responses." *J. Projective Techniques and Personality Assessment,* 1963a, *27* (4).

————. "On the Social Psychology of the Psychological Experiment." *American Scientist,* 1963b, *51* (2), 268–283.

Rosenthal, R., Persinger, G. W., Vikan-Kline, L., and Fode, K. L. "The Effect of Early Data Returns on Data Subsequently Obtained by Outcome Biased Experimenters." *Sociometry,* 1963, *26* (4).

Schein, E. "Management Development as a Process of Influence." *Industrial Management Rev.* (School of Industrial Management, M.I.T.), 1961, *2* (11), 1–19 (Reprint).

Scott, W. R. "Field Methods in the Study of Organizations." In James G. March, ed., *Handbook of Organizations.* Chicago: Rand McNally, 1965.

Seashore, S. E. "Field Experiments with Formal Organizations." *Human Organization,* 1964, *23,* 164–170.

Seashore, S. E. and Bowers, D. G. *Changing the Structure and Functioning of an Organization; Report of a Field Experiment.* Monograph No. 33. Ann Arbor: Survey Research Center, Institute for Social Research, 1963.

Selltiz, C., Jahoda, M., Deutsch, M., and Cook, S. W. *Research Methods in Social Relations.* Rev. ed. New York: Holt, 1959.

Shepard, H. A. "Basic Research and the Value System of Pure Science." *Philosophy of Science,* January 1956, 48–57.

Sofer, C. *Organization from Within.* London: Tavistock Publications, 1961.

Solomon, R. L. "An Extension of Control Group Design." *Psychological Bull.,* 1949, *46,* 137–150.

Spires, A. M. "Subject–Experimenter Interaction in Verbal Conditioning." Unpublished Ph.D. dissertation, New York U., 1960.

Stouffer, S. A. "Some Observations on Study Design." *American J. Sociology,* January, 1950, *40,* 353–361.

Strauss, G. "The Set-up Man: A Case Study of Organizational Change." *Human Organization,* 1954, *13,* 17–25.

Taylor, F. W. *The Principles and Methods of Scientific Management.* New York: Harper, 1911.

Tolman, E. C. and Brunswik, E. "The Organism and the Causal Texture of the Environment." *Psychological Rev.,* 1935, *42,* 43–77.

Tooley, J. and Pratt, S. "Who Will Watch the Brain Watchers?" "Letters to the Editor," *Behavioral Science,* 1964, *9,* (3).

Trist, E. L. *Wider Organizational Networks and Their Environments* (Mimeo).

Trist, E. L., Higgin, G. W., Murray, H., and Pollock, A. B. *Organizational Choice.* London: Tavistock Publications, 1963.

Trist, E. L. and Bamforth, K. "Some Social and Psychological Consequences of the Longwall Method of Coal Getting." *HR,* 1951, *4* (1) 3–30.

Vikan–Kline, L. "The Effect of an Experimenter's Perceived Status on the Mediation of Experimenter Bias." Unpublished Master's Thesis, U. of North Dakota, 1962.

Whyte, W. F. *Money and Motivation.* New York: Harper, 1955.

Whyte, W. F. *Pattern for Industrial Peace.* New York: Harper, 1951.

Woodward, J. *Management and Technology.* London: Her Majesty's Stationery Office, 1958.

3

The Comparative Study
of Organizations

Tom Burns

University of Edinburgh

THE PURPOSE OF COMPARATIVE STUDIES

For a sociologist the use of the adjective "comparative" to qualify the "study of organizations" is something of a pleonasm. Comparative study is the fundamental sociological method and has been since Montesquieu. This is true even for research which has a single community, tribe, or organization as its object. In such studies the social anthropologist (as against the ethnographer) or the sociologist (as against the historian or the reporter) is faced from the outset with the need to eliminate or reduce the uniqueness of the actual people, actions, relationships, and settings he observes. To do this, as S. F. Nadel (1951) has pointed out in the case of social anthropology, the social scientist must reduce his essentially narrative record to terms which are applicable to a wide range of quite different collectivities; he must then go on to reconstruct what he has observed in a way which will reflect both his own actual research experience and the similarly analyzed and reconstructed experience of other students. In all this, comparison is fundamental, if implicit. More particularly, in case studies of all kinds, one relies on the initial novelty of the situations observed, one's unfamiliarity with what is routine behavior for the actors, the apparent idiosyncrasy of the criteria by which certain individuals or acts are labeled deviant, to alert one's critical understanding.

113

At the most elementary methodological level—that of the early Chicago school, say, where R. E. Park's injunction to aim at being a good journalist seems to have served as a governing principle—the distinction between sociological researchers and reporters lies in the self-conscious attempts in the former to relate their research observations to common experience and to other observers' findings in an explicit rather than implicit way.[1] The difference is all-important. It reflects the obligation to explain.

Comparative studies fall clearly on the *diagnostic* side of the dichotomy proposed by Zetterberg (1962) for social research—the other side consisting of *model-construction*. In other words, comparative studies are concerned with the answer to the question "what is it?" rather than to "how does it work?" For scientific inquiry, the second question is the operational point of departure for field and laboratory experiment, with which may now be associated simulation. These are the topics dealt with in other chapters of this book. This chapter is concerned with ways in which the first question, "what is it?" may be answered. Of course, the social scientist is dealing with matters of general knowledge and common observation. This means that the social scientist is necessarily concerned with the assumptions which prevail among the people he studies—and which, as a "citizen," he shares. But he is concerned with these assumptions only in pursuit of a higher order explanation. To paraphrase a previous statement (Burns, 1962), the purpose of comparative studies of organizations is to achieve an understanding of organizations which is different from that current among the people through whose conduct the institutions exist: different, new, and better.

The *praxis* of comparative studies is therefore to criticize: to criticize or question assumptions about the meaning of behavior, and claims about the value of achievements. It is the business of social scientists to conduct a critical debate, in this sense, with society at large about its equipment of social institutions. In so far as sociology, at least, is effective, it has been effective in this way from Marx and de Tocqueville, and from Booth and Giddings, on. And not only in sociology. It is Paul Lazarsfeld who has underlined the critical, assumption-questioning purposes of so much social science, and his classic illustration is still worth repeating. In his "exposi-

1. The distinction is very fine even in the best of the studies—e.g., Zorbaugh's *The Gold Coast and the Slum* and Donovan's *Saleslady*—but is none the less there and, I think, valid. Reporting must direct itself to a public that possesses a very specific and strictly contemporary accumulation of experience and a degree of insight and understanding; the reporter levels with his reader. The social scientist must, however crudely, relate his report to an accumulating, organized body of knowledge independent of him and his reader. In order to learn about one institution, as Goffman remarks, "we would be well advised to look at others" (Goffman, 1961, p. 3).

tory review" of *The American Soldier* (Lazarsfeld, 1949, pp. 177–178), he lists a number of conclusions which most people would probably dismiss as obvious:

1. Better educated men showed more psycho-neurotic symptoms than those with less education. (The mental instability of the intellectual as compared to the more impassive psychology of the-man-in-the-street has often been commented on.)
2. Men from rural backgrounds were usually in better spirits during their Army life than soldiers from city backgrounds. (After all, they are more accustomed to hardships.)
3. Southern soldiers were better able to stand the climate in the hot South Sea Islands than Northern soldiers (Of course, Southerners are more accustomed to hot weather.)
4. White privates were more eager to become noncoms than Negroes. (The lack of ambition among Negroes is almost proverbial.)
5. Southern Negroes preferred Southern to Northern white officers. (Isn't it well known that Southern whites have a more fatherly attitude toward their "darkies"?)
6. As long as the fighting continued, men were more eager to be returned to the States than they were after the German surrender. (You cannot blame people for not wanting to be killed.) B, 561.

We have in these examples a sample list of the simplest ways of interrelationships which provide the "bricks" from which our empirical social science is being built. But why, since they are so obvious, is so much money and energy given to establish such findings? Would it not be wiser to take them for granted and proceed directly to a more sophisticated type of analysis? This might be so except for one interesting point about the list. *Every one of these statements is the direct opposite of what was actually found.* Poorly-educated soldiers were more neurotic than those with high education; Southerners showed no greater ability than Northerners to adjust to a tropical climate; Negroes were more eager for promotion than whites; and so on.

The central position occupied by the comparative method in social psychology and sociology and the way in which this is related to the essentially critical (assumption-testing) nature of the science are part of the continuing experience of social research. My own experience in organizational studies is, I believe, characteristic, and may serve as a paradigm of the learning process which such research essentially is.

Most studies of organization depend a good deal on interviews with managers; and one begins these interviews traditionally with questions about the particular job one's respondent does and how it fits in with other people's. The next step is to examine the discrepancies between the picture one gets from different respondents of the organization in which they all participate. There are always discrepancies; but, of course, the question presented by such internal inconsistencies is not "Which version is right?" but "How do these differences arise?" "How is it that these different versions of the same set of social circumstances have arisen in the minds of persons who have to cooperate with each other in the very circumstances they view so differently?" The need to account for these differences marks the first stage beyond description.

Some years ago, at the outset of one such inquiry (Burns and Stalker, 1961), I encountered a major difficulty even before this first comparative stage had been reached. A whole series of interviews with managers followed a rather disconcerting pattern. In answer to my first question, they would say, "Well, to make all this clear, I'd better start from the beginning," and then proceed to give me an account of their careers in the firm. This account would be lucid, well organized, and informative, but would stop short at some months beforehand. I would then ask again what they were, in fact, doing now. After a pause, they would go on to explain, equally lucidly, what they would be doing when the present reorganization was over and their department could settle down to work as it was now planned. After a succession of such occasions, I was fairly certain that I had encountered the sociologist's poor substitute for the natural scientist's "discovery"—the feeling that what had looked like solid, commonsense ground was turning into rather liquid assumptions. Had other managers, in more stable concerns, been recounting history too, without my being aware of it? If it came to that, what did those not supervised by a foreman or by a manager "do"—on what activities did they spend the hours of the working day?

These questions, taken a little further and looked at in the light of previous research, formed the starting point of a study of a hundred top executives in ten British companies (Burns, 1954, 1957). In the context of the present discussion, one particular aspect of the study is worth mentioning in detail.

It will be apparent that the "comparative method" as we have hitherto considered it, is a method of generating questions (e.g., "hypotheses"). R. K. Merton (1959) in his prefatory essay to *Sociology Today* quoted Aubrey, Darwin and Agnes Arber to remind us that, as the last of these has said, "the difficulty of most scientific work lies in framing the questions rather than in finding the answers." What is not so often insisted upon is that questions do not suggest themselves. They arise from doubt. Doubt, in turn, arises from the existence of an alternative where none was previously suspected; it arises from a discrepancy between facts, or between preferred interpretations, or between facts and assumptions. The studies of ten companies were founded on the discrepancy between the assumption that managers know what their job is and the evident inability of a number of managers to describe their jobs. At the end of each of the ten studies (which resulted from the confrontation of the managers in the first firm with this discrepancy, and their decision to cooperate in a study to "ascertain the facts"), there was an accumulation of data consisting of their own minute-to-minute records, on standard time-sheets, of all they had done which could be described as "work for the firm," or even as "time spent on the firm's behalf." The concluding task was, first, for each to give an estimate of how he had distributed his time among the subjects which, by agreement, made up the total management function; and, secondly, to give a similar estimate for the top-management group (self-defined and numbering eight people on an average, managing director included).

Taking the estimates made by individuals of the whole group's activities, and comparing them with the actual figures, the most noticeable effect was the wildly different conceptions offered by different members of top management groups of how the efforts of the group were directed.

Accuracy can hardly be expected from estimates by one person of how a whole group, even one in which he works, spends its time. The point of these estimates was that they represented, in crude terms, the assumptions each person had about the context of organized activity in which his own work was being done; they showed the kind of weight he thought was being given to each subject by the rest of the management group.

Even among heads of concerns, there was a widespread tendency to overestimate attention to production, to underestimate the claims of outside interests on time; but the discrepancies were far fewer than those encountered among their subordinates. One technical manager and his deputy thought that their colleagues must be spending 70 percent of their time on current production problems as against an actual 12 percent. A production manager thought of sales and attention to customers' needs as claiming 5 percent of the whole group's time as against 23 percent.

By far the greater number of individual recorders overestimated grossly the proportion of all management time spent on current production. This was true, for example, even of works managers and works supervisors; three of them thought that production matters bulked twice as large as they in fact did.

Comparison of individual recorders' estimates of their own time with the actual figures reinforces the conclusion that there is a general tendency to overestimate the proportion of time spent on clearly defined or "important" subjects of production, costs, accounts, and to underestimate time taken up by personal matters, general management policy discussions, and the like. This may indicate either the deflection of managers from the central tasks of management by the emergencies of problems concerning people and by time-consuming discussions of future uncertainties, or it may reveal genuine misconceptions of the direction of management effort.

To ascertain that there is a sizable difference between the pattern of behavior which is conceived as normal, and which even acts normatively, and that which is actually followed is, of course, only the beginning. There are varieties of difference, qualitative and quantitative, and the interpretation eventually focuses on the variation. But the point I wish to establish here is that explanation, which is the object of comparative studies, is here arrived at by the critical comparison of the actual and the assumed patterns of action.

THE DILEMMAS OF TAXONOMY

The object of comparative study is to provide answers to the question "What is it?"—answers that are more comprehensive, more meaningful, and, eventually, more useful than those in common currency. The procedure of comparative study is to analyze the object of study—an organization—into components, and then to translate the question "what is it?" into two others: "What is it like?" and "What is it not like?" The reasoning process is essentially analogical.

Analogical reasoning has for some time been regarded as scientifically rather disreputable; the traditional view—now largely exploded—of the process of scientific discovery as being founded on inference, and the confusion between proof and methods of study has relegated analogy to the status of "spurious explanation" (Reichenbach, 1951, pp. 5–26). It is only recently that renewed interest in the empirical study of scientific investigation of the roles of metaphor and analogy in it (Pepper, 1942; Schon, 1964) has suggested that there is more than one mental process involved, that there is a sequence of stages, and that each stage has its attendant and appropriate form of intellectual operation. In fact, the model we now have seems remarkably close to the picture Whitehead (1929, p. 5) gives in his famous aperçu:

> The Baconian method of induction . . . if consistently pursued, would have left science where it found it. What Bacon omitted was the play of a free imagination, controlled by the requirements of coherence and logic. The time method of discovery is like the flight of an aeroplane. It starts from the ground of particular observation; it makes a flight in the thin air of imaginative generalization; and it lands again for renewed observation rendered acute by rational interpretation.

Still bound by the traditional dismissal of analogical reasoning as unscientific, social scientists have tended to regard comparative studies as taxonomic and as justified only insofar as they lend themselves to the creation of a classification system. And this in spite of the fact that the history of sociology, from Montesquieu through Spencer, Marx, and up to Weber himself, is littered with the debris of ruined typologies that serve now only as the battleground for that academic street-fighting that so often passes for theoretical discussion. Most of the discussions of the group concerned with comparative studies at the Ford Foundation Seminar turned (somewhat centrifugally, however) on the problem of taxonomy. At the outset, it was argued that preoccupation with problems of classification was central to the group's concern (which was assumed to be the feasibility of making statements about organizations in general). And, although it was claimed that taxonomy (which was an appropriate end product of comparative studies) differed from typology (which was not), the distinction, if it exists,[2] was not particularly evident most of the time.

The existence of powerful support for the notion that comparative studies of organizations have the construction of some system of classification as their end product, and the way in which the notion constantly reappears in various guises in the discussion of organizational analysis require some examination of the taxonomic procedures that seem to be available. We can begin with two major attempts, made almost simultaneously, to elucidate a single major taxonomic principle for the classification of organizations of all kinds.

TYPOLOGIES BASED ON A SINGLE TAXONOMIC PRINCIPLE

In some ways, at least, social scientists, and especially sociologists, are nothing if not open-minded. Any consideration of the subject of this section has to deal with two books published some years ago within a few months of each other: Amitai Etzioni's *A Comparative Analysis of Complex Organizations* (1961) and P. Blau and W. R. Scott's *Formal Organizations: A Comparative Approach* (1962). Read separately, each is useful, illuminating and compendious. Taken together, they sow doubt and confusion from their opening paragraphs on. The first sentence of Etzioni's book reads, "The comparative study of organizations is a much neglected field." Blau and Scott prefer the alternative gambit. Introducing the bibliography appended to their book they remark, "The more

2. We may well obliterate the suggestion that there is any real difference between these two terms as merely adding to confusion by introducing a false dilemma. The *Shorter Oxford Dictionary* gives a variety of meanings for the two words, of which the following are clearly appropriate to the present matter: *taxonomy:* Classification, esp. in relation to its general laws or principles; that department of science, or of a particular science or subject, which consists in or relates to classification. *typology:* Archaeol. The classification of remains and specimens according to the type they exhibit and its evolution, etc.

than 800 items in the bibliography which follows represent a third of the bibliography which we have compiled."

Scott (1965, p. 485), in his contribution to R. E. L. Faris' *Handbook of Modern Sociology*, rubs in the same point of difference: "Organizations being ubiquitous, sociological explorations in virtually every substantive area have been compelled to take account of their presence. While the analysis of organizations is the stock in trade of the industrial and military sociologist, the last two decades have seen the investigation of organizations or organizational phenomena in such diverse areas as criminology, mental health, medicine, secondary and higher education, religion and social welfare." It could be argued that the comparative study of organization is not necessarily identical with the study of organizations on a comparative basis, but it is clear that both Etzioni and Blau and Scott aim at, first, a taxonomy of organizations in general (i.e., at the elucidation of elements or characteristics of organizations which are clear, distinct and qualitatively invariant), and, second, a typology of organizations in terms of these elements or characteristics.

The spectacle of two formidably elaborate and almost concurrent attempts to arrive at reasonably watertight classifications, which nevertheless employ utterly different criteria and result in irreconcilably disparate typologies, raises a number of questions. For our present purposes, it is enough to consider whether the construction of such classificatory schemes is, in fact, the central object of comparative studies, however wide ranging.

To resolve this question, and to consider the consequential matter of the status of organizational studies by comparative methods, it is necessary to make a rather closer examination of methodological foundations than is afforded by the customary deferential nod in the direction of Cohen and Nagel, etc., for classificatory systems which this kind of study turns up are clearly much more than the cognitive maps they pretend to be. They are Darwinian rather than Linnaean, seeking to explain rather than merely to identify. But to explain by subsuming particular instances of relationships, or of social norms or routines, under more general headings involves discriminating between different modes of variables. And it is here that language itself proves so deceptive.

To explore the studies of Etzioni and Blau and Scott a little further: each makes use of a single principle according to which the major species of the class—"organizations"—are defined. For Etzioni this major principle is compliance, the other half, so to speak, of the notion of authority; since Simmel pointed out that the logic of the social relationship of power and authority, from coercion to persuasion, involves submission and compliance as necessary complements, it is permissible, though perhaps a little perverse, to treat varieties of authority and influence in terms of their mirror images, i.e., as varieties of compliance. But Etzioni goes on to compose an orthogonal series of variants out of three "degrees of involvement"—moral, calculatory and alienatory. Only too clearly, these stand for the kinds of sentiment relevant to the degrees of compliance corresponding to three modes of exercising power—persuasion, reward, and coercion.

The outcome of this exercise in higher tautology is, not surprisingly, a three-by-three scheme of nine organizational types which resolves itself into three "congruent" types, with the other six "incongruent" types representing various degrees and directions of abnormality. And, further, we have a "dynamic hypothesis" postulating that "congruent types are more effective then incongruent types. Organizations are under pressure to be effective. Hence, to the degree that the environment of the organization allows, *organizations tend to shift their compliance structure from incongruent to congruent types and organizations which have congruent compliance structure tend to resist factors pushing them towards incongruent compliance structures*" (Etzioni, 1961, p. 14).

All of which prompts three questions: First, if there is so much pressure towards congruence, how do organizations get to be "incongruent" in the first place? Second, what is the "environment" doing in there if it is not to afford blanket cover for all contingencies which might weaken or wreck the hypothesis? And, third, for whom and for what are organizations to be reckoned "effective"?

This last question provides one connection of substance with the typology devised by Blau and Scott. The taxonomic principle in their case is to determine the kind of prime beneficiary served by an organization—owners, members, "public-in-contact" (clients), or public-at-large. In this, they are following Talcott Parsons (1956) fairly closely; the difference between their "prime beneficiary" and Parsons' "type of goal or function" is largely a matter of a variant reading of Parsons' basic concept of "output." In addition, they halt the Parsonian analysis at the societal level and consider the instrumental function of organizations only, rather than follow him and classify organizations in terms of the ways in which these functions are construed internally.

Blau and Scott see in their *cui bono* principle a way of introducing meaningful distinctions between types of organization and also of explaining something of the nature of organizations as a class. Their criterion sorts organizations into four subclasses: "(1) 'mutual-benefit associations,' where the prime beneficiary is the membership; (2) 'business concerns,' where the owners are prime beneficiary; (3) 'service organizations,' where the client group is prime beneficiary; and (4) 'common-

weal organizations,' where the prime beneficiary is the public-at-large"
(1962, p. 43).

Thus we seem to have a satisfactory way of distinguishing business
concerns, trade unions, hospitals, and police forces. But do we? As the
authors go on to remark, following Berle and Means (1932, p. 14),
"public corporations transform owners into mere stockholders and vest
controlling power in the hands of top-level employees, enabling them to
govern the enterprise in their own interests." And does such a shift
"constitute fundamental transformations of business concerns into distinctly different types of organization" (Blau and Scott, 1962, p. 44)? In
what sense was General Electric in the 1930's distinctly different as an
organizational type from, say, the Ford Motor Company, in which the
stock was still largely in the hands of persons who saw themselves, and
were regarded, as owning the business? For that matter, how justified is
it to regard a hospital operated as a business enterprise by a consortium
of medical practitioners as an organization fundamentally different from
a hospital publicly maintained or privately endowed? Different, yes, but
surely not in the sense in which Blau and Scott have devised their scheme
of organizational types.

Cui bono? is in fact not a simple question to answer. Quite apart from
the different replies the question can elicit for organizations that are
palpably similar in type, a simplistic assumption lies behind the question
itself. This assumption is that the goals of an organization—e.g., the
purposes it serves or, again, the individuals or groups for whom it exists
to "do good"—are explicit, stable, and coherent. But, as Howard Becker
(1963, p. 7) has pointed out in a very different context: "The question
of what the purpose or goal of a group is, and, consequently, what
things will help or hinder the achievement of that purpose, is very often
a political question. Factions within the group disagree, and maneuver to
have their own definition of the group's functions accepted. The function
of the group or organization, then, is decided in political conflict, not
given in the nature of the organization."

More precisely (and with none of the ambiguity arising from Becker's
indiscriminate equation of "group" and "organization," or of "goal,"
"purpose," and "function"), Cyert and March (1963, p. 28) have found
it necessary to discard the common sense notion that organizations have
clear, fixed, and characteristic goals: "Agreement on objectives is usually
agreement on highly ambiguous goals; . . . behind this agreement on
rather vague objectives there is considerable disagreement about subgoals, [and] organizations appear to be pursuing different goals at the
same time. . . . Since the existence of unresolved conflict is a conspicu-

ous feature of organizations, it is exceedingly difficult to construct a useful, positive theory of organizational decision-making if we insist on internal goal consistency."

The trouble with the attempt to devise a taxonomy of organizations from first principles, as political theorists discovered long since with that more limited, more specific, but equally elusive notion—the State, is that, as Bavelas (1959–60, p. 498) has remarked, "Human organizations are not biological organisms; they are social inventions."

In lapsing into the fallacy of misplaced concreteness, social science follows common usage, as it usually does (Burns, 1958), and seeks to justify it. The justification lies in the definition of organizations as "social units oriented to the realization of certain goals" as Etzioni's definition runs (1961, p. 79). Yet the definition, as we have seen, is spurious; it defines—i.e., limits the kinds of things the words refer to—only if we conveniently forget that organizational goals are often, indeed usually, in dispute.

COMPREHENSIVE CLASSIFICATORY SYSTEMS

Granted that organizations are social inventions and not organisms or real objects, yet, it might be agreed, they seem credited by everybody, social scientists included, with a fair number of the attributes of reality and independent existence. If prisons, factories, government departments, labor unions, ships, air transport companies, and hospitals are organizations, then a good deal of hard material is incorporated in them, and they represent substantial facts of life for those in them and for those who have to deal with them.

Taking this straightforward, pragmatic line, it should be clearly feasible to list a number of attributes of organizations which will vary quantitatively or qualitatively between different organizations, and which would, when ordered, correlated, and contrasted, yield a simple classification of organizations that might of itself contribute to an understanding of them, and that would certainly provide extremely useful basic data for intensive studies within restricted fields or samples. Industrial and business organizations are, in fact, classified for many administrative purposes by a limited range of variables, such as number of employees, issued capital, turnover, project turnover, rate of growth, type of product, rate of investment in research and design (R & D). Such classification has, moreover, been exploited and supplemented to good effect by economists for generations.

It was with this in mind, although it was not explicitly stated, that the attempt was made, at the Ford Foundation Seminar, to construct a list of variables that would characterize organizations and that might be used to develop a classificatory system. Reconstructed, and amplified a little, the list reads:

Economic Dimension
1. Number of employees
2. Capital investment
3. Number of clients, customers, subscribers (i.e., nonemployed members)
4. Horse-power ratio (or some other measure of proportion of inanimate power to manual labor force)
5. Direct labor costs in proportion to total costs.

Administrative Dimension
6. Proportion of managers and supervisors to total personnel
7. Number of administrative levels
8. Number of different job titles and distribution of personnel between them
9. Line-staff ratio
10. Degree of geographical concentration or dispersal of resources, personnel, and destination of output
11. Method, frequency, and direction of communication within the organization
12. Form of control exercised over staff or members
13. Span of control (number of subordinates per supervisor)
14. Responsibility (relative frequency of monitoring by superiors)

Institutional Dimension
15. Degree of specificity, in quantifiable terms, of goals and output, e.g., profit, remuneration, hours of work, in the case of businesses, as against effectiveness of hospitals as judged by patients, professional press, staff, sponsoring body
16. Extent (number, comprehensiveness, particularity) of formal rules
17. Degree of specification of jobs (or some other measure of extent to which performance is programmed by central or higher administration)
18. Specialized training requirements, educational qualifications, etc.
19. Complexity and duration of job cycle
20. Degree of segmentation (i.e., extent to which persons with different job titles work in the same unit) or segregation
21. Frequency and nature of interaction with people and places outside the organization

22. Visibility of individual's performance in comparison to that of others in organizations
23. Variation (e.g., ambiguity, conflict) in requirements and assessment of individuals.

The list does not, of course, pretend to be complete. More seriously, once one is outside the category of economic variables in familar use, the items become increasingly difficult to render into operational terms; questions of the units and instruments of measurement are posed that are inherently difficult to answer and one is almost bound to find different answers in different situations. Some of the variables, again, are operational and others conceptual. But the basic difficulty is that the individual items appear to be specific to different kinds of organization. Capital investment, for example, is not particularly relevant (or easily discernible) to government departments or labor unions, although it is of prime importance for business concerns.

The list, in fact, represents a selection of the kinds of data that are available to investigation or that might be obtained in different organizations. The question arises, whether, instead of attempting to compile an exhaustive catalogue of such variables (which would certainly be extremely unwieldy and of dubious value), it might not be more profitable to turn to research studies themselves, examine the variables adduced in them, and devise a means whereby the data might be standardized or rendered comparable for purposes of secondary analysis.

This possibility is not so much modeled on, as suggested by, the Yale Human Relations Area File and the Yale Technology Project. The Human Relations Area File consists of a very large compendium of abstracted and original monographs and reports by social anthropologists on primitive communities. It was created during the 1930's and exists as a body of data that can be used by social scientists as comparative data for secondary analysis. The Yale Technology Project was set up to study the implication of modern technological development for industrial organizations, individuals, and society at large (although this last stage was not fully realized). What eventuated was about thirty case studies of firms and plants of varying size. The studies were reported in a good many books and papers, many of which achieved a substantial reputation. The original data remain, however, rich sources of information and insight, comprising for each concern:

a) Background material: newspaper clippings, house journals, etc.
b) Information from respondents: open-ended interviews, but following a common patter—"Tell me about your job. . . ." "What kinds of headaches. . . ?" "What do you like about it. . . ?" "What do

you think an ideal company would be like. . . ?" Some questionnaire material is also deposited.

c) Official company and documentary material: (1) on organization
structure and regulations (organization charts, personnel rosters,
organization manuals); (2) technology (formal descriptions of
technical resources)

d) Observations: time diaries and other raw data; interoffice communications; records of meetings

e) Research findings, conclusions, descriptions of research methods.

The general problem of ordering such data, as against the Human
Relations Area File, is that, by a generation ago, social anthropologists
were satisfied that they had developed an adequate and coherent theory
of social structure; this is not true of social scientists for organizations.
The purposes of an attempt to create a large repository of research data
on lines such as the Yale projects [3] indicated would be:

1) To provide more adequate empirical reference or support for statements in the field of organizational theory

2) To widen the range of statements which it is possible to offer about
specific objects of study

3) To provide a data archive facility

4) To provide data for secondary analysis, on the same lines as those
developed in the field of political sociology, possibly, like the latter,
on the cross-cultural as well as national basis.

The merits of any such archives are entirely dependent on the effectiveness with which retrieval procedures yield data of the kind the
original researchers used and relied upon. It is, in some ways, a concrete
or symbolic representation of the general problem of using secondary
data (i.e., other people's research) for comparative studies.

At the present stage of development in the social science of organizations, it does not seem feasible to contemplate developing a matrix of
organizations into which original data could be separated out according
to their empirical attributes (such as those listed on pp. 124–125). There
are, then, two methodological problems. The first is the design of a
system (actual or notional) of storage and retrieval for research data on
organizations comparable to those already devised for space technology
and the like, and, more generally, for new library systems, and for
language translation. The second, is the elucidation of the criteria
relevant to ordering data for such a system.

We are, it will be noted, back to problems of classification, but with a

3. Udy, who put forward the general proposal under discussion, is engaged on the
further exploration of the material of the Yale Human Relations Area File and the
Yale Technology Project for comparative purposes.

difference. The objects for classification are not organizations or parts or attributes of organizations but analytical concepts and frames of reference within which methodological procedures can be designed and comparative studies usefully made. The classificatory scheme that is now envisaged points in the direction, not of typologies—of a natural history of organizations—but of the effective extension of studies of organizations by providing ready access to comparative data.

AN ANALYTICAL SCHEMA FOR COMPARATIVE STUDIES

The valid guides for comparative studies, it is suggested, are analytical rather than empirical or methodological. What is necessary is the composition of a system of categories by which research data, the analytical methods applied to the data, and findings can be identified; such a system has to be reasonably logical, but the criteria of adequacy (serviceability) is its comprehensiveness. The appropriate paradigm, in fact, is a thesaurus. One of the objections to the catalogue of empirical (methodologically determined) data listed in the previous section is that it is admittedly incomplete and would almost certainly remain so however determinedly residual and potential types of data were hunted down. At the other extreme, the listing of social forms—structural, institutional, or collective—can be equally open-ended; unless one accepts the boundaries imposed by a particular theoretical system, the ordering of data for comparative study under such headings as status system, peer group, reference group, and managment style has to be regarded as subject to revision in terms of the theoretical (and methodological) requirements of individual researchers and is, as a series, constantly liable to prove incomplete.

If one begins afresh, as the Ford Foundation Seminar group did, by considering the practical realities of organizational research, it looks as if a useful distinction could be made between the kind of observations, records, and statements applying clearly to individuals, those applying to categories or groups, and those applying to an organization as a whole. Unfortunately, as soon as one considers these divisions as other than sources of data, the division breaks down. It is a basic assumption of social science that social structure influences the behavior of individuals; but this influence can only be inferred from the behavior of individuals; but this influence can only be inferred from the behavior of individuals. At first sight, indeed, survey research, which is always concerned with individuals, would seem to follow exactly the classic model of induction. Characteristics of groups, sections and categories, and probabilistic "laws" applying to a population or collectivity are inferred from the study of individuals and used as principles to explain individual behavior. It is certainly difficult and almost certainly impossible, therefore, to distinguish sociologically relevant data about individuals from data that apply to groups or larger collectivities. In the last resort, all social research data apply to individuals.

As soon as one moves into analytical categories anything in the nature of a schema of categories in terms of a quantitative order becomes impracticable. If the object of study is individuals and individual behavior, it will almost always be necessary to obtain information about work groups and sections and about the organization as a whole, since these at least impose constraints on the possible range of behavior in which individuals can engage; similar qualifications apply if the object of study is work groups or the organization as a whole.

Beyond this, there are extra-organizational factors which limit the possibilities open to the organization as a whole and, consequently, the groups and individuals within it: economic factors, the educational system, cultural values, the level of technology, and the like. Ultimately, "economic factors," "educational system," "level of technology" and similar terms are also reducible to the attributes of individual people and their behavior; but explanatory propositions about any particular set of individuals ordinarily require the treatment of aspects of the behavior of other individuals in terms of such abstract entities. It is necessary, that is, to "close the system" one is studying in a more or less arbitrary manner (Gluckman and Devons, 1964), substituting abstractions for the individuals external to the system, abstractions which may be treated as variables in the extent to which they impinge on the individuals within the system defined for study.

In doing this, the student of organizations adopts, in a more or less articulate way, the mode of thought and the assumptions which prevail among individuals in any collectivity. In so far as one individual's actions are dependent on those of others, he has to regard them as institutionalized and therefore predictable. Each individual works within a framework of the institutionalized activity of others and contributes to the framework of institutionalized activity within which others work. The degree to which institutionalization "governs" behavior (in the sense of its following presumptive laws and, therefore, being predictable) is related not only to the uniformity or nonconformity of the behavior of individuals themselves but also to the social distance from the closed system of action which is the object of attention at the time. So "the government" is habitually treated as virtually a constant if one is studying the behavior of a school board, "technology," as a constant if one is occupied with the behavior of shoe-salesmen. Similarly, in the reverse direction, the *variation* in the behavior of school boards may, for most purposes, be ignored in a study of the behavior of government officials concerned with education, and of shoe salesmen, in a study of a research laboratory in a footwear plant.

Institutionalized complexes like "the formal organization," "the market," "labor union policy" are treated as abstractions, therefore, when they lie outside any closed system of action that is the object of study, and the variance within the closed system that is ascribed to their influence is a function both of the degree to which the action they represent is institutionalized, and of their remoteness.

These elementary and ineluctable features of the study of social behavior have to be rehearsed because we are searching for a system of categories that will not alter as we shift attention from one closed system of study to another. With this in mind, we can attempt to list a number of elements of social action relevant to organizational studies that, taken together, both characterize organizations and provide analytical categories for comparative purposes. The condition set out in the preceding paragraph acts as a general constraint and as a principle by which analytical categories may be generated. For, to begin with, it is clearly necessary to examine, analyze and account for the *interchanges of all kinds which take place between the largest "closed system" among the possible objects of study*—be it industry or defense system, single plant, branch of an organization, work group or class of individuals—*and relevant institutional elements on the outside.*

At this point, a second analytical dimension makes itself apparent. There are, in fact, three models of analysis which have been applied to precisely the functional relationship between an organization, regarded as a closed system, and its environment. Two of these are becoming fairly fully articulated and are often contrasted with each other as dichotomous; the usual labels are "system theories" and "factor theories." Both, however, allow the notion of interaction and mutual influence between organization and environment which the third, "response theories," does not.

These three models are also relevant to what is topically the next level of analytical categories: those which apply to the *events and the actions within the closed system which derive immediately from the nature and variety of its interaction with the environment*. A system theory model tends to represent these major events in terms of the primary and secondary tasks generated within the closed system, and the distribution of these tasks among groups and individuals, as a more or less unstable equilibrium requiring constant surveillance (i.e., management). Factor theory models represent major events in terms of goals, subgoals, and the system of expectations and performances that between them contribute to the operation of the closed system. Response theory models are appropriate to accounts which are couched in terms of the division of labor, management systems, role systems, and the like.

The closed system (i.e., the field of investigation) is now visible as a complex array of human and technical action. The coordination of these activities in terms of a socio-technical system serving the tasks of the total organization is effected by a *network of communication* conveying information and instructions.

The communication network operates effectively in the service of the closed system insofar as the information and instructions are attended to because (a) they are "authoritative" and (b) responses called for are appropriate in terms of the commitment of the individual. Logically sequential to the analysis of communication structure, therefore, are sets of analytical categories relevant, first, to the *authority structure* and the varieties of authority and, second, to the commitments of individuals to relationships which involve compliance with authority.

For the most part, commitment to membership of a closed system in which authority relationships obtain is resolvable into two kinds: a contractual or quasi-contractual *engagement* of effort in return for rewards, material and immaterial; and *involvement,* dedication to effort over and above engagement, separate from it, or directed to other kinds of objective. There are, then, three types of analysis following and dependent upon that which applies to the communication network. They are concerned with: authority; engagement (and rewards); involvement (and responsibility).

This series of analytical categories applies to a set of relationships and to attributes of action that, together, may be regarded as the institutional apparatus within which *individual behavior* occurs. This apparatus may be formulated according to three different theoretical models. It can, according to a response theory model, be seen as a prescription of behavior—in the sense in which social structures, situations and the evaluative definitions applied to certain social positions may be said to prescribe roles and role behavior. Or, in terms of factor theory, it may be regarded as a set of constraints within which the individual operates in a sufficiently institutionalized (and therefore dependable) way. Or, in terms of a system theory, it may be seen as a set of conventions in continual interplay with the ways in which individuals define their occupational and other kinds of behavior. The choice of theoretical model is available at the last as at the previous levels.

The list of analytical categories themselves is, or should be, exhaustive. Taken together, that is, they serve to distinguish organizations from other institutions. They are:

1) Relationships between the organizations and its environment
2) Definitions of tasks and division of labor
3) Communication system
4) Authority structure
5) Systems of engagement and rewards
6) Involvement (responsibility)
7) Definition of individual social identities in organizational settings.

ORGANIZATIONS IN SOCIETY

Although the analytical schema we have outlined begins by studying the categories relevant to examining the relationship between the organization and its social, economic, technical, and political context, it treats the relationships from the point of view of the organization itself. This is orthodox enough, and unexceptionable, if one adopts the orientation to the subject that prevails almost universally among social scientists concerned with the study of organizations. Yet the point of view is widely questioned among European social scientists, who have in recent years shown a growing disquiet at the way in which social science, and especially sociological theory, has become more and more enclosed within a set of analytical concepts pertaining exclusively to the internal structure and dynamics of social, psychological, political, or economic systems. For sociology and social psychology, this is explicable perhaps in terms of the metaphysical climate prevailing among older, more influential and better-known disciplines; economics, social anthropology, and psychoanalysis, for example, showed similar proclivities during the second quarter of the century. They tended to work increasingly within the boundaries of equilibrium theory, structural functionalism, and libidinal organization. But these are all now showing clear breaks with their past.

This inward-looking direction of social science [4] is most clearly evident when one considers Gouldner's (1959a, p. 404) contrast of "natural systems" models with "rational" models as representing the "two distinct approaches to the study of complex organizations." Gouldner cites Selznick's work as the best contemporary exemplar of the first; for the second, in which the organization is treated "as a rationally conceived means to the realization of expressly announced group goals" (ibid.), he clearly points towards the work of Simon and the Carnegie Institute of Technology school of organizational analysis. Yet how large or important is the distance between them? Selznick moved from his early treat-

---

4. For a critical examination of this tendency in sociological theory, see G. Poggi, "A Main Theme of Contemporary Sociology: Its Achievements and Limitations," *British J. Sociology,* 1965, *16,* 283–294.

ment of the organization as one kind of environment for interaction to a consideration of organizations themselves as adaptive systems; common to both kinds of study is a latent analytical distinction between system and circumstance and a preoccupation with the conditions under which the system can persist as a viable entity; in short, the mode of thinking is as biologistic as that of nineteenth-century social philosophers was "geologistic," and is determinedly *introspective* throughout. Simon (1958) is no less concerned throughout his work with the optimum conditions for goal-attainment, which is implicitly equated with survival. If one contrasts his rendering of the role of innovation with, say, Schumpeter's, the identification of Simon's analytical methods and approach with the interests of the individual organization is strikingly evident. Gouldner's two models are, in fact, variations on the same dominant theme.

What is needed, not to replace this approach but to supplement it, is a conceptual scheme relating the organization to society in a way that will not relegate the latter to the position of "environment" or of biological "culture." This involves the development of analytical categories that (a) identify organizations as functioning elements of society and (b) apply to the positive and negative consequences for society of the nature and operation of organizations.

Thus, the set of analytical categories suggested in the previous section needs to be supplemented (for many research purposes), by two further categories, one logically anterior and the other logically posterior. The implication is, of course, that the two sets are connected, although not necessarily in a one-to-one relationship. The organization itself, in the present theoretical setting, is seen as acting as a transducer between the two sets of factors and, in itself, as a pattern of institutional forms organized by entrepreneurs or by administrators (i.e., "organizers") out of the first set of factors, called here "institutional generators" and in conformity with their perception of the second set, the "action consequences."

The logical initial presumption is that organizations are started and kept in being because of some demand arising either (a) in society at large (for goods or services of specific kinds, such as are provided by productive industry, merchants, business, welfare agencies; or by government departments and agencies, police forces, armed forces), or (b) in a set of individuals (for activities in which they can engage only if they are planned ahead and engage other appropriate persons; churches and recreational and sports groups fall into this category, though perhaps not exclusively, and another subgroup would include political parties, labor unions, criminal gangs, and dramatic societies). Demand, to be an effective "institutional generator," must clearly exist above a particular threshold in the preference ordering of the variety of wants existing among the members of large and complex societies.

Labor force and capital resources are obvious constituent elements in the process of forming and maintaining an organization. The point of view adopted here, however, presents them as active "generators." Since the Keynesian revolution, the maintenance of "full employment" has been an explicit policy of Western states and was before then axiomatic for socialist societies. And almost any period of history can show instances of organizations set up only and merely to provide work. These are, however, the extreme cases of the requirement in organized society that livelihoods be provided. Capital, as representing the continually accumulating value produced by labor and technical progress, acts also as a generator insofar as it "requires" profitable investment or useful application. The material resources available to society, in particular localities or sectors of activity, serve as generators in the same way.

Demand and resources are formed and articulated to the point at which particular organizations and kinds of organization may be generated in accordance with three sets of institutional elements in society: "value system," "educational system" and "technological system." The last two may be taken as self-explanatory, but the first, it should be said, relates to the conventional system of norms, upheld by beliefs, which enters into the institutional forms that can be utilized in generatory organizations. Marcuse (1956, 1964), for instance, has written at length about not only the universality of alienated work in both Freudian and Marxian terms, but of the even more striking phenomenon of the virtually universal acceptance of alienated work as a normal condition of life in Western society. H. A. Simon, in discussion, has made much the same point of the "extraordinariness" of workers actually performing tasks demanding a high degree of skill and involvement that are utterly remote from their personal interests and the rest of their cognitive field.

Variation and developmental change in the value system of society, as in the educational system and the technological system, manifestly affect profoundly not only the institutional pattern and structure of organizations, not only the capacity of society to meet demand and use resources, but the *kinds* of organization which may be brought into being and the social characteristics of the entrepreneurs and administrators who try to start organizations and run them.

Action consequences are of the same conceptual order as institutional generators and may be more briefly indicated. The two sets of elements are:

Institutional Generators	*Action Consequences*
Demand	Payoff to members, supporters, users, public
Labor force	Capital formation or depletion
Capital	Formulation or reformulation of demand
Material resources	Bearing of rigid or elastic strategies on value systems and educational systems
Value system	Technological contribution
Educational system	Growth, stability, or decline in the number and variety of inputs and outputs
Technological system	

There is no special symmetry to be imputed to the two sets of categories, but it will be noticed that the final item (concerning variation in the flow and nature of inputs and outputs) directly affects demand, which is the first. It is feasible therefore, within limits, to regard outputs as a category which is both specific to organizations and also most indicative of the relationship between organization and society.

Stanton Wheeler, in discussion, and independently of the conceptual apparatus outlined above, suggested that organizations were brought into being in order to operate certain "processes" on behalf of society in an effective—i.e., organized—way. Organizations were, in short, divisible largely into those which processed *things* (manufacturing industry) and those which processed people (that is, which existed so as to effect changes in people who pass through them). There seemed to be an uncomfortably large residual category of organizations like churches, political parties, and sports teams that clearly belong to neither division, but, if the schema is elaborated, it is unexpectedly fertile in developing categories of relationship between organizations meaningful for comparative purposes. One possible formulation is given in Figure 1 with examples inserted in each cell.

ORGANIZATION AND CHANGE PROCESSES

The previous section began by drawing attention to the preoccupation with the internal structure and processes of organizations, and pointing out that in this regard sociologists and social psychologists were working within walls knocked down some time since by other social scientists.

There is one other set of limits to theoretical perspectives, however, which the sociologists and social psychologists have apparently been able to break out of as soon as their colleagues or, at least, to see the need for so doing. These have to do with the incapacity of structural equilibrium theories to deal adequately with the dynamics of human behavior. The presumption has been that we have to begin analysis of the complexities of behavior by analyzing "the state of the system at a given moment" and then move on to accounting for changes in the system through time. It is, fortunately, unnecessary to rehearse arguments I have given at length elsewhere (Burns, 1958), since it is now fairly generally accepted that to work from concepts which assume, first, that behavior, relationships, purposes, functions, and causal sequences are frozen into immobility at a given moment and, secondly, that this paralyzed anatomy is then open to inspection by researchers is to desert the ground of empirical reality too abruptly and to forgo any real chance of relating theoretical explanations to even common experiences of social change. As Scott, in discussion, remarked, the study of behavior over time in terms of process was almost entirely neglected because of the lack of conceptual apparatus. "Functional role," "work group," "administrative system," he suggested, were, at best, partial concepts. What was needed were concepts which incorporated the notion of process—learning, socialization, influence, reward processes, for example. These and other ideas related to generic social processes to which the terms used in social

FIGURE 1

Organizations and Outputs

	Organizations Concerned With Change Processes		Organizations Concerned With Maintenance Processes	
	Things	People	Things	People
Internal to Organization	Manufacturing Industry	Hospitals Schools	Public Utilities	Established Churches Health Services
External to Organization	Research and Development	Evangelical Churches Political Parties	Distribution	Police

FIGURE 2

Types of Comparative Study

A complete analytical schema for the comparative study of organizations along the lines we have discussed would have to be realized in terms of three sets of variables. In tabular form, it can be represented in this fashion:

Analytical Categories	Diachronic Studies			Synchronic Studies		
	System Theory Models	Factor Theory Models	Response System Models	System Theory Models	Factor Theory Models	Response System Models
Organizations in Society	1	2	3	4	5	6
Relationships between the Organization and its Environment	7	8	9	10	11	12
Definitions of Tasks and Division of Labor	13	14	15	16	17	18
Communication System	19	20	21	22	23	24
Authority Structure	25	26	27	28	29	30
Systems of Engagement and Reward	31	32	33	34	35	36
Involvement (Responsibility)	37	38	39	40	41	42
Definition of Individual Social Identities in Organizational Setting	43	44	45	46	47	48

Handwritten annotation over "Diachronic Studies": Historical content

Handwritten annotation over "Synchronic Studies": Cross-cultural topography—administrative system, work group—were irrelevant. This involves, moreover, going beyond the methodological procedure of examining structural changes over time. What counts is not the measurement of changes in structure and scale (important as these may be), but the identification and analysis of the effect of intervening variables which work out in sequential, tree-like processes. Gouldner (1954) in his study of the different forms of bureaucratic organization, in fact studied changes in the nature and structure of organization as a process occurring via management succession. At a different level of comprehensiveness the present writer has recently been engaged in the study of the personality changes consequent upon engagement and involvement in occupational roles (Burns, 1965).

The claim that the system outlined in the previous section is exhaustive is easy enough to make. But this property may easily exist because of the elasticity of some of the categories (notably the last: "definition of individual social identities") and the dubious durability of the threefold classification of theoretical models actually in use. Its utility doubtless rests, first, on the extent to which individual students can resolve ambiguities—a problem faced by all cataloguers and index-makers—and introduce refinements to suit their needs, secondly, on the degree of consensus prevailing among users, and, thirdly, on the logical necessity, and therefore degree of universality, attaching to refinements. What is immediately obvious is that certain of the cells in the table are extremely well populated and others practically empty, and that, roughly speaking, the density of research data would increase as one moved from the top left-hand to the bottom right-hand corner.

The second half of this chapter is devoted to a review of instances of comparative studies. Necessarily, they are characteristic of the way in which different approaches have developed and become exploited rather than characteristic of this or any other formal schematization of the comparative method applied to organizations. What any review of actual studies reveals is that, far from falling into logically coherent patterns, they seem to be continually and almost obstinately departing from them. Like any other kind of inquiry which has a history and an establishment, organizational studies seem at the time to be pursuing not so much the right kind of knowledge as the right kind of questions; not definitive information but fresh hypotheses; not exploring and mapping new territory but staking claims and prospecting.

Given that the purpose of comparative study is properly analytical explanation (or critical understanding), the schema is aimed at producing categories of relevance for using material for comparative purposes rather than a classificatory system of comparative studies. Comparative studies themselves, of course, are a different matter, since they tend to restrict themselves to a single, or a few, comparative categories and to develop these in refined and complicated ways. In what follows, therefore, both comparative studies and studies of particular relevance to the comparative method are arranged only tentatively according to the sequence of analytical categories; and no attempt has been made to find specimens to fit every box. The review also concentrates on the variety of approaches applicable to the first two analytical categories, which relate especially to the study of organizations as a whole.

DIACHRONIC STUDIES OF ORGANIZATIONS IN SOCIETY

Historical contrast is the classic method of comparative studies, indeed of sociology. There is therefore a special appropriateness in starting with long-term comparative studies. It was used systematically, almost exclusively, by Marx. In effect, the purpose of using historical comparison in this way is to arrive at an understanding of the contemporary social situation by examining its origins.

The understanding thus arrived at is twofold. First, and most important, the common perception of the contemporary situation, however systematized and uniform that appreciation may be, is seen for what it is: a snapshot of a process. This revelation, though, has its limitations, and Carl Becker's (1932, p. 19) remark on historical explanation carries both implications: "We can identify a particular thing only by pointing to the various things it successively was before it became that particular thing it will presently cease to be."

Secondly, the terms and concepts applied indiscriminately to each and every stage of the existence of an institution may be shown to conceal changes of a fundamental kind. A classic example of this is Marx's statement on the effects of the factory system and the new technology on the organization of labor:

> Along with the development of the factory system and of the revolution in agriculture that accompanies it, production in all the other branches of industry not only extends, but alters its character. The principle, carried out in the factory system, of analysing the process of production into its constituent phases, and of solving the problems thus proposed by the application of mechanics, of chemistry, and of the whole range of the natural sciences, becomes the determining principle everywhere. Hence, machinery squeezes itself into the manufacturing industries first for one detail process, then for another. Thus the solid crystal of their organisation, based on the old division of labour, becomes dissolved, and makes way for constant changes. Independently of this, a radical change takes place in the composition of the collective labourer, a change of the persons working in combination. In contrast with the manufacturing [i.e., handicraft] period, the division of labour is thenceforth based, wherever possible, on the employment of women, of children of all ages, and of unskilled labourers, in one word, on cheap

labour, as it is characteristically called in England. This is the case not only with all production on a large scale, whether employing machinery or not, but also with the so-called domestic industry, whether carried on in the houses of the workpeople or in small workshops. This modern so-called domestic industry has nothing, except the name, in common with the old-fashioned domestic industry, the existence of which presupposes independent urban handicrafts, independent peasant farming, and above all, a dwelling-house for the labourer and his family. That old-fashioned industry has now been converted into an outside department of the factory [Marx, 1906, Chap. 15, Sec. 8b].

The transformation undergone in the division of labor, work roles, productive organization, and the relationship of home and family to occupation to which Marx points, all lies concealed under an unchanging terminology. In the same way terms like "bureaucracy," "organization chart," "technology," "R & D" tend to conceal fundamental changes that have occurred during the last twenty years in the perception and operation of the practical activities and social institutions to which they refer.

For any writer on social institutions in the nineteenth century, explanation seems to have been conceivable only in terms of historical contrast. Even Tocqueville's *Democracy in America* contains implications of a basically historical contrast, the method he employed elsewhere. It is difficult, now, to appreciate how revolutionary was Durkheim's development of comparative analysis on a contemporary, cross-cultural basis.

The Durkheimian revolution was possibly too successful. In terms of organizational studies, the analytical possibilities offered by the change in institutional forms, roles, and beliefs from one generation to another (which is what Marx was concerned with) have remained curiously unexploited. This is true despite the notable achievement of the one major study in this field, Berle and Mean's *The Modern Corporation and Private Property*. Widely quoted as their findings have been by students of industrial and business organizations, the neglect of longitudinal comparative studies, especially those involving historical research, seems to have led to a failure to incorporate their insights into the body of writings that makes up contemporary organization theory. There is no reference to the book, for example, in what is probably the most widely-used text of all—March and Simon's *Organizations*. Yet no work bears so closely on the topic which so many writers have made of central importance—i.e., goals, and the way in which they are formulated by and for organizations.

Their thesis is that, during this century, there has developed a separation between ownership and control, between the holding of shares and the control of the policies and activities of a company by a management that may or may not hold a minority of shares. This tendency is held to be as inherent in the structure of large-scale enterprise as is the tendency towards monopoly, arising as it does out of the division between ownership and the use of property. Power has been passing into the hands of the managers of enterprises and out of those of the multitudes of small shareholders, among whom ownership is now usually dispersed and whose joint influence cannot, in practice, match that of the single compact minority interest of the board. Further, and more generally, the technical, financial, and administrative complexities of a modern large-scale enterprise have transformed the relationship between the shareholding owner and the manager of productive capacity.

Elton Mayo (1949, p. 32) remarked upon—but nobody has examined—one of the implications of the emergence of the large-scale enterprise: "Instead of the life of a business coming to an end in two or three generations, we have, by improving industrial organisation, conferred upon such business a 'species of immortal life' which must be maintained by the community at its peril." Again, the implications that this has for the relationships between the corporation and specific environmental fields (labor supply, governmental agencies, labor unions) have been remarked upon (for example, by Celier, 1959 and by A. T. M. Wilson, 1961) but not investigated—at least by sociologists or social psychologists.

The most general examination of historical contrasts can bring to light new and revelatory perspectives of social change. It is years since Galbraith (1959) produced his now celebrated historical aperçu concerning the new and insecure relationship between production and market which has appeared as production in America and elsewhere has caught up and overtaken spontaneous consumer demand. This provided a theoretical rationale for the stimulation of the propensity to consume by advertising, styling, and consumer research. It also suggested a causal basis for the development of industrial research and development as a permanent entrepreneurial activity. Since this explanation is at least reasoned, it is to be preferred to the current acceptance of this quite fundamental change in the ideology and operation of productive and other organizations as a function of scientific progress itself or, to sound the depths of tautology, of "social change." It has received very little attention from students of organizations.

Keirstead (1948), again, used his explorations of economic history to point to the fact that when one introduces time into the discussion of the profit-maximizing assumption, it is obvious that for the modern corporation almost every consideration, including maximizing profit, becomes subordinate to survival. This has obvious connections with the Berle and Means' thesis:

> Directly, that is, the realities of industrial enterprise are organised in terms of the firm rather than of the entrepreneur, then almost any profit terms upon which the firm can survive become preferable to grosser

profits on which it might possibly not survive. There is, in fact, no change in the logical basis, but merely in the way in which it works: (a) through individual mortals, (b) through corporations which are relatively potentially longer-lived. For an individual entrepreneur, profit-taking can be maximized for any period of time however short, since the rewards will certainly be a substantial help towards his own survival. Moreover, for the individual the random sector of circumstances affecting his strategies increases enormously with time. And he makes hay, therefore, when the sun shines, and a bird in the hand is worth two in the bush. For the Corporation, randomness does not increase at anything like the same rate. And survival means only survival of the firm. The birds in the bush, which are tomorrow's or the next ten years' production, are just as important as that in the hand [Burns and Stalker, 1961, p. 35]

While it is American lawyers and economists who have made most effective use of historical comparison in analyzing the current relationships between organizations and their social and economic environment, and have thereby pointed to the major influences on the internal structure and on the formulation of the policy-aims of organizations, what little exploitation of historical comparison as a research method has occurred in other social sciences has been done in Europe. Alain Touraine's (1955) study of automobile workers, to take one instance, has been considerably enriched by the comparison he has drawn between the situation of workers in modern, large-scale, technologically advanced plants and that which prevailed earlier. The erosion or rejection of supervisory relationships based on direct subordination, for example, is seen as a consequence of the development of specialized management systems, in which the individual's work behavior is governed by a variety of functional specialists, all exercising impersonal kinds of authority.

Almost identical conclusions were reached by Janowitz (1960) in his study of U.S. Army and Navy officers. Apart from the historical sample of 760 generals and admirals "developed for the purpose of analyzing trends in social background and professional careers," extensive use is made of the writings of professional soldiers in the past and present to illustrate the change in forms of authority from those based on domination to those involving manipulation. My own studies of industrial organizations have depended increasingly on the enlightenment which a historical perspective not only brings of itself, but forces one to search for. At its simplest, it becomes impossible to regard the bureaucratic form that is now conventionally accepted as the ideal type of rationalistic organization as something towards which past ages have been struggling, or as a perfect model that stands as a Platonic idea behind all the imperfect representations actually present as working organizations.

The notion of organizations as developing and changing in time is

<u>critically important</u>, especially in any attempt to perceive the relationships between them and the historical situation of society in, by and for which they are created. The fact that organizations change so profoundly in institutional character and structure from one generation to another while still serving virtually the same ends both for their members and for society calls for a more thorough-going explanation of the structure and function of the organization as it is now; it provides comparative material to aid that explanation; and it enforces considerations of the general societal forces and conditions which are at work. Crozier's (1963) study of the postal check clearing section of the French post office and of a number of plants in the tobacco monopoly was comparative not only in the obvious sense but in that the general findings were related to the historical circumstances of administration, governmental and industrial, in France.

SYNCHRONIC STUDIES OF ORGANIZATIONS IN SOCIETY (CROSS-CULTURAL)

It seems reasonable to draw a parallel between long-term historical and large-scale cross-cultural studies. The parallel is meaningful in more than one sense; just as historical comparison requires a wide-ranging historical competence, so does the cross-cultural study demand more than the application of identical research procedures in different societies. We are in danger, as Hans-Paul Bahrdt (1961) has suggested, of creating a "sociological man" out of the measurable variables yielded by studies of voting behavior, industrial morale, wage-payment system, bureaucratic organizations, and leisure, a sociological man just as unreal and, eventually, just as big an obstruction to theoretical development as "economic man" proved to be.

It is in this respect that Weber presents so eminently laudable and dangerous a methodological model. The placing of his work within the context of cross-cultural studies rather than comparative historical studies is justifiable on the grounds that historical material is used as often to point contrasts between the institutional apparatus of very different forms of social organization prevailing in different historical epochs as to trace the processes which changed value systems, structures, and organizational forms. What gives his work [5] its character is the alliance between outstanding intellectual powers and immense scholarship.

Weber was concerned with the way in which social values and normative images of social organization develop as a kind of mental

5. In particular, *Wirtschaft und Gesellschaft* which traces the relationship between various forms of economy and the dominant types of authority, of religious beliefs, of organization and legal systems; and *The Protestant Ethic and the Spirit of Capitalism* (Weber 1964; 1930).

equipment with which men fashion an acceptable or workable frame-work of institutions. He is constantly reiterating his purpose of establish-ing the subjective, cognitive, structures with which men impart meaning to their social actions. Indeed, the force of the concept of ideal types lies not in its analytical applications, but in the way in which it reflects this normative rendering of the structures the individual reads into and at-taches to the social circumstances of his life, and to which, eventually, he strives to make these circumstances conform.

Ideal types, in fact, represent a normative extreme of system theoriz-ing, in that the shared value elements which inhere in the parts and maintain the system are, so to speak, maximized. It is, therefore, inap-propriate to convert the elements Weber itemizes in his description of bureaucracy as an ideal type into autonomous factors which it is reasonable to convert into variables and then to seek for correlations between them as though they were independent.

The difference may be sufficiently displayed by citing two widely different excursions into cross-cultural analysis: the comparative studies made by Bendix (1956) of management ideologies in the course of indus-trialization in Europe and America and Udy's taxonomical analysis of data on the organization of work drawn from the Human Relations Area Files at Yale.

Bendix's book is a carefully documented account of the value systems of entrepreneurs and managers, and the counter-systems of workers' be-liefs in England during the primary and secondary phases of industrializa-tion, in Russia during the development of its industrial system under capitalism, in the United States during this century, and in East Germany since 1945. He pays consistent attention to the contextual system of values and beliefs in the polity and in the organs of society related to the industrial enterprise. In this he is, of course, immensely aided by the circumstances of his own career that make him free of primary and secondary sources in German and English. The section on Russia, signifi-cantly, relies very heavily on secondary material, notably Vasili Klyu-chevski's *History* and a German history of Russian manufacturing industry published in 1900. He makes the Weberian principles followed through-out quite clear in a preliminary statement:

> Studies of ideologies imply a neglect of persons and private beliefs. I shall treat entrepreneurs and managers as "members" of a social group by virtue of their position in economic enterprises and by virtue of the common problems and experiences to which such positions expose them. And I shall attribute to this group ideologies of management which have been articulated in response to the logic of authority relationships in economic enterprises. While the publicly expressed ideas of a social

group frequently reflect a range of views rather than a single, fully developed ideological position, even this range of views will *not* do justice to the diversity of personal beliefs or attitudes of the group members. As I see it, this is not a serious defect, dictated though it is by the questions I have asked and by the nature of the materials available for study. For the attitudes of individuals do not become the public opinion of a group merely by the process of addition. Instead, public opinion is formed through a constant process of formulation and reformulation by which spokesmen identified with a social group seek to articulate what they sense to be its shared understandings. A study of ideologies deals with these formulations and reformulations and hence with those attitudes which have proved strong enough to gain adherents [Bendix, 1956, pp. xxi–xxii].

Udy (1959a and b) drew on data in the Human Relations Area Files relating to the organization of manufacture and production generally (i.e., including hunting and collecting food) in 150 different nonindustrial societies. In his paper, Udy took seven characteristics of bureaucratic organization from Weber's description of bureaucracy as an ideal type and found that, whereas there was a positive correlation within each two clusters of three and four characteristics, there was no association between the clusters themselves. The first cluster comprised (1) a hierarchy of at least three levels of authority, (2) functional specialists in the organization not engaged in manual work, and (3) differential allocation of rewards. The second cluster consisted of (1) specification of goals as the production of goods, (2) rewards differentiated by performance, (3) participation by a form of contractual relationship, and (4) distribution of rewards by those in higher authority to subordinates.

The first cluster of characteristics, Udy claims, refers to the hierarchic ordering of authority, and the second to principles of rationality—the two major components of Weber's ideal type; the conclusion is that, empirically, and outside the special circumstances of Western industrial societies, there is no necessary connection between the two. But, as Scott (1965, p. 499) rightly comments, "The absence of any association between the hierarchical and rational elements is possibly due to an inclusion within Udy's sample of a considerable number of organizations in which a previously existing political hierarchy had been imposed on a production situation (through 'custodial recruitment'). In these situations, role assignment was based on ascribed political status, rewards were not likely to be distributed according to performance, and organizational objectives were more often diffuse than specific." Leach (1960) has drawn sufficient attention to the dubiousness of the basic data, and to the risks of this kind of analysis of them; the point of Scott's remarks in the present connection is to reinforce the prescription mandatory for cross-cultural analysis or organization (at least in the contemporary situation): that, in comparing social institutions, it is essential to insure, not only that the units are equivalent, but that the context of the cultural situation and of the social system at large does not contain factors which render comparison of the institutions under study invalid. This prescription is, of course, additional to the general considerations affecting the treatment of system theory models as if they were complexes of independent variable factors.

Bendix used comparative analysis to establish a general thesis concerning the necessary relationships between managerial ideology and the organization of industrial production, that is, variations in the substantive and systemic properties of the one were shown to be reflected in changes in the substantive and systemic qualities of the other. Udy's work is, in essence, an attempt to test the necessary coherence of the elements said by Weber and his followers to compose the mode of rational organization towards which industrialization tends. A quite distinct purpose and methodological approach is visible in the attempt to elucidate the components of a system by changing the cultural context— an attempt that may be generated, as in the case of French's Norwegian study (French, Israel, and Ås, 1960) by an initial failure of research findings established in one cultural situation to replicate themselves in another. This kind of check can lead the investigator either to abandon the second project, or the whole series, as invalid or methodologically unsound, or it may give rise to the kind of questioning suggested earlier as the critical stage in research: the questioning that must preface research design and the collection and analysis of data that are to supply the answer, but that can arise only from doubt.

Cross-cultural studies provide opportunities for this kind of fertile difficulty in generous measure; they have, however, to be matched by research opportunism and imagination. French's Norwegian study supplies an instance of the way in which the "failure to replicate" in a different cultural setting may be used to reconstruct the hypothesis and reinterpret the finding of the original research so as to strengthen their validity and widen their application. While he was at the Oslo Research Centre, French undertook a replication of the well-known "resistance to change" experiment (Coch and French, 1948) in an entirely different cultural setting. It will be remembered that, in the original field experiment, three groups of workers were constituted to follow different procedures, labeled "no participation," "participation through representation," and "total participation" in accomplishing a technical and product change. In the event, the third group demonstrated higher-level job satisfaction, lower turnover, and, most important, higher productivity. The Norwegian plant manufactured rubber footwear instead of pyjamas, but "the factory there was similar to the American factory. . . . The work was also on piece-rate. In this particular Norwegian factory, there was an additional point of similarity to many American companies: the company president talked a good game of participation but he obviously did not practice it" (French, 1964, p. 36). There was also a basic similarity between the ideology and form of government characteristics of both countries.

Yet the experiment did not replicate the original findings. Labor-management relationships improved (or rather, mutual understanding and the perception of management-labor relationships as cooperatively rather than competitively based was greater) more in the "total participation" groups than in the "control" groups and there was a tendency for more participation to produce satisfaction, but both these dimensions were less susceptible to measurement (and, in the original study, were the subject of "incidental observations" rather than measurement). In the critical variable related to productivity, "there was essentially no difference between the experimental and control groups in the level of production following the experiment" (ibid., p. 41).

This negative result led to a review of the assumptions concealed within the original formulation. "We are," says French "trying to become more refined in our thinking and participation." He makes a distinction between psychological participation ("the extent of influence on a jointly made decision which the participant *thinks* he has") and objective participation ("the amount of influence on the decision he *actually* has"). But, more important, an entirely new variable (new, that is, in the context of this particular study) is introduced to take care of the discrepancy: "We said to ourselves 'if the experiment comes out differently here in Norway than it did in the United States, what might account for the differences?' Our answer to this question is contained in the following hypothesis: To the extent that participation is considered legitimate, it will have favourable effects on the dependent variables of satisfaction, labour-management relations, and productivity . . ." (ibid., pp. 37, 38).

Legitimacy, in fact, turns out to be the normative controls on output, familiar since the Hawthorne bank-wiring room studies, and not unknown to F. W. Taylor. But to point this out is not to criticize the experiment or the experimenters; the context of social norms governing commitment to work methods improvement, cooperation with bosses, value placed on high earnings, their plans or groups of plans, and so on was clearly constant for the first experiment. The procedure appropriate to science is to observe complete conceptual parsimony in framing hypotheses and to introduce factors only under compulsion.

This procedure is implicit in the fourth variety of cross-cultural comparison, which is properly termed "exploratory." It is a procedure increasingly practiced in pragmatic terms among economists concerned with the conditions under which economic institutions, certain specific entrepreneurial activities, or large-scale construction or development schemes may expect to succeed in the emergent countries. The procedure, simple enough in methodological terms, is to examine the structure, constitutent parts, functions of comparable institutions or processes in similar countries, where they exist, and the social, economic, and cultural conditions that appear to make for success or failure. Naturally, in most cases, true parallels are rare, and it is usual to have to resort to a search for the constituent elements and functions and for the relevant contextual conditions as they exist in partial or embryonic form. This is the procedure adopted by Thorsrud and Emery (1965) in their examination of the institutional forms and conditions essential for the success of a new social apparatus of industrial democracy in Norway.

There is one final development in the use of cross-cultural comparison that deserves mention here, although it is concerned with organization as a methodological instrument rather than as a field of study. It is evident that since the war the lines of theoretical development, methodological practice, and research interest of the social sciences in different countries (previously so different as to often amount virtually to different disciplines though sharing the same name) have tended to converge. Just as the social sciences themselves, from economics on, have emerged and developed as part of the response system of individual societies to the process of industrialization and the social, economic, political, and psychological change processes associated with industrialization, so the increasing *community* of experience among advanced industrial societies in the present third phase of industrialization has conditioned the approximation of sociology, social psychology, and behavioral science in general. The approximation has meant largely a convergence on American models, but this has been due as much to the common belief that social pressures and social changes follow the American pattern as to the academic hegemony of American behavioral science during the past twenty years.

During the 1960's, however, as European societies have emerged from the traumatic experience of the 1940's, the variety of interaction between what is common in international experience and national cultures has made itself apparent. The assumption of the convergence of advanced industrial societies is now very much in question. The growth of interest in Europe and America in cross-cultural studies during the 1960's is, therefore, no historical accident.

It is the special circumstances that surround the contemporary interest in cross-cultural studies that renders the comparative study of organizations in this context of special importance and interest. International organizations, political and economic, operate for the most part in the context of different national societies according to organizational models and practices that are, in principle, uniform for all their national subsidiaries or branches. Where this is the intention, it may be assumed that the differences in structure and in practice, where they exist, reflect national differences in the institutional forms appropriate to the task, in industrial and organizational ideology, and in norms of achievement and competence—differences, that is, going beyond manifest economic, technical and other variations, and underlying assumed uniformities. This, at all events, is the strategy underlying the current research of Willener into the role of middle management in identical functional positions in steel plants in the Coal, Iron, and Steel Community countries, and the studies being mounted by Burns and Trist into the problems specific to large international corporations.

RELATIONS BETWEEN ORGANZATION AND ENVIRONMENT

At this next level of analysis, the observation post of study is stationed within the individual organization, looking outward, so to speak. The shift of position and orientation is already expressed in the identification of society at large and institutional elements in society as "environment."

Emery and Trist (1965) have produced a preliminary analysis of the interrelationship between system and environment in terms of four basic types of environment. The suggestion is that organizational systems are formulated largely by their competent (i.e., appropriate) modes of behavior in different types of setting. They state "the following general proposition":

> that a comprehensive understanding of organisational behaviour requires some knowledge of each member of the following set, where L indicates some potentially lawful connection, and the suffix 1 refers to the organisation and the suffix 2 to the environment:
>
> $$L_{11}, L_{12}$$
> $$L_{21}, L_{22}$$
>
> L_{11} here refers to the processes within the organisation—the area of internal interdependencies; L_{12} and L_{21} to exchanges between the organisation and its environment—the area of transactional interdependencies from either direction; and L_{22} to processes through which parts of the environment became related to each other—i.e., its causal texture —the area of interdependencies that belong within the environment itself [p. 22].

The authors go on to postulate four states that the environment can assume and to note the appropriate character of organizational response.

1. "Placid, randomised environment," corresponding to Simon's (1957) idea of a surface over which an organism can locomote, and which is mostly bare but has in it widely spaced, randomly deposited heaps of food. This would represent the market situation of classic economic theory, and best tactics are continual trial and error.

2. "Placid, clustered environment," corresponding to the economists' state of imperfect competition in which learning can take place—i.e., "the clustering enables some parts to take on roles as signs of other parts." The appropriate organizational response is a rudimentary strategy based on discerning some locations as potentially richer.

3. "Disturbed-reactive environment," a type 2 environment in which a number of other similar organizations coexist. "One has now not only to make sequential choices but to choose actions that will draw off the other organizations."

4. "Turbulent fields," in which dynamic processes (e.g., increasing pace of technological development as a response to competition) arise within the environment to create significant variances for the organizations.

The four types, and the behavior of organizations in response to them, are illustrated by synopses of case studies.

The general thesis bears some resemblance to that developed in connection with studies of the electronics industry (Burns and Stalker, 1961, Chap. 5). Here, four types of systemic response to states of market and technical environment were distinguished and labeled "organization within a stable program," "organization for change," "organization for a constant or predictable rate of novelty," and "organization in the least predictable conditions." These four levels of response were reduced to two ideal types, mechanistic and organic, which represent appropriate responses to a relatively stable or relatively changing market and technical environments. Crozier arrives at much the same differentiation of ideal types of environmental-organizational relationship (Crozier, 1963, pp. 370–371). Woodward (1958) in a study of over 200 industrial concerns related organizational system to technology or, more generally, to varieties of "situational demand." The theoretical model is explicitly of the response system kind:

> Organisation appeared to grow in response to a number of stimuli. The "organisation conscious" firms tended to draw on the concepts of management theory, irrespective of how appropriate they were to the technical situation. Fashion was another important factor. Materials

controllers and industrial engineers were becoming popular at the time of the research, and it was interesting to see how they spread from one firm to another. Moreover, organisation had been modified to some extent in every firm to accommodate individuals—"empire builders" who distorted the pattern in their search for status, and misfits for whom sinecure had to be found. These distortions often continued long after the people concerned had died or left the firm.

But although "situational demands" did not determine formal organisation, they appeared to have considerable influence on spontaneous or informal development. In a number of firms formal organisation did not satisfy "situational demands" adequately, while informal organisation did [p. 38].

She concludes: "The systematic analysis of 'situational demands' might well be used to predict the effects of technical changes on management structure" (p. 39).

Goffman (1961) eliminated the interactive processes that obtain between all organizations and their social environment to establish a category of total institution which included prison, hospital, homes for the incapable, barracks, boarding schools, and monasteries. The interesting feature of this celebrated essay in the present context is that, although the separation of "staff" and "inmates" is stressed, the specifically boundary-maintaining function of the directors of such institutes is deliberately left out of the account. In addition, of course, the differing instrumental prescriptions of these institutions by society are also omitted. Despite—or rather because of—this, it is a brilliant instance of the establishment of an analytical category that cuts across common usage classifications. It gains not only from the critical undertones implicit throughout in the matching of characteristics between hospitals and prisons, but from the explanatory force of the comparative method when used to demonstrate similarities and even identities in social systems, social controls, and role-performances in what are ordinarily regarded as utterly different physical, social, and moral situations.

DEFINITION OF TASK AND DIVISION OF LABOR

This section composes the very large body of work concerned with the way in which the purposes of our organization are defined within it and the consequent distribution of the total tasks among groups and individuals. It is at this point, not surprisingly, that a sharp distinction occurs between the theoretical models which different students have developed and exploited.

There is a sense in which the development of the social sciences depends on the constant conversion of the substantively qualitative into the substantively quantitative. Apart from this, in the case of the most recalcitrant qualitative material, Barton and Lazarsfeld (1955) have argued (and it is a theme to which Lazarsfeld frequently recurs), codification is necessary to point out dangers, indicate neglected possibilities, and support improvements. Even at this level, one of the major contributions of factor theories makes itself felt—that which comes from the obligation to order concepts, to distinguish them to insure that they maintain the definition given to them in the first place throughout the analysis and that the set of terms is adequate to the task of analysis. It is at this stage that concepts may be, and often have to be, reformulated after consideration (Goode and Hatt, 1952, pp. 49–50) of the meaningful elements of the concepts actually employed, of the variety of usages of the terms in the literature and of the variety of other terms used for the same phenomena. "Respecification of the concept," claim the authors, "always leads to more fruitful hypothesis." Reordering the concepts, according to analytical procedures such as representation of material in matrix form, can also lead to more fruitful analysis. At the very least, it can lead to the consideration of material with "a fresh eye," lending a kind of binocular vision to the theoretical insights the researcher has developed. This is, indeed, the great merit of mathematical models, fruitless though they may have been so far in advancing the substantive content of the social sciences.

Since the Barton and Lazarsfeld paper appeared there has been an immense change of front even among the most qualitative-minded schools of research to quantitative analytical methods, which must be considered separately from the mathematical developments proper that have affected and occurred with the social sciences. The last ditches defended by such slogans as "those who count, don't" have all been surrendered—almost all, that is; there are still memorable engagements being fought (Schlesinger, 1962). Research orthodoxy now requires the translation of impressionistic or case study procedures, still the necessary prelude to most empirical research projects, into survey procedures, for validation if for nothing else.

Few statistical procedures are specific to the study of organizations, and the development of quantitative techniques in the comparative analysis of organizations as a whole has lain mostly with economists. If once the processes of interaction between the environment and the organization can be satisfactorily itemized, the construction of a matrix of quantitatively expressed variables from which component analysis ("latent structure" analysis) can be made becomes possible, as Barton's (1961) pioneer attempt has shown. R. R. Blake has developed a simple matrix formulation out of two variables—"concern for people" and "concern for production." The resulting grid allows for the positioning of any individual concern (relative to others previously studied) and for recording progress through the change process which the research team or consultant is involved in promoting (Blake and Mouton, 1964). Chapple and Sayles (1961) employ task, structure, and technology as variables in an approach, fundamentally different in ideology, and much more sophisticated analytically, but not dissimilar in conception.

There is a sizeable and familiar difficulty, however, standing in the way of a wholesale move into quantitative procedures. Once one deserts the accepted common ground of "administrative sociology" and economic statistics in which one is either dealing with units which are the accepted currency of analysis at any level of study—registered companies, money values, production quantities, number employed, capital value of equipment, turnover, labor costs, and change rates in them; or occupational status, earnings, educational qualifications, labor turnover, age of employees, number of skills, and functional specialties—it becomes extremely difficult to define variables and units of measurement in any but an entirely ad hoc manner, and this largely destroys the value of quantitative procedures. This, it should be added, is a failing attributable to social theory, not to formal analysis. Power (or its converse, compliance), for example, which features so large in the theoretical analysis of organizations, is an extremely refractory term to render into useful quantitative formulations (for an example, the curiously naive reduction by Fromm cited in Barton's standard paper on "Property-Space" (Barton, 1955, pp. 52–53). The concept of power is, in fact, extremely complex and various; Emmet (1954), in an illuminating paper, lists five major types, each containing two or three subtypes—and all excluding coercion. The observations made by two contributors in a discussion at the Operational Research Conference in Cambridge in 1964 express the general difficulty in succinct terms:

> The scientist's problem, said Stansfield, was to describe what he observed in nature, and relationships between the phenomena, in terms which were as precise as possible while remaining understandable to others. A great deal of information in any situation has to be condensed through the use of symbols. The symbols used are words, as used in definition, and mathematical symbols. He did not see that Rapoport's paper, at least in its earlier section, said anything more than that the most precise and economical way of describing nature was in terms of mathematical relations. If this was so, it was something which was assumed at the outset of any scientific career; he personally had done this during his first year at this university, but had had to spend his next five years contending with the difficulties of definition. One began by thinking one knew what an atom was, and then spent several years in discovering how much experience and consensus had built up over several generations in such a way that other people knew what one was talking about, a way, moreover, that would take several volumes

to spell out at length. The difficulty in social science was that this common experience and consensus did not exist. He himself was uneasy about the devotion of so much attention to the development of a mathematics for the social sciences, in the absence of a common understanding of what the mathematics could possibly stand for. . . . Gayner reinforced the doubt raised by Stansfield by pointing to the history of the natural sciences. It was true that mathematics served as the common language of sciences, but the progress in any individual natural science had been dependent on theoretical formulations related to the specific content of these sciences. Mathematics could hardly have served as the language of chemistry without the prior existence of such terms as element, atom, molecule, valency, atomic weight. These were verbal terms with a firm and virtually universal definition without which one would not know what the mathematics was about [Burns, 1964].

METHODOLOGICAL APPROACHES IN DIACHRONIC CASE STUDIES

In principle, there should be no difference between long-term diachronic studies and short-term ones. Obviously, studies which make use of historical data require the investigator to do more than explore the part of the institutions to which his special interest attaches. To treat history as a rummage box that will surely produce (and it unfailingly does) evidence to support theories with ambitions beyond anything which the available contemporary evidence or research material will support is reckless amateurism, which draws its just retribution from the professional. Nevertheless, apart from adding this extra academic dimension to himself, the student of organizations comparing institutional differences over generations (as with Boulding, 1953), or centuries (as with Bendix, 1956), is treating time as a major, independent variable in much the same way as the student of organizational change compares system states over a period of months, or a year or two. The object is to use the contrast between two conditions of the same system separated by time as a basis for comparative study, or to study the process aspect itself of institutional activity.

In Gouldner's (1954) study of a gypsum mine, the different forms taken by the organization at the beginning and end of the period were the result of the predominance of first one and then another distinct bureaucratic pattern. These forms took their shape from the intentions, cognitions, and aspirations of the chief manager, on the one hand, and, on the other, from the counter-system devised by subordinates by way of response. The two forms of "representative bureaucracy" and "punishment-centered bureaucracy" were suggested by the opportunity of actually watching the transition from one to the other over the "succession crisis," when an outsider took over the chief executive position.

This is something, therefore, akin to field experiment—the difference being, of course, that the change is generated within the system under observation, not imposed or introduced. There is no sense in which changes in the system are controlled, and no sense in which they can be checked and measured by comparison with the course of events in a "control" group unaffected by the induced change. Short-term longitudinal studies are, therefore, methodologically more primitive than field experiments. This is revealed, incidentally, in the remarks which Gouldner (1954, p. 259) offers in defense of his "violating the canons of good interviewing": "Before a miner was going to tell us anything about *his* feelings, he wanted to know about *ours*." Nevertheless, he adds, "we were all convinced that our best data was [sic] obtained during such moments of real interaction."

Much the same point is made, rather more elaborately, in the remarks on interviewing in *The Management of Innovation* (Burns and Stalker, 1961). The interviews were lengthy, lasting anywhere from one hour to a whole working day, developing along "fairly free lines" after the opening, which was usually conducted on formal, routine lines. During the later stages,

> it proved possible to create a more productive relationship than can be constructed on the basis of one person's seeking information from another. The conventions governing such interviews and the limits of the information regarded as admissible or relevant are nowadays prescribed fairly strictly. To go beyond these limits, it is not enough to demonstrate interest or even sympathy; in the writers' experience, an informant will get to the point of formulating and presenting his experience, beliefs, opinions, anxieties, and criticisms only when there has been established a relationship which is reciprocal in some genuine sense; when there is some point for the informant in going further than the needs of courtesy, and compliance with an undertaking by the firm to co-operate with the researcher, seem to require of him. Thus the researcher has to make the relationship "real"; one in which he is prepared to behave on his side as what he declares himself to be. This can only be done by showing how he is making use of the information he is receiving; by the occasional interpretation of a situation in terms which are both derived from his perception of the situation as an outsider and as a sociologist or psychologist, and which are also appropriate to his informant's ability or preparedness to comprehend. From then on, whether the interpretation is accepted or not, there is a freer, more satisfactory quality about the interview, a stronger desire to recruit and present facts, examples, views. There are no interpretations and appraisals contained in any part of this report which have not been communicated at some time or other to persons involved in the situations at issue. Invariably, also, we have found our own ideas being amended, extended, or corrected by such traffic [pp. 13–14].

I am now inclined to be less defensive about this kind of interviewing procedure ("All this," I wrote, "is very far removed from any method of investigation which could possibly be called scientific!"). This particular study involved not merely examining a technically and socially complex system in process of change from one situation, undefined and possibly obscure or misrepresented, to another. The new state of the system (the emergence of which, the study had been designed to observe) was not in some cases realized at all or in anything like the terms envisaged by those involved. The process of change, moreover, occurred according to a complex of variables that could only be identified as (or after) they produced their effects. All this requires—to use an old-fashioned word—a "cybernetic" relationship between researcher and subject. Research becomes, in fact, a true search process among the experience of individual members of the social system, in which hypothesis and deduction become a serial process. There is a sense in which, in their eagerness to achieve "scientific detachment," social scientists have cut themselves off from their main resource—the ability of human beings to memorize and report their own experiences.

The need for this fairly highly sensitized interaction was, in fact, particularly acute during the principal phases of this study. The purpose of the study was, as originally conceived, simple and straightforward. Earlier studies has suggested that there were two distinct systems of management practice: one "mechanistic," appearing to be appropriate to an enterprise operating under relatively stable technological and market conditions; the other, "organic," appearing to be required for condition of change. The main phase of the research began when it appeared possible to study the experiences of a number of engineering firms interested in entering new fields of electronics research and development and thus moving from relatively stable conditions to a situation of fairly rapid technical and market change. The presumption was that it would be possible to observe the processes of organizational adaption from a mechanistic to an organic system in a variety of contexts. In the event, hardly any firm succeeded in accomplishing the change, or, indeed, in realizing its intentions. In half the cases, laboratory groups were disbanded by management or were disrupted by resignations. Others were converted into test departments, "troubleshooting" teams, or production departments. The research project as originally conceived, therefore, was a disappointing failure. On the other hand, seen in terms of the quite unexpected problem of why the working organization of the firms did not change as their circumstances changed, the project become immediately far more interesting theoretically.

A third procedure that may be subsumed under this heading of short-term diachronic studies is the "tracer" method developed by Woodward. In essence this is similar to the illuminating pursuit of the "stages through which an actual problem proceeded in an actual company" observed and recorded in the classic "Observation of a Business Decision" study by Cyert, Simon, and Trow (1956). Marples' (1960) tracing of a design from inception at a management committee to finished production is reported in more detail than the Cyert, Simon, and Trow study, but follows essentially the same pattern. These two latter examples are necessarily diachronic, but are concerned specifically with the delineation of decision-making paths; the comparison is between actual patterns of decision-making and presumed or traditional patterns. The Carnegie Institute group's distinction between "programmed" and "non-programmed" decision-making provided the foundation for much of the behavioral and simulated behavioral studies issued from the same school since (see Newell and Simon, 1961). Marples' elucidation of the tree-like development of decisions which constitutes the formal structure of events as conceived by traditional management thinking reveals multifarious loops, false leads, and restarts; this study, too, shows a close kinship with the development of models of the development process on which Critical Path Analysis techniques are founded.

Woodward's use of tracer methods is directed more specifically to institutional analysis. It is "based on the assumption that when the management of a firm makes a decision to manufacture a product, or series of products, a control system is brought into existence." The research comprised three case studies of production orders in three firms: for an analogue computer; for a batch of receivers forming part of a comprehensive aircraft communication, navigation, and direction finding system; and for a four-week production program for a brand of soap. "The 'tracer' approach implies a very detailed study of part of a firm's total activities over a period of time: the methods used were based on social anthropology, the direct and prolonged observation of the daily behaviour of people towards each other until patterns of interaction were 'identified' " (Woodward and Eilon, 1964, p. 4).

As in the earlier tracer studies, comparative analysis is directed towards the contrast between the formal system of control designed or intended by management and the actual behavior of the organization. Thus, the more formalized a control system, the less possible it is to measure achievement standards by anything other than the relative degree of failure; the study follows the implications of this observation for information flow, for internal political activity, and for the individual management role—and career. Researchers in each firm were given "guide lines to indicate the ground they were expected to cover," (ibid., p. 5) but, beyond this, were free to develop their case studies as they wished.

Woodward and Eilon's remarks on the utility of their fully articulated exploitation of the tracer method are worth quoting in full:

> All three research workers felt that the use of a "tracer" was helpful in finding out what happened inside a factory. Its disadvantage, particularly relevant to Case II, where the main control problem was to fit a number of different orders into an overall production programme, was that the concentration of one order meant losing some of the significance of the different orders on each other. This was outweighed by its advantages, however. The first of these was that it was possible to compare objectives and attitudes at all levels of the hierarchy and between line and staff departments in relations to the same task, and to see how the same task created different problems for and offered different satisfactions to the various individuals and groups concerned with it. Secondly, the "tracer" provided a valuable reference or "homing" point for the research workers themselves during a long and complex investigation. It would have been impossible to make such a detailed study and to ask the same questions of the same people so many times without having this reference point to which the answers could be related.
>
> Thirdly, following the "tracer" through the firm at the pace at which it was being made enabled the research workers to see the envolvement of the control system and the relationships associated with it in a "real" time context. The fact that an individual, asked at a progress meeting to follow up a certain component, did so on the morning before the next progress meeting, could have significant implications not only for the control system itself, but also for the human relations associated with it. It was also possible to see how time ebbed away in the politics of decision-making, and how and when a sense of urgency was introduced into the control-system. In this respect, the "tracer" method has advantages over the more generalised organisation study and gets round the difficulty so often encountered in attitude surveys of relating what is said to the events taking place in the factory at the time the survey is being carried out [1964, p. 9].

COMMUNICATION SYSTEM

Probably greater advances have been made methodologically and theoretically in this area of study than in any other directly concerned with organizations and organizational behavior. This is largely due to the work of H. A. Simon and his colleagues, work that has been directed more and more towards the articulation of mathematical models of organizations themselves, but that has, so far, had its greatest impact on the way in which organizations and organizational behavior are perceived and conceptualized.

Of fundamental importance is the distinction established early in the work of the group between programmed and non-programmed decision-making (Cyert, Simon and Trow, 1956; Simon, 1958; March and Simon, 1958). Work within an organization takes place—and can only take place —on the assumption that other work processes are taking place around it. This is not a matter of simple routines: in programmed decisions the choice made is to some extent a forgone conclusion, although it may be necessary to perform a complicated series of calculations before a single choice is actually made. Simon (1958) instances driving a car to a destination, which involves almost exclusively programmed decision-making, although a good deal of computation (most of which is done "unthinkingly") takes place based on information obtained through the eyes. Experience in driving counts, but the more experienced the driver, the nearer the approach to a fully programmed series of decisions—i.e., he knows what to do "automatically" on every occasion of choice. There is no substantial dissimilarity, says Simon, between this and what happens in practice when a monthly schedule is planned in a factory.

Programmed decision-making is what it is because of the existence of an institutional framework around the individual. "The pattern of behavior in a business firm in which this particular decision [the choice of an aggregate production rate for a factory] represents one small detail, may be regarded as a mosaic of such decision-making programs. . . . So far as any of the programmed decision-making processes is concerned, all the other programs that surround it are a part of its environment" (p. 53). In non-programmed decisions the alternatives of choice are not given in advance, but must be discovered by a rational process of searching. Not that in non-programmed decisions the chooser is compelled to calculate in terms of expectations and his degree of belief in them; Simon suggests that such searches for alternatives are conditional upon a higher level of aspiration, when satisfaction will have to be sought outside the routine, habitual, programmed courses of decision-making.

To a very large extent, the processes which we have in mind as specific to work organizations are reducible to cognitive apparatuses of these two kinds; moreover, the organization processes referred to as specifically managerial are reducible to non-programmed decision-making and especially to the design of new or amended programs, which will, of course, include the provision of subroutines for monitoring and controlling the output of programs or parts of programs. Conversely, it could be said that the social scientist, in studying organizations, and therefore in elucidating the patterns of communications and of behavior, is concerned to determine the programs—the institutional mosaic—within which work and other role-behavior takes place, and, further, to find out who, among managers, peer-groups, former generations, reference groups, powerful or influential groups or individuals or trade unions, write the programs.

Less methodologically exotic, but fairly closely related to behavioral studies in general orientation is a series of what might be termed "behavioral recording studies." Walker, Guest, and Turner's study (1956) based on observations of foremen's activities and communications and their very detailed recording is familiar, but self-recording studies have been comparatively little exploited until very recently, when a number of researches using this technique appears to have started concurrently in England and America.

Self-recording techniques merely exploit a little more thoroughly and a good deal more ruthlessly the more familiar of all elements in social research methodology—the fact that people can be asked to report all kinds of information about themselves and will frequently oblige by answering. This amounts to social scientists having the inestimable advantage of turning the very subjects they wish to study into observational and recording posts.

In 1948 Sune Carlson was conducting a small seminar composed of the presidents of a number of Swedish business and manufacturing companies. At one point it became clear that it would be interesting, and perhaps profitable, for them to study how they spent their time. The ensuing study lasted four weeks for each member who participated (a number dropped out, and complete records were eventually obtained from five). Records were made by the subject and his secretary of all communications and worktime contacts with other people, by correspondence, notes and memoranda; by telephone, conference, and meeting; by conversation; the information content of the communication was classified under a number of headings; the names and organizational locations of the others involved in communication were recorded; and action was classified in terms of purpose—obtaining information, making decisions, giving orders.

My own study used a similar recording method, but was applied to the top executive group in each of a number of firms. All of them recorded during the same period (four or five weeks in most cases). The project was designed as a comparative study. Ten concerns and ninety-eight executives, members of self-defined "top management groups" were included in the study.

The method, as then established (Burns, 1954), has been followed subsequently with few variations (Burns, 1957; Horne and Lupton, 1965; Burns and Sinclair, 1963; Butler, 1960). The method is to arrange for records of how they are spending their time to be kept simultaneously by a number of people over a period of some weeks.

The standard recording form has six divisions showing:

Time   (taken for the episode)
Persons   (communicated with or present, if any)
Mode   (of activity—e.g., conversation, reading or writing or dictating letters)
Place   (i.e., in which part of the workplace the episode took place— own office, office block, assembly department, home, outside factory, traveling)
Subject   (the functional category of task or problem which formed the subject of the episode)
Purpose   (giving or receiving information or advice, both or neither; giving or receiving instructions or decisions, both or neither)

The results bear on many other matters than the distribution of individual and group managerial time or the substantive content of their functional roles—which, indeed, is the least interesting part of the results. More important is the picture—the moving picture—such studies give of the management system, seen as a communication network. And the production of this information itself yields comparative data of considerable interest. For seven manufacturing concerns, to take one instance, the proportion of all management time spent in spoken communication (all forms, from conferences to telephone conversations) ran as follows:

$$80\text{--}71\text{--}68\text{--}56\text{--}55\text{--}44\text{--}42 \ (\text{percent})$$

The order is significant. The firms are arranged from left to right also in terms of their investment in R & D—i.e., their susceptibility to environmental (technological and market) change. Moreover, the direction of communication changes. In the first firm, slightly more than half of all communication was lateral—i.e., with colleagues—this proportion dropped until, in the seventh firm, virtually all communication was vertical in direction.

AUTHORITY STRUCTURE

Study of the nature and legitimacy of authority and social controls has been familiar since the Hawthorne experiments (Roethlisberger and Dickson, 1939). The Bank-Wiring Room Study still remains the most strikingly successful attempt to elucidate the rationale (i.e., the cognitive structure) of the complex system of guides and rules governing work behavior. The Hawthorne study has been, in fact, the starting point of all organizational studies of work behavior in terms of either conformity or nonconformity with managerial direction and supervision.

There is a large number of comparative studies that regard the structure, form and behavior of the work groups as dependent on the single variable of management or supervisory "style." The best known is the series of studies by the Survey Research Center of work groups relating variations in productivity to differences in supervisory behavior. Supervisors of high production groups were men likely to show concern for their subordinates, to spend time in planning and other facilitating activities, and less likely to supervise closely (Kahn and Katz, 1953). These conclusions, nevertheless, have been challenged by studies mounted as replications by Argyle in England (Argyle et al., 1959), a circumstance which is connected with French's "discovery" of the operation of legitimacy and the discussion of Blau and Scott of the development of a normative framework within which supervisory control operates (Blau and Scott, 1962, pp. 141–143; Gouldner, 1954).

It will be remembered that the establishment of the behavior patterns in the Bank-Wiring Room was rendered possible through the perception by the research team of differences not only between the rules imposed by and expectations of management and the rules and norms of the work groups, but differences within the work group itself. A study of the institutional structure and characteristic behavior of management cliques and cabals in a factory began with casual observation of minor behavioral differences (Burns, 1955).

The identification and analysis of the normative controls developed within groups by explicit and implicit comparison with those imposed by organizational requirements as interpreted by senior executive authority has, for many years, been a major theme of organizational studies, ranging through medical students (Becker et al., 1961), post office workers in Holland (Van Beinum, 1963) and France (Crozier, 1965), textile workers in Norway (French, Israel and As, 1960), engineering operatives in England (Baldamus, 1961), industrial scientists in the United States (Kornhauser, 1962) and in Britain (Burns and Stalker, 1961), prisoners (Sykes and Messinger, 1960), and social workers (Blau, 1955).

SYSTEMS OF ENGAGEMENT AND REWARD AND INVOLVEMENT

Comparative studies at this level are at present in a rather more dynamic phase than appears to be the case with the analysis of authority structure. Comparative studies by Behrend (1959), by de Bal (1964), and by Lutz and Willener (1960) of wage and incentive schemes, based on wide-ranging surveys have all pointed to the complex interaction between (a) the perception of earnings as a return for work, appraised in terms of normative standards developed by individuals and categories of workers by comparison with others (reference groups) and (b) the perception of wage and bonus payment systems (used by individuals as well as by organized groups as the outcome of a bargaining procedure between workers and managers.

More generally, there are three directions in which studies of the individual within the organization have developed. One is sufficiently illustrated by the analysis of the varieties of role structure prescribed by different work situations. Adapting the "system theory" concept of role-set (Merton, 1957) to operational use in analytical procedures, Kahn et al. (1964) collected data on the different demands made within the organization, on supervisors by immediate and other superiors, peers, and subordinates, and construed them in terms of the possibilities of the integrated role, role-dilemma, or role-conflict that they presented to the individual. In rather different terms, I have studied the commitments of individuals to the organization, to their departmental colleagues, to their age-grade, to their own careers, and to a professional ethos within the contexts of a broadcasting organization and a large hospital. Out of these commitments, it is argued, are constructed the variety of social systems that coexist within the social milieu of work—the most important being the working organization itself, the system of internal politics, and the career system (Burns, 1965).

More interesting methodologically is the development of the theory of human decision-making (Newell, Shaw, and Simon, 1958) to the point at which it is possible to identify the operationally relevant information, the kind of information processing, and the rule for combining the kinds of information processing involved in the decision-making of individuals in specific circumstances and for specific ends.

> Within this framework the problem of constructing a model of some specific decision behavior becomes a problem of uncovering the basic rules of operations employed by the decision maker to lead him to the particular decisions under consideration. If the decision process is one which is frequently employed by the individual, questions about the procedure followed, the records consulted, the information that is processed and the output can provide a rough picture of the more important parts of the decision process. These interviews are frequently more rewarding if there is one person to ask the questions while another takes notes. It must be noted, however, that this approach asks an individual to describe and in some sense justify why he behaves as he does. To the extent that many people are unable to describe how they reached a particular decision the information gathered in this manner must be regarded with some caution.
>
> A more reliable guide to decision processes is a protocol of an individual's decision behavior. A protocol is a tape recorded transcript of the verbalized thoughts and actions of a subject who has been

instructed to think or problem solve aloud. Since a protocol is a description of what a person does, it avoids some of the problems inherent in the interviews and questionnaire techniques.

A variant on the interview approach is to ask the individual to write out a decision routine which he thinks will accomplish the task at hand. By questioning him to construct routines of this type and then asking relevant questions, e.g., "But what happens if . . . ?" he may be led to expand and alter what he has written before [Clarkson and Pounds, 1963, p. 22].

The consequential development of the procedure in terms of a model appropriate for writing a computer program to simulate the decision processes of a given individual belongs to the discussion of the development of simulation as a research tool, but the opportunities the procedure promises for analysis in just those situations which have been studied through survey methods and open interview by the Michigan group and by Burns are obvious.

SOCIAL IDENTITIES

Payment and incentive schemes relating to individual workers clearly involve consideration of groups, norms, and organizational settings. Even F. W. Taylor, who, as Friedmann (1955) has insisted, was bent on treating the individual worker as far as possible as an isolated individual and maximizing productive efficiency in terms of each separate worker, observes that there exists what he called "systematic soldiering," or shirking; he remarks on a kind of tacit agreement among workers in a firm, perhaps in a whole neighbourhood, about the amount of work they should do (Taylor, 1911). A number of comparative studies have concentrated on this "outer framework" of normative principles within which the individual's *occupational identity* (involving all the roles into which a person enters and role-behavior he manifests in his capacity as member of the productive system of society) forms itself. Popitz identifies six "images of society" which enter into the varieties of the worker's attitudes to the enterprise as a system to which he is expected to become committed as a participant member as well as engaged as resource: static order, progressive order, structural dichotomy (of class and power) as collective fate, dichotomy as individual conflict, progressive or reforming social order, and class struggle.

Conversely, the specific nature of the occupational role of the chief executive enters into the analysis of the boundary-maintaining processes, which are his operational province. Selznick (1957) posits a categorical difference between the leadership and the executive role. "A new 'logic' emerges" (p. 3). Drawing on comparisons and analogies between leaders in business, governmental and military organizations, he suggests that the institutional role of the leader is defined by his key tasks of: defining the goals in the light of the commitments of the organization; building policy into the social structure of the organization; maintaining values, distinctive identity and integrity; and ordering internal conflict. From a different point of departure, similar prescriptions are reached from an analysis of the situation and behavior of the chief executives in sixteen companies (Burns and Stalker, 1961, Chap. 10). Here the role is initially defined in terms of its major characteristics of social isolation. There are, in principle, it is suggested, four ways of dealing with this social isolation: exploiting it, escaping from it, and, in either case, resorting to means which are either organizationally legitimized or not. This, in turn, gives four kinds of relationship with the members of the concern, each of which promotes a specific array of responses and thus acts as a determinant of the organizational structure (or at least of the way in which that structure behaves).

Crozier (1965) has followed the line of Chinoy (1955) and of Andrieux and Lignon (1960) in relating the occupational and leisure identities of white collar workers.[9] In the discussion of his results, he suggests that individual office workers themselves confront a problem of boundary maintenance between the occupational world and its environment (i.e., in this case, other social milieux of which they are members). It is at this point that studies of organizations and the individuals in them go into reverse, so to speak. The selves which are partitioned into social identities so as to accord with the specifications written out by the varieties of social organizations they take part in are, in these studies, recomposed in an attempt to identify and describe the total social situation and behavior pattern of the individual.

COMPARATIVE RESEARCH AS A RESEARCH STRATEGY

The tools, conceptual and methodological, that social scientists work with are extremely crude and easily blunted. Statistical procedures afford the most precise and rigorous methods generally available, and statistics are a way of oversimplifying; if the procedures and results are probabilistic, statistics often distort as well.

There is, therefore, a good deal to be gained from applying the concept of comparative study to methodology as well as to subject matter. The very useful exercise which Goode and Hatt (1952) called re-conceptualization is, in fact, no more and no less than an attempt to take a fresh look at material and methods, a deliberate escape from the limitations any particular method among those available to social scientists imposes.

The self-recording technique described above, for example, was de-

9. This is also the theme of Zweig's (1962) study of workers.

vised as a rather desperate resort to obtain entirely fresh data and an entirely different formulation of a research problem which was then new to me and appeared utterly intractable; the adequate description and analysis of a concern which was to all appearances flourishing and expanding, but which was rife with conflict and frustration and broke all the most elementary rules of orthodox management practice, down to the refusal—as a matter of management policy—to define managerial roles or to have an organization chart drawn.

Major developments in research techniques and methods have emerged, in fact, from endeavors to mount an assault on a research problem from an entirely different angle of approach. Bavelas' creative experimental work with small groups stemmed from his effort to recompose the early Lewinian interpretation of the dynamics of interaction within groups in entirely different conceptual terms, with entirely different kinds of observational data, analyzed with entirely different instruments. Survey research itself involves, or should involve, a reformulation of the aperçus which develop in the impressionistic observations and open-ended interviews of the pilot phase into the quite different conceptual framework of an experimental design.

It is something of a tragedy that the "binocular" vision the dualistic strategies thus developed can bring to research is so often lost because of the tendency of each new departure to become a specialized field of study, autonomous and academically segregated. The great merit and strength of simulation is that it enforces a reconsideration of data and processes and analysis in totally different terms from those in which problems are presented; yet such merit and strength as the method has brought to the social sciences are being dissipated by its exploitation in terms of business games and of a new specialism.

It may be worthwhile for social scientists to address themselves to the problem of developing research expertise in more than one branch of methodology and of combining them in research strategies that will not merely offset disadvantages inherent in one branch but, of themselves, develop more penetrating and more reliable methods than can be hoped for from each pursued in isolation.

REFERENCES

ABBREVIATIONS

ASR   American Sociological Review
HR   Human Relations
JAP   Journal of Applied Psychology
JASP   Journal of Abnormal and Social Psychology
MS   Management Science
SSR   Sociology and Social Research

Andrieux, A. and Lignon, J. L'ouvrier d'aujourd'hui. Paris: Riviere, 1960.
Argyle, M., Gardner, G., and Cioffi, F. The Measurement of Supervisory Methods. London: Oxford U., Institute of Experimental Psychology, 1957 (Mimeo).
Bahrdt, H.–P. "Zur Frage des Menschenbildes in der Soziologie." European J. Sociology, 1961, 2, 1–17.
de Bal, M. B. "Crise, mutation et depassement de la rememeration au rendement." Sociologie du Travail. April–June 1964, 6, 113–134.
Baldamus, W. Efficiency and Effort. London: Tavistock Publications, 1961.
Barton, A. H. "The Concept of Property-Space in Social Research." In P. F. Lazarsfeld and M. J. Rosenberg, eds., The Language of Social Research. Glencoe, Ill.: Free Press, 1955.
Barton, A. H. Organizational Measurement and Its Bearing on the Study of College Environments. New York: College Entrance Examination Board, 1961.
Barton, A. H. and Lazarsfeld, P. F. "Some Functions of Qualitative Analysis in Social Research." Frankfurter Beitraege zur Soziologie, 1955, 1, 321–361.
Bavelas, A. "Leadership: Man and Function." Administrative Science Qtly., 1959–60, 4, 491–498.
Becker, Carl. The Heavenly City of the Eighteenth Century Philosophers. New Haven: Yale U. Press, 1932.
Becker, H. Outsiders. New York: Collier–Macmillan, 1963.
Becker, H., et al. Boys in White. Chicago: Chicago U. Press, 1961.
Behrend, H. "Financial Incentives as the Expression of a System of Beliefs." British J. Sociology, 1959, 10, 137–147.
Bendix, R. Work and Authority in Industry. London: Chapman and Hall, 1956.
Bendix, R. Max Weber, An Intellectual Portrait. Glencoe, Ill.: Free Press, 1960.
Berle, A. A., Jr. and Means, G. C. The Modern Corporation and Private Property. New York: Macmillan, 1932.
Blake, R. R. and Mouton, J. The Managerial Grid. Houston: Gulf Publishing Co., 1964.
Blau, P. The Dynamics of Bureaucracy. Chicago: U. of Chicago Press, 1955.
Blau, P. and Scott, W. R. Formal Organizations: A Comparative Approach. San Francisco: Chandler, 1962.
Boulding, K. E. The Organizational Revolution. New York: Harper, 1953.
Burns, T. "The Directions of Activity and Communications in a Departmental Executive Group." HR, 1954, 7, 73–97.
_____. "The Reference of Conduct in Small Groups: Cliques and Cabals in Occupational Milieux." HR, 1955, 8, 467–486.

————. "Management in Action." *Operational Research Qtly.*, 1957, 8 (2).

————. "The Idea of Structure in Sociology." *HR*, 1958, 217–228.

————. "The Sociology of Industry." In A. T. Welferd, *Society*. London: Routledge and Kegan Paul, 1962.

————. "The Systems Concept as a Common Frame of Reference." In *Operational Research and the Social Sciences*, Proceedings of Operational Research Society Conference. Cambridge, England, 1964; London: Tavistock Publications, 1966.

————. "Ambiguity and Identity." Department of Sociology, U. of Edinburgh, 1965 (Mimeo).

Burns, T. and Sinclair, S. *The Child Care Service at Work*. Edinburgh: H.M.S.O., 1963.

Burns, T. and Stalker, G. M. *The Management of Innovation*. London: Tavistock Publications, 1961.

Butler, W. P. "A Study of Communication." *Personnel Practice Bull.*, 1960, *16* (3).

Celier, C. "The Social Sciences and the Changing Role of Management." Paris: OEEC, 1959, 31–40.

Centers, R. *The Psychology of Social Classes*. Princeton: Princeton U. Press, 1947.

Chapple, E. D. and Sayles, L. R. *The Measurement of Management*. New York: Macmillan, 1961.

Chinoy, E. *Automobile Workers and the American Dream*. Garden City: Doubleday, 1955.

Clarkson, G. P. E. and Pounds, W. F. "Theory and Method in the Exploration of Human Decision Behaviour." *Industrial Management Rev.*, 1963, 5 (1), 17–27.

Coch, L. and French, J. R. P., Jr. "Overcoming Resistance to Change." *HR, 1,* 1948. Also in D. Cartwright and A. Zander, eds., *Group Dynamics*. 2d ed., New York: Row, Peterson, 1960, 319–341.

Crozier, M. *Le phenomène bureaucratique: Essai sur les tendences bureaucratiques des systemes d'organisations modernes et sur leurs relations en France avec le systeme et culturel*. Paris: Editions du Seuil, 1963.

Crozier, M. *Le monde des employés de bureau*. Paris: Editions du Seuil, 1965.

Cyert, R. M. and March, J. G. *The Behavioural Theory of the Firm*. Englewood Cliffs: Prentice Hall, 1963.

Cyert, R. M., Simon, H. A., and Trow, D. B. "Observation of a Business Decision." *J. Business* (University of Chicago), 1956, 29, 237–248.

Donovan, F. R. *The Saleslady*. Chicago: U. of Chicago Press, 1929.

Eisenstadt, S. N. "Bureaucracy and Bureaucratization." *Current Sociology*, (Blackwell), 1958, 8 (2).

Emery, F. E. and Trist, E. L. "The Causal Texture of Organisational Environments." *HR*, 1965, *18*, 21–32.

Emmet, D. "The Concept of Power." *Proceedings of the Aristotelian Society New Series*, 1954, *54*, 1–26.

Etzioni, A. *A Comparative Analysis of Complex Organizations*. Glencoe, Ill.: Free Press, 1961.

Everett, E. H. *On the Theory of Social Change*. Homewood, Ill.: Dorsey, 1962.

French, J. R. P. "Laboratory and Field Studies of Power." In R. L. Kahn and E. Boulding, eds., *Power and Conflict in Organisations*. London: Tavistock Publications, 1964, 33–51.

French, J. R. P. and Coch, L. "Overcoming Resistance to Change." *HR*, 1948, *1*, 512–532.

French, J. R. P., Israel, J., and As, D. "An Experiment in Participation in a Norwegian Factory: Interpersonal Dimension of Decision-Making." *HR*, 1960, *13*, 3–19.

Friedmann, G. *Industrial Society.* Glencoe, Ill.: Free Press, 1955.

Galbraith, J. K. *The Affluent Society.* London: H. Hamilton, 1958.

Gluckman, M. and Devons, E. *Closed Systems and Open Minds.* Manchester, England: Manchester U. Press, 1964.

Goffman, E. "On the Characteristics of Total Institutions." In *Asylums.* New York: Doubleday (Anchor Books), 1961.

Goode, W. J. and Hatt, P. K. *Methods in Social Research.* New York: McGraw-Hill, 1952.

Gouldner, A. W. *Patterns of Industrial Bureaucracy.* Glencoe, Ill.: Free Press, 1954.

————. "Organization Analysis." In R. K. Merton, L. Broom, and L. S. Cottrell, eds., *Sociology Today.* New York: Basic Books, 1959a.

————. "Reciprocity and Autocracy." In L. Gross, ed., *Symposium on Sociological Theory.* New York: Row, Peterson, 1959b, 241–270.

Hoggart, R. *The Uses of Literacy.* London: Chatto and Windus, 1957.

Horne, K. and Lupton, T. "The Work Activities of 'Middle' Managers: An Exploratory Study." *J. Management Studies,* 1965, *2*, 14–35.

Janowitz, M. *The Professional Soldier.* Glencoe, Ill.: Free Press, 1960.

Kahn, R. L. and Katz, D. "Leadership Practices in Relation to Productivity and Morale." In D. Cartwright and A. Zander, eds., *Group Dynamics.* New York: Row, Peterson, 1953, 612–628.

Kahn, R. L., et al. *Organizational Stress: Studies in Role Conflict and Ambiguity.* New York: Wiley, 1964.

Keirstead, B. S. *The Theory of Economic Change.* London: Macmillan, 1948.

Kornhauser. *Scientists in Industry.* Berkeley: U. of California Press, 1962.

Lazarsfeld, P. F. "The American Soldier: An Expository Review." *Public Opinion Qtly.,* 1949, *13*, 380.

Leach, E. R. Review of S. H. Udy's *Organization of Work. ASR,* 1960, *25*, 136–138.

Lefebvre, H. "Perspectives de sociologie rurale." *Cahiers Internationaux de Sociologie,* 1953.

Lockwood, D. "Social Integration and System Integration." In Zollschau and Hirsch, eds., *Explorations in Social Change.* London: Routledge and Kegan Paul, 1965, 244–257.

Lutz, B. and Willener, A. *Neveau de mecanisation et mode de remuneration.* Luxemburg: (Mimeo) C.E.C.A., 1960.

March, J. G. and Simon, H. A. *Organizations.* New York: Wiley, 1958.

Marcuse, H. *Eros and Civilisation.* London: Routledge and Kegan Paul, 1956.

————. *One Dimensional Man.* London: Routledge and Kegan Paul, 1964.

Marples, D. *The Decisions of Engineering Design.* London: Institute of Engineering Design, 1960.

Marx, K., *Capital.* Trans. by E. and C. Paul. London: Swan, Sonnenschein, 1906.

Mayo, E. *The Social Problems of an Industrial Civilisation.* London: Routledge and Kegan Paul, 1949.

Merton, R. K. "The Role-Set: Problems in Sociological Theory." *British J. Sociology*, 1957, 8, 106–120.
————. "Problem Finding in Sociology." In R. K. Merton, L. Broom, and L. S. Cottrell, eds., *Sociology Today*. New York: Basic Books, 1959.
Michels, R. *Political Parties*. Trans. by E. and C. Paul. London: Allen and Unwin, 1914.
Nadel, S. F. *Foundations of Social Anthropology*. London: Cohen and West, 1951.
Newell, A. and Simon, H. A. "The Simulation of Human Thought." In W. Dennis et al., *Current Trends in Psychological Theory*, Pittsburgh: U. of Pittsburgh Press, 1961.
Newell, A., Shaw, J. C., and Simon, H. A. "Elements of a Theory of Human Problem-Solving." *Psychological Rev.*, 1958, 65, 151–166.
Parsons, T. "Suggestions for a Sociological Approach to the Theory of Organisations." *Administrative Science Qtly.*, 1956, 1, 63–85 and 225–239.
Pepper, S. C. *World Hypotheses*. Berkeley: U. of California Press, 1942.
Poggi, G. "A Main Theme of Contemporary Sociology; Its Achievements and Limitations." *British J. Sociology*, 1965, 16, 283–294.
Popitz, H., Bahrdt, H. P., Jueres, E. A., and Kesting, A. *Das Gesellschaftsbild des Arbeiters*. Tübingen: Mohr, 1957.
Reichenbach, H. *The Rise of Scientific Philosophy*. London: Cambridge U. Press, 1951.
Roethlisberger, F. J. and Dickson, W. J. *Management and the Worker*. New Haven: Harvard U. Press, 1939.
Schlesinger, A. "The Humanist Looks at Empirical Social Research." *ASR*, 1962, 27 (6), 768–771.
Schon, D. *The Displacement of Concepts*. London: Tavistock Publications, 1964.
Scott, R. E. "Theory of Organizations." In R. E. L. Faris, ed., *Handbook of Modern Sociology*. Chicago: Rand McNally, 1965.
Selznick, P. *Leadership in Administration*. New York: Row, Peterson, 1957.
Shaw, C. R. *The Jack Roller*. Chicago: U. of Chicago Press, 1930.
Simon, H. A. *Models of Man*. New York: Wiley, 1957.
Simon, H. A. "The Role of Expectations in an Adaptive or Behaviouristic Model." In M. J. Bowman, ed., *Expectations, Uncertainty and Business Behaviour*. New York: Social Science Research Council, 1958.
Sykes, R. and Messinger, S. "The Intimate Social System." In *Theoretical Studies in Social Organizations*. New York: S. S. R. C., 1960.
Taylor, F. W. *The Principles of Scientific Management*. 1911. Reprinted in *Scientific Management*. New York: Harper, 1947.
Thorsrud, E. and Emery, F. E. *Industrial Democracy*. London: Tavistock Publications, 1965.
Tocqueville, A. de. *Democracy in America*. Ed. by P. Bradley. New York: Vintage Books, 1954.
Touraine, A. *L'Evolution du travail ouvrier aux Usines Renault*. Paris: C.N.R.S., 1955.
Udy, S. *Organization of Work*. New Haven: HRAF Press, 1959a.
————. "'Bureaucracy' and 'Rationality' in Weber's Organization Theory." *ASR*, 1959b, 24, 791–795.

Van Beinum, H. J. J. *Summary of "Een Organisatie in Bewegung."* Privately published by author, 1963.

Walker, G. and Turner. *The Foreman on the Assembly Line.* New Haven: Harvard U. Press, 1956.

Weber, M. *The Protestant Ethic and the Spirit of Capitalism.* Trans by T. Parsons. New York: Scribners, 1930.

_____. *Wirtschaft und Gesellschaft.* Ed. by J. Winchelmann. Kiepenheuer und Witsch, 1964.

Whitehead, A. N. *Process and Reality.* Cambridge: Cambridge U. Press, 1929.

Willener, A. *Images de la société et classes sociales.* Berne, 1957.

Wilson, A. T. M. "The Manager and his World." *Industrial Management Rev.,* (M.I.T.), 1961, 3 (1), 1–26.

Woodward, J. *Management and Technology.* London: H.M.S.O., 1958.

Woodward, J. and Eilon, S. "A Field Study of Management Control in Manufacturing Industry." Paper contributed to Operational Research Society Internation Conference, *Operational Research and the Social Sciences,* Cambridge, England: 1964.

Zetterberg, H. L. "Theorie, Forschung und Praxis in der Soziologie." In R. Konig, ed., *Handbuch der Empirischen Sozialforschung.* Stuttgart: Ferdinand Enke V., 1962, I, 65–104.

Zorbaugh, H. W. *The Gold Coast and the Slum.* Chicago: U. of Chicago Press, 1929.

Zweig, F. *The Worker in an Affluent Society.* New York: Heinemann, 1962.

4

Computer Simulation Models for Organization Theory

THORNTON B. ROBY

Tufts University

This chapter is concerned with potential uses of the computer simulation model as a conceptual tool in the development of organization theory. The objective of the chapter will be to highlight methodological issues and, whenever possible, suggest lines along which these problems might be resolved. No attempt will be made to survey the current state of computer simulation except insofar as existing models are used for illustrative purposes; moreover the discussion does not enter into the details of computer programing.

One reason for this treatment of the topic is that there are already a number of very competent expositions of existing simulation efforts and of programming procedures (for example, Orcutt et al. (1961); Borko (1962); Green (1962); and Feigenbaum and Feldman (1963). These are not all directly relevant to organizational applications but they do repre-

Partial support for the completion of this chapter was obtained under Contract NONR 494 (15) with the Office of Naval Research and under Contract AF19(628)2450 with the Decision Sciences Laboratory (Electronic Systems Division), Air Force Systems Command, United States Air Force.

The general outline of this chapter was formulated and developed in discussions with Professors Geoffrey Clarkson, Robert Joyner, Kenneth Knight, Frederick Munson, and Anthony Obershall at the 1964 Pittsburgh Conference on Organization Theory. The suggestions offered by that group during the conference and in subsequent correspondence are greatly appreciated. Remaining errors of omission or commission are the exclusive responsibility of the author.

171

sent an impressive fund of ingenious and effective techniques that may be adapted to the latter area. Thus there does not, at the present time, seem to be a pressing need either for a survey or for a how-to-do-it manual. Instead, it is attempted to assess the probable impact of computer simulation on the construction of organizational theory and to consider how computer simulation might be used with other techniques now at hand.

Computer development has occurred at a pace unprecedented in previous technological innovations. During this growth period of not more than ten years or so, most of us have been either too engrossed or too aloof to develop a useful perspective on what has happened. It may still be too soon to assess with confidence the influence computers ultimately may have on the development of organizational theory; it is clear that computer techniques represent a distinctly new approach and, although they should not alter the ground rules of scientific procedure, they may profoundly change the tactics. Perhaps it is not too soon to speculate on some of the implied tactical changes.

The emphasis of this chapter then is programmatic: beginning with a general consideration of the purpose of computer application in organizational theory, we single out as the special focus of this chapter the use of the computer simulation model as a novel and unique theoretical tool. The next section is concerned with the basic ingredients of a computer simulation model. Three aspects of this problem are considered: the initial nucleus from which the model is refined and elaborated; the substantive elements or building blocks of which the model is constructed; and the language in which the model is couched. The next topic examined is the process of testing and revising the computer model, and of relating it to empirical data. A rather Utopian four-stage testing process is outlined: internal testing, initial testing of ad hoc validity, generalization to new substantive areas, and, finally, process evaluation. A final section goes on to venture possible applications of computer simulation in the future, recognizing that these applications are not presently feasible.

VARIETIES OF COMPUTER APPLICATION

Although this chapter is directly concerned with the application of the computer in developing simulation models it will be useful to begin with an examination of possible computer uses that lie outside the strict definition of computer simulation. This survey will help to establish by exclusion exactly what is intended by the term "simulation model," but in addition it will be pointed out that many of these not-quite-simulation studies may be closely related to, or ancillary to, simulation studies proper. It is of course hoped that with obvious changes many of the methodological remarks that follow will apply to these related uses of the computer.

AS AN AID IN DATA REDUCTION OR STATISTICAL ANALYSIS

Here the function of the computer is largely to help interpret or digest empirical data obtained through other means, such as field studies or laboratory experiments. Typically the computer programs employed for such investigations do not contain any special features that mark them as applying to the organizational problem as opposed to, say, problems in agriculture or medicine. The emphasis is on the statistical technique itself and the syntax of the program is derived from the statistical procedure employed. Although this is clearly a non-simulation use of the computer, even this application may impinge on true simulation in one direction not explored extensively to date: generation of distributions for determining the significance of certain results that may occur in an empirical set of observations—that is, the establishment of purely statistical bench marks without intrinsic substantive interest. Thus if the investigation concerned the incidence of communication between individuals in a group or the distribution of sociometric scores in a group, the computer could be used to determine what the chance distribution should be, given the obtained marginal score distributions. Any observed set of scores could then be evaluated against this base line and a precise probability could be placed on any interesting deviations that occurred in the empirical data.

More generally, if the means and variances are available for a number of performance measures that have been obtained in an observational situation, the statistical base line model may be used without substantive hypotheses to obtain distributions for expected profiles of the dependent variables and to determine with what frequency such profiles could be expected to occur if the variables are essentially unrelated.

DERIVING THE CONSEQUENCES OF AN ACCEPTED THEORY

Here the emphasis is not on theory construction as such but on the application of theory which has already been at least tentatively accepted. The theory may be scientifically or logically well founded, as it is in much of operations research, but it could as well be based on folklore or common sense. In this sort of application the computer is an associate consultant, a consultant with the unique advantages of being able to reckon with many variables and a comparative freedom from bias as to what answers the vice-president may wish to hear. This may, therefore,

be an extremely effective use of computers but it is not a scientific enterprise. The objective is to provide well-considered answers to specific
problems or optimal decisions on policies, rather than to generate or to
test hypotheses.

PROVIDING SOLUTIONS FOR A MATHEMATICAL MODEL

Often it is possible to describe a system in great detail and subtlety
with a mathematical model, but the eduction of numerical or precise
qualitative consequences may be very difficult indeed. Richardson's
(1948) War Moods model, although it leads to some almost testable
propositions, obviously contains many more implications than can be
developed by ordinary analytical techniques. The computer can be employed to derive numerical estimates suitable for empirical tests from
such a model but this is a rather different application from a true computer simulation program. The principal difference is that the structure
of the indicated process is here dictated by the standard procedures of
numerical computation (such as iterative solutions of differential equations) rather than by dynamics hypothesized for the system under
investigation.

The boundary may be very fuzzy. In fact it is easy to imagine mixed
models in which certain processes are represented by mathematical functions and others, by a more literal attempt to simulate actual organizational dynamics; however, it will be emphasized below that the latter
objective is always the ultimate goal of a simulation model in the strict
sense.

AS AN ADJUNCT TO THE LIVE STUDY OF ORGANIZATIONS

In this application the simulation program is designed to provide an
environment for organizational behavior. The simulated environment
may involve only the external world within which the investigated organization is assumed to operate or it may include part of the organization
itself. In the latter case one would be studying individual or subgroup
reactions to organizational conditions.

There are impressive advantages in the use of the computer for this
purpose. It offers the possibility of control over a virtually unlimited
number of exogenous variables and conditions. It makes it possible to
build response-contingent relationships into the environment so that
rapid and realistic feedback can be provided to the live subjects whose
behavior is being tested. And finally the data can be recorded and
processed directly and in great volume. This application requires on-line
access to a computer, but the costs of such access are no longer pro-
hibitive.

The chief reason for distinguishing between this application and the pure simulation objective again lies in the criteria that are most relevant. In the present use, one is primarily interested in realism as it affects the live participant in the organization study. The question is not so much whether the simulated component is anatomically similar to its real world counterpart as whether it is similar enough to elicit and sustain the illusion of reality and to elicit representative behavior on the part of live subjects.[1]

PROGRAMMING EXERCISE

The primary objective here is to show what a computer can do when used with a little ingenuity. The emphasis is on verisimilitude of performance rather than on producing results that can be compared rigorously with empirical data; and the customary canons of scientific parsimony tend to be put aside for a sort of kitchen sink approach that rivals the prodigality of nature itself. In spite of the slightly derogatory flavor of the title given this application, it may have real didactic and propaedeutic value. It permits the exploration of computer capabilities in a somewhat freer way than do more restrained procedures, and in a way possibly congenial to persons with an intimate knowledge of substantive processes but a distaste for the rigors of more austere theory construction. Thus it is possible that this application may, at last, provide a bridge between the rich intuitions of psychological practitioners and the hallowed methods of scientific theory construction.

As a tool of preliminary theoretical formulation, the above procedure seems to be a rather good form of the well-known *Gedankenexperiment*. As compared with the customary practice of following through a set of postulations in one's imagination, the computer offers several benefits: first, it has led to a language—in simplest form, the flow diagram—which is particularly useful for elaborating complex interrelations and processes. In addition, the prospect of obtaining a volume of palpable, though fictitious, results may counteract the sense of futility that tends to be associated with a purely hypothetical formulation of conditions.

REAL SIMULATION MODELS

The aim of real simulation models is to use computers to derive testable and generalizable consequences from a set of constructs that are internally consistent, have explanatory power, and are themselves susceptible to further analysis and test. Thus the objectives and criteria are

1. According to "Turing's Test" (Turing, 1950), the latter criterion should be valid for either application. Our position in this matter is developed in a later section on process correspondence.

essentially the same as those of the familiar hypothetico-deductive method. From this point of view, the computer simulation model is a candidate for membership in the powerful team already including the more abstract mathematical or logical model, on the one hand, and laboratory or field research, on the other. The principal concern of the following discussion is to examine ways in which computer simulation models may be integrated most effectively into this team.

FORM, CONTENT, AND LANGUAGE

This section will examine three interrelated topics. The first concerns the general structure of simulation models; the second concerns the building blocks or terms that are used; and the third topic is the symbolic expression of this content. Emphasis throughout will be placed on the initial choices made by the theorist in formulating the model. It is assumed that the ensuing processes of testing and revision may modify or reverse many of these initial choices.

OVERALL ARCHITECTURE

In the initial attack upon any significant problem in organization theory, it is clear that some type of simplifying assumptions must be appealed to. These assumptions are best made quite explicitly so that the theorist will be alerted to the probable kinds of error threatening his findings. Thus the most important typology of first approximation models seems to be in terms of the guiding fictions introduced at their launching.

The first of three types of guiding fictions to be described will be labeled *organismic*. Models of this type attempt to incorporate the entire system under consideration and to represent all of the important interactions between components of the system, but in gross aggregative or statistical form. The model achieves *prima facie* descriptiveness at the level of overall system behavior, then adjusts and refines the definition of constituent processes to satisfy the requirements of fine structure descriptiveness. Although none of the approaches to be described is the monopoly of any scientific discipline, the organismic approach has been followed typically by sociologists.

The *idealized* model may also attempt to deal with the total system with respect to substantive components, but it deliberately simplifies the assumed functional relations among the components. Examples are the assumption of strict rationality of decision processes or perfect community of interests and objectives among organizational members. Here descriptiveness is sacrificed for sharpness of functional implications much as in the analogous ideal laws of physics. Further development of models of this type must entail enrichment of their dynamics with auxiliary influences—for example, social prejudices and partially conflicting goals. This initial approach has been associated with economists.

A third angle of attack will be labeled *segmental*, and it deals with the substantive components of an organizational system singly and in isolation. Ordinarily the components examined in this way will be individuals, but subgroups, roles, or other organizational building blocks might be used. The assumption is that a thorough explication of the behavior of such units within an organization will indicate clearly how they fit together: refinement must then consist in making amends for this assumption which is, in practice, simplistic. Social psychologists are perhaps the most prominent advocates of this approach.

It is easy enough to characterize these approaches in terms that establish any one of them as the path of righteousness and set the others beyond the pale. The first approach is bold and holistic; the second is incisive and elegant; and the third is sound and methodical. Alternatively, the first approach is pretentious; the second is perversely formalistic; and the third approach is pedestrian and niggling. As a matter of record, however, comparatively successful theories have been developed starting from each of these approximations and none of them is inherently self-defeating. The optimal approach for a particular problem depends both on the ultimate objectives and upon the state of knowledge at the time of theorizing. Undoubtedly it depends too on the particular tastes and skills of the modeler.

Still at the level of overall architecture, a second distinction may be based on the objective of study in the model. Here again a three-way classification is suggested. The first type of problem is the so-called developmental system, concerned with the changes in the organization itself as a result of its interaction with the task environment. A second object of study concerns the performance of an organization at a given level of development, typically at maturity. The third object of study is the effect of the organization on the behavior of constituent individuals.

Although this distinction differs from the earlier one, it is not entirely unrelated. The organismic model may lend itself most naturally to the study of group development, to the overall transformation of organizational characteristics. The idealized or normative model is not usually concerned with development except to specify the asymptote towards which the development may proceed; on the other hand, the normative model is perhaps the approach of choice for the study of group performance. Finally, the segmental model, which focuses on the individual participant in the group, is perhaps best suited for the investigation of effects of organizational participation on the behavior of individuals.

ILLUSTRATION

In order to provide a concrete reference for the distinctions made above and a framework for later illustrative material, we shall consider a problem in the theory of organization permitting various approaches. The problem concerns the nexus of relations between the external activity of an organization and its internal communication processes. It has attracted both theoretical and experimental attention.

An approach to this problem beginning at the organizational level and using the organismic approximation may be based on the Homans' (1950) model. This model is built around four variables: friendliness, interaction, activity, and imposed "task load." In the present case, the task load describes the environmental input, interaction is an observable process variable, friendliness is a measurable but not directly observable system-state variable, and activity is the output variable. These distinctions among variables will be described in more detail below.

Simon (1957) has translated this model into a system of differential equations and has based a number of interesting analyses on a "phase space" treatment of the model. Most of his conclusions, however, relate to the asymptotic behavior of the system and to shifts in asymptotic behavior as a function of changes in the basic parameters. Translation of Simon's differential equations into a Monte Carlo simulation model might permit an investigation of several aspects of the problem that would be impractical to study analytically, for example, a more detailed investigation of nonlinear cases and functional relationships involving three or more parameters. Even more beneficial would be the derivation of quantitative results that could be compared with field or laboratory data.

Proceeding from these investigations at the aggregative level, the model can be articulated further to yield a more detailed picture of group behavior, as Simon (1957, p. 113) has indeed suggested. In fact, the same parameters used to describe organizational characteristics can be indexed more specifically to refer to the activity, interaction, and sentiments of subgroups within the group or, finally, to the individuals in the group. Thus, without essentially changing the model, and beginning with an organismic approximation, it is, in principle, possible to simulate organizational behavior in any degree of detail.

Representative of the idealized approach to this problem would be the paradigm suggested by Roby and Lanzetta (1956) for investigating the information exchange in work groups in which individual group members have comparatively stable and distinct task responsibilities. Briefly this formulation assumes that task responsibilities can be defined in terms of the classes of information which they generate or which they require for successful execution of instrumental responses. The normative communications between various persons in the group can be estimated by matrix multiplication.

Here again, although some progress can be made using conventional mathematical techniques, a much greater range of problems might be treated by expressing the functional relations in probabilistic terms and studying the resulting Monte Carlo simulation. Refinement of this model would obviously take a different course than the foregoing organismic one. In this case, the factor of interpersonal attitudes has been omitted deliberately in the first approximation, and it must somehow be introduced in later phases to achieve any degree of realism. Possible procedures for successively modifying simulation models are discussed in detail in a later section. For the present it will be noted that the modification may, in this case, take the form of a correction for attitudinal factors in the basic functions of a normative model or, alternatively, of direct superimposition of a secondary system of socially oriented communications on those predicted by the task-defined normative system.

To illustrate the segmental approach to a model of organizational communication, one might begin with a program of individual interaction behavior such as that developed by the Gullahorns (1964). This model (also based on formulations of Homans [1950]) investigates the probability of specific types of communications to specific persons as a function of current needs and of past reinforcement for communication; thus, the task inputs would be treated as generating current needs for information and the behavior of individuals in seeking out sources of information might be simulated by some streamlined version of the Homunculus model.

For any of these approaches, the focus of interest may be on the way in which a group changes over time, on the productivity or effectiveness of the group as a social unit, or on the effect of participation in the organization on the behavior and attitudes of individual group members. It is apparent that these three processes interact and that none of them can be thoroughly understood without taking the others into account. But it is equally evident that there are differences in time scale and emphasis among the three problems that justify looking at them in comparative isolation.

INGREDIENTS

This section will attempt to make a set of terminological distinctions concerning the substance of a simulation model and will later illustrate these distinctions using the message problem discussed above. Some of these distinctions may seem painfully copybook and most of them are not new. However, it seems important to reexamine the terminology which is used in more conventional scientific approaches. One reason for this is that a new layer is added to the investigative process. In conventional behavioral research the experimenter is clearly part of the environment. He may modify the organization in specific ways, but some part of the organization is always inaccessible to direct manipulation. In simulation studies, however, the experimenter pulls all the strings even if they are so tangled that he does not know in advance what they will do. From this standpoint the variation in a simulation model is wholly exogenous to the system under investigation.

The distinctions made below attempt to capture this point and also to indicate the kinds of decisions the theorist or experimenter makes, to what extent these decisions are arbitrary, and to what extent they are constrained by the logic of the problem. An attempt is made to put all this in a reasonably tidy framework, but the framework is less important than the aim to make explicit the issues involved.

Figure 1 provides a rough schematization of the total program specification as here considered. This specification describes both the system model itself, and the steps taken to test the model. For the present, chief attention is focused on the latter aspect of the program.

Summarizing the sequence briefly, a particular initial configuration, consisting of initial states and an event schedule, is entered, either explicitly or as part of an imbedding program. The configuration interacts with the system dynamics—defined by the system syntax statement—to produce certain intervening states and events. The process continues until it is terminated by instructions which may or may not be contingent upon outcomes. In either case, the interval covered is a simulation cycle. Even though a vast number of different measures may be taken, the recorded results of a simulation cycle constitute a single "observation" of the model because the entire process is dependent on the particular initial configuration.

Sampling instructions then indicates the next initial configuration to be investigated. The new initial configuration may be determined in advance or may be in part contingent upon the outcome of the preceding simulation cycle. The program run concludes when all relevant initial configurations have been sampled.

FIGURE 1

Schematic Description of Program Specifications for
a Computer Simulation Model

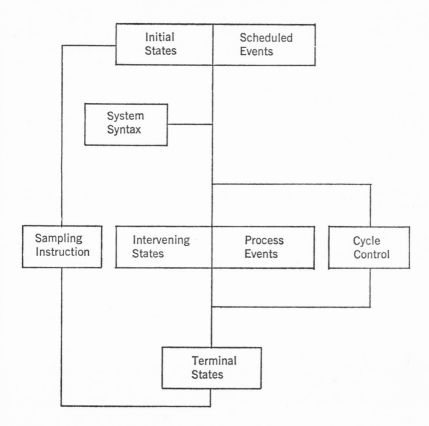

Printout (or other display) will ordinarily consist of terminal states, process events, or a summary of these results. In addition, it may include initial states in order to identify simulation cycles and intervening states to aid in interpretation.

Three types of decision are highlighted by this cursory account. One class of decisions concerns the length of a given simulation cycle and the conditions for terminating it. The cycle may be permitted to run until a certain terminal state is reached or, alternatively, it may be run through a certain fixed set of scheduled events (for example, a given budget of problems that a committee is to solve). A second class of decisions concerns the "sampling" process: the density of observations in the vicinity of a given initial configuration and the range of initial configurations that is covered during the entire program run. A final decision concerns the volume and type of data preserved and recorded.

These decisions are considered again within the context of specific tests for the model. Before reaching that point, however, it will be necessary to examine in more detail the ingredients of the model itself. Some of the distinctions made here are assumed to be inherent in the situation or in the conceptualization of the process. Others are of a more arbitrary character. Generally speaking the distinctions listed first are more essential ones and distinctions made later are more elective.

1. Explicit Entry–Computed Result

As already noted, everything that happens in a simulation model happens at the dictate of the simulation-theorist and the results are, strictly speaking, tautological. There is, however, a useful psychological distinction to be made between the terms and values explicitly entered into the model and those which ensue after a sequence of computations and which motivate the simulation study.

This distinction is one of degree and it is useful to specify four stages: first, those terms entered explicitly by the simulation-theorist; second, terms generated as a direct function of explicit entries (for example, the expression of event probabilities in actual event occurrences); third, intervening variables or processes obtained primarily to fractionate and simplify the problem of programming; and, finally, system performance measures and states presumably comparable with empirical data.

2. Functional Status

A second distinction concerns the causal or variational properties of terms in the system: three broad classes of terms may be defined. *Syntactic* statements incorporate the assumed mechanisms that are operative—all relationships among substantive terms. It is assumed that these statements are an inherent part of the description of a model and are modified only by express intention. *Parametric* terms are constant for a data cycle; they may affect other terms of the system or govern functional relationships but are not themselves modified. However, they may be modified in successive simulation cycles as part of a systematic "sampling" process designed to test the model under a variety of conditions. *Variable* terms are those subject to modification as determined by syntactic statements in the model and the values assumed by system parameters or other variables.

3. Environmental-Organizational (Exogenous-Endogenous)

The distinction here is between those aspects of the model referring to the task environment within which the organization is operating and those aspects referring directly to the human component of the system—that is, the organization itself. As a number of theorists have noted (Simon, 1957, Chap. 1) when the interaction between the environment and the organism is closely reciprocal, the cause-effect relationships between exogenous and endogenous elements may be obscure. Even so, the distinction has sufficient descriptive and heuristic value to be worth maintaining.

The three distinctions introduced above refer to the functional status of terms in the model. The next three distinctions are concerned with the substantive properties or referents of the model. They all revolve around the concept of "aggregation" as it has been used in social theory. From the present standpoint aggregation is itself an aggregative term, is a matter of degree, and refers to several aspects of possible compression or elaboration of descriptive terms.

Any variable term referring to an organization may be adequately tagged by three indices—one specifying the substantive referent, a second specifying the persons involved, and a third specifying the time of description in relation to other events. These three indices, and the related axes of extension or elaboration, will be referred to as *hyletic*, *locative*, and *temporal* respectively. Aggregation then takes the form of lumping along any of these axes and elaboration is the degree of specification along one or more of the axes.

4. Hyletic Aggregation-Elaboration

This index might describe the environmental referent of a certain message, the affect reflected in a specific interpersonal attitude or the ostensible purpose of a certain act. Clearly the qualitative breakdown of these substantive categories may be carried as far as measurement permits and as theoretical precision requires. A crucial consideration here is that the category systems for the various terms should be defined in such a way as to simplify the expression of functional relations among the terms. For example, action categories should, if possible, bear a clear relationship to specific classes of environmental states or events, as should communication category systems. Even interpersonal attitudes should ideally be developed with reference to the other hyletic specifications in the model. Thus the appropriate degree of extension along this axis depends in large part on the definition of the task logic and of the functions which represent the organizational operating procedures.

5. Locative Aggregation-Elaboration

Variables or events may be tagged in various ways with respect to the individuals concerned. In the case of messages (or attitudes), an ordered pair of persons is involved; for actions, only the responsible agent need be named. Although the index is in this case discrete, it does not follow that locative aggregation is an all-or-none matter. To illustrate, the representation of interpersonal attitudes in a group may specify the persons bearing the attitudes or the persons toward whom those attitudes are directed or it may contain no individual identification. In the latter case, the mean or other statistics describing the distribution of attitudes may be given.

6. Temporal Aggregation-Elaboration

The temporal specification of variable states or events may be given on an absolute time axis or with reference to other events or states. A temporally aggregative description of a given set of events might consist of a simple frequency count or of a more detailed statement of the temporal distribution. An aggregative description of state variables can be given in terms of mean level over time or it may include specification of the range of variation, trends, or periodicities.

A third set of distinctions among the terms of the model similarly concerns the mode of representation. However, where the above distinctions bear on the amount of system information retained, this last set of distinctions is more a matter of the most efficient or perspicuous way of representing a particular aspect of the system.

7. State-Event

In principle there are state descriptions of a system such that, if the initial state is given, any subsequent state description will summarize adequately the incidence of intervening system events. Conversely, if the initial state is given together with the exact chronology of system events, the new system state is determinable. Thus, in principle, state and event descriptions may be informationally equivalent.[2] In practice, though, any attempt to express physical reality in uniform state or event terms is at best awkward and may greatly increase the difficulty of conceptualization.

Some types of variables lend themselves more naturally to description as states or conditions while other terms are described naturally as events or processes. There seem to be no methodological drawbacks to basing this decision on convenience and custom for each term of a system individually as long as it does not complicate functional relations between terms.

2. An able and provocative discussion of the philosophical background and the current status of this distinction is contained in Whitrow (1961). The picture that emerges is one of a dichotomy of thought originating with Parmenides and Archimides (states or existents) on the one hand, and Heraclitus and Aristotle (process or flux) on the other.

8. Determinate-Stochastic

This distinction is again a familiar one and the choice is one of conceptual convenience. Philosophical questions aside, any stochastic system may be thought of as based on an underlying set of determinate laws, and any determinate system may be regarded as the limiting case of a stochastic system.

9. Scale Units

This distinction concerns the scale assumptions that are incorporated in a model. At one extreme there may be only nominal classifications with no order relationships among terms. Intermediate scale levels incorporate counting and ordering operations. The strongest scale assumptions are of continuous measurement with interval or ratio scale properties.

It may be debated whether this distinction is arbitrary in quite the same way as the two preceding ones. Very briefly, the pro argument would be that the gain in quantitative information obtained by expressing measures on a continuum is in general offset by the loss in qualitative information entailed in specifying the continuum.

AN ILLUSTRATIVE MODEL

In order to illustrate the distinction introduced above, a model will be described that treats the relation between communication and performance in an organization. For the sake of concreteness it will be supposed that the problem under investigation is the relation between the degree of specialization or departmentalization in small retail establishments and resulting productivity, morale, and interpersonal attitudes.[3]

The assumed functional relations are schematized crudely in Figure 2. Directed lines indicate causal influences and the small circles indicate confluence or interaction of causal effects. The meaning of the various terms is explained in greater detail in the following paragraphs. A glance at the figure suffices to show that the approach is organismic. It should be emphasized that this formulation is designed to provide instances of the distinctions suggested above; it is not offered as a contribution to organization theory. The intention is to show the range of choice that is possible, possible bases for making a choice one way or the other and the effect of choices made at one point on other terms of the model. The discussion is summarized in Figure 3.

The first term, *task logic,* concerns the entire set of functional rules

3. Compare Rome and Rome (1962) or Siegel et al. (1964) for models at approximately this level of comprehensiveness.

FIGURE 2

A Schematic Description of Functional Relations for
the Illustrative Simulation Model

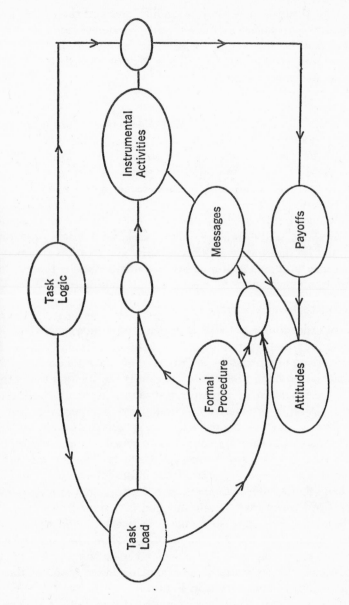

FIGURE 3
Terminological Classification for an Illustrative Simulation Model

	A. Task Logic	B. Task Load	C. Formal Procedures	D. Attitudes	E. Messages	F. Instrumental Activities
1. Entry-Result	Static entry	Generated entry	Manipulated entry	Static entry and result	Intervening variable	Result
2. Causal Role	Syntactic	Parametric	Syntatic	Variable	Variable	Variable
3. Reference	Environment	Environment	Organization	Organization	Organization	Organization and environment
4. Hyletic Elaboration	Economic	Customer demands	Positions	Affect	Personal or task	Task function
5. Locative Elaboration	—	Point of Input	Task assignment, channels, jurisdiction	Attitude bearers	Who to whom	Agent
6. Temporal Elaboration	Imposed priorities	Diurnal fluctuation	Priorities, phasing	—	—	Lag
7. State-Event	—	Event	—	State	Event	Event
8. Determinacy	Mixed	Stochastic	Determinate	Determinate	Stochastic	Determinate
9. Scale	—	Category	—	Interval	Category	Category

that are postulated for the effective environment within which the organization operates. In the present case these rules could presumably be derived from the study of marketing economics. Task logic is an explicit entry and is concerned with a syntactic description of the environment. The specific causal role of task logic in this model has two aspects. First, it determines the task load imposed on the group. In life, the load would be affected by group activity also, but this feedback loop is omitted in the model. A second capacity in which the task logic acts is in setting a utility score on various instrumental activities, depending on the time of their execution. These contingencies are reflected in the hyletic and temporal elaboration of the task logic.

Task load in the illustrative model is not entered explicitly in detail but is instead generated from certain parameters of the task logic. It is therefore considered as a parametric term and is of course descriptive of the environment. Task load may be elaborated in all three modes. Here the hyletic elaboration consists in the specification of customer demands. The locative elaboration indicates the physical points (for example, service counters) at which inputs occur. Temporal elaboration specifies the fluctuations in task input rate during a given day, week, or year. Strictly speaking, these elaborations are built into the task logic itself, but it is rather more natural to identify them with the substantive term. In relationship to the final three distinctions, task load is expressed as a succession of discrete random events. An alternative expression would suggest the continuous rates that are a determinate function of task logic parameters.

Formal procedure is the organizational counterpart of the task logic and, like the latter, is a syntactic term. Unlike task logic, the formal procedure is manipulated systematically in order to study the effects of specialization. Formal procedure is quite extensively elaborated in the illustrative model. There is a specification for the particular task units clustered together and the standard reaction to particular task load items. The allocation of tasks to persons or departments is stipulated, and formal channels of communication and lines of authority are indicated. Temporal elaboration includes a statement about the priorities of task load items in case of conflict, and the normal succession of informational and instrumental processes. Formal procedure is described here as determinate since all prescriptions are given in categorical form. As with task logic, the state-event and scale distinctions are not directly applicable to this syntactic statement.

Attitude covers the social climate of the organization and the job-related morale of participants. At the beginning of each simulation cycle a certain value is entered as part of the initial configuration, and the final value is printed out as one of the dependent variables of interest. Attitudes are identified by their affective content such as job satisfaction and liking for other members of the organization, and the bearer of the attitude is specified. There is no special need for temporal specification except to indicate the terminal value. In terms of the final three distinctions, attitudes are represented as part of a state description of the organizational members and they are assumed to be measurable on an interval scale; thus conceptual operations such as superimposition of attitude modifiers and averaging are presumably justified. Attitudes are hypothesized to vary as a determinate function of the number of messages from other team members and of the payoff from instrumental activities. An alternative would be to represent attitudes as categorical states governed by certain transition matrices (cf. Cohen, 1958).

Messages are wholly dependent on other existing state variables of the system and on the task load. In the model we suppose they are not of direct interest and are not recorded, hence occur only as ephemera in the simulation process, for use only by the theorist in conceptualizing the model. Messages may be specified in terms of content to any extent required; here it is assumed sufficient to identify them as task or social messages. Locative elaboration specifies the source and receiver, and temporal elaboration describes their time of occurrence.

In this model social messages are considered as occurring with a certain probability determined by the existing friendship attitudes between persons, and task messages as governed by task load and by organizational procedures. To illustrate the latter, suppose person A receives a certain customer order; he then contracts persons B, C, etc., in a certain priority specified in organizational procedure. Since task load is a stochastic variable, it is natural to consider messages as stochastic. Alternative treatments of messages are possible; for example, the mean rates of message transmission between persons can be regarded as state variables varying continuously and rigidly determined by interpersonal attitudes and task load inputs.

The *instrumental activities* of the organization, or some criterion measure thereof, constitute the basic results of the simulation study. They are organizational variables insofar as they describe the activity of the system, but in some cases—for example, sales—they are also assumed to have a direct environmental effect. The elaboration of instrumental activities entails a substantive account of their economic function and identification of the responsible agents. A form of temporal elaboration would be to measure the lag between occurrence of a task load element —for example, a customer demand—and execution of the corresponding instrumental activity. These detailed elaborations would not ordinarily be preserved in the printout, but would be represented by summary indices.

Instrumental activities in the illustrative model occur as a determinate function of task load or associated messages, and are expressed as discrete events in category form. Like the other event-type variables in the model, instrumental activity might be alternatively expressed as continuously varying profiles, specifying the momentary expenditure of effort on each task-relevant dimension.

This synopsis is based on a tentative framework for describing terms of a simulation model. Undoubtedly the distinctions illustrated here will require further revision when they are put to use. They will have served their present purpose if they suggest, first, the kinds of options open to the theorist in formulating a model and, second, the potential advantage of placing the required decisions within the context of an explicit, systematic framework.

SIMULATION LANGUAGE

The foregoing paragraphs have placed a heavy emphasis on the latitude which the theorist has in formulating a model. It should be observed that, in the present era of computer simulation, the actual choices made seem to be based as often on the affinity between certain programming languages and the respective poles of description as they are on purely conceptual or scientific grounds. Such affinities undoubtedly exist; as an obvious example, the list-processing languages lend themselves well to categorical description while algebraic languages are more convenient for continuous or graded formulations.

Of course the choice of a programming language may itself have been based on a judgment as to its scientific suitability for the problem at hand, but such judgments are also susceptible to historical accident and to convenience. Moreover the programming languages most used at present in simulation models are not well suited to mixed formulations even though such hybridization may be strongly indicated. To illustrate, observations of groups suggest that their learning is often characterized by relatively gradual adjustment and consolidation, interspersed with dramatic modifications in procedure. The former aspect of group development may be very conveniently characterized by continuous functions, but the latter aspect suggests that this continuity should be taken with a grain of saltation. Existing computer languages seem to nudge the theorist in one direction or another and to discourage these mixed formulations.

Perhaps the most important thing to stress at this point is that the terminological choices that are made—for whatever reason—are not inconsequential from a psychological standpoint, even in those cases where two phrasings are equivalent in the informational or logical sense. First, there is the question of how rapidly and smoothly the model will mature as a function of the initial formulation. Even if the ultimate description of a real world process is not seriously affected, the initial formulation certainly influences the rate at which errors are detected and corrected. For example, it seems likely that minor logical flaws or small substantive discrepancies may find lurking-places more easily in stochastic models than they do in deterministic models, other things being equal. In another area of investigation, there must presently be several dozen rival stochastic learning theories that connot be dislodged by existing empirical evidence (Galanter and Miller, 1959). This does not, of course, detract from the usefulness of stochastic models but it suggests that processes should not be assumed aleatory if they can be formulated as well in deterministic fashion.

A more serious danger is that the initial formulation may in some way lead to a cumulative Whorfian distortion of the picture that emerges of the underlying dynamics of the system. As remarked above, the symbolic language employed affects the sort of intervening variables and explanatory constructs that are likely to be posited. To the extent that these are hypostatized, they may become very difficult to eradicate from later versions of the model. In this connection a particular risk is imposed by the process of aggregation. The familiar pitfall here is the assumption of organizational characteristics having no well-defined basis in the behavior of individual organization members (e.g., "group mind," "group cohesiveness").

The most secure safeguard against conceptual errors that may creep in through the choice of a programming language, or of specific terminological alternatives, is a systematic testing procedure; an attempt to specify such a procedure is offered below. In addition, however, it would seem that some very worthwhile methodological research might be conducted in the translation of existing models from one terminological framework to another one as different as possible. As examples, it would be interesting to see whether the General Problem Solver (now couched in IPL V) or the WANG algorithm model (now in Lisp) could be expressed, however clumsily, in a Fortrantype programming language.

As a final cautionary note on this topic, it should not be forgotten that, quite apart from the choices open to the theorist in selecting a simulation terminology, the basic nature of the digital computer may impose certain ineluctable constraints on the kinds of hypotheses that are examined and on the ways in which variables are expressed. Even with loops and parallel processing capabilities, computer programs imply a sequential ordering of processes that to some extent violates nature. It would be most unfortunate if a generation of theorists were, themselves, being subtly programmed by this seemingly compliant *factotum*.

TESTING THE COMPUTER MODEL

This section will describe a multistage testing procedure and discuss the modifications which may result from such tests. Four stages of testing are suggested: internal tests; preliminary empirical tests, secondary validation, and process comparison. For each stage of testing several questions are considered: the breadth of sampling of the explicitly introduced independent variables; the intensity of sampling, that is, the number of data runs that are obtained at particular points; the sort of output which should be examined; and the nature of tests and criteria to be applied. It should be understood that the rather pedantic ordering of the tests here given is for expository purposes only; in practice the tests described might be combined in various ways, might be finessed entirely, or might occur in a different order from the one here followed.

INTERNAL ANALYSIS

As here understood, internal analysis concerns not only logical properties of the model but also the general behavior of the model independent of its correspondence with any specific set of data. Many of the discrepancies in this respect will ordinarily be disposed of during the initial formulation and programming of the model. However, even this automatic culling should be more effective if there is a specific check-list to keep in mind.

Important tests are as follows: (1) Are the postulated functional relationships mutually consistent? (2) Are processes unambiguously defined over the relevant domain of independent variables? (3) Do the functional relationships conform to the general pattern intended? and (4) Are substantive invariances and boundary conditions preserved? The first two questions are essentially logical, and the second two are quasi-substantive, although they can be investigated without any direct comparison with data.

Each of the suggested tests points to certain critical sampling regions, that is, distinct configurations of explicit input variables that should be studied. For example, in order to examine mutual compatibility of the assumptions, as well as the degree to which boundary conditions and invariances are preserved, the critical point of test would seem to be at extreme values of the independent variables. Any tendency for a model to come apart at the seams or to exhibit runaway growth processes is most apt to be revealed at these extreme points. A second consideration, however, is that something should happen over the normal operating range of the model; a model is unlikely to be fruitful or suggestive if it makes differential performance predictions only for extreme values of the input variables. From this standpoint, then, it is desirable to investigate the interior of the domain; an additional reason for exploring intermediate values is to determine whether functional relationships observed for extreme values tend to be monotonic. Still a third consideration is that the model should be scrutinized with particular care at those points for which the results can most easily be evaluated by common sense reasonings or with the aid of analytical mathematical models. If the simulation model behaves appropriately in these more comprehensible regions, there is some cause for confidence in its behavior under more complex conditions. The net implication of these remarks may appear to be that one should test the model everywhere. Fortunately this is almost literally possible with computers, the limiting factor being the willingness of the theorist to examine and digest the results once obtained. In any particular case, however, one or the other of the foregoing considerations should take precedence and guide the selection of independent conditions.

Having established an appropriate sampling range, it remains to specify the intensity of sampling, that is, the number of simulation cycles obtained in the vicinity of a particular initial configuration. Here the question of interest might be the standard error of estimate of dependent variables or, in some cases, the continuity of functional relationships at certain points. Under special conditions it may not be necessary to obtain more than one estimate of each independent configuration. For example, if there is a known linear relation between some independent variable and the output, then the standard error of estimate can be obtained in the form of deviations from linear regression. In general, if functional relationships are continuous, the error of estimation may be judged by deviations from best-fitting curves.

The variability of estimates enters into an evaluation of the model in several ways. If the computed output varies inordinately relative to the degree of jitter explicitly introduced in the input variables, the model is unlikely to be stable enough for useful prediction. In addition, some foreknowledge of the variance is important in a test of the model's validity. This is particularly true if the variance is not uniform over the range of input configurations—that is, if there is inherently greater variability in the output data at certain regions of operation.

For the sake of concreteness a few representative internal tests may be suggested for the communication-performance problem discussed above:

1. The model presumably contains functional relationships describing frequency of communication in terms of task input and also relating

frequency of communication to interpersonal attitudes. One obvious test is whether the predictions from these functional relationships are in conflict at any point—that is, whether there is "play" enough for both factors to operate.

2. There are natural limits on the maximum message rates for individuals and the maximum message rates possible for the organization as a whole. For example, no one person may be talking more than 100 percent of the time and no channel may be used more than 100 percent of the time. There must be provisions in the model to insure that these limits are not violated.

3. The model should guarantee that the number of people in the group, the number of messages transmitted and other discrete items will remain equal to, or greater than, zero.

4. If the relationship between communication and task load is assumed to be positive over all levels of the latter, it should be determined whether this, and similar relationships, do obtain in the simulated data.

PRELIMINARY EMPIRICAL TESTS

The tests suggested here compare the simulation with a set of empirical target data which has been available during the construction of the model. It should be accepted in advance that, insofar as any postulates built in the model are ad hoc with respect to these data, this cannot be taken as a confirming test of the model. It is a necessary rather than a sufficient test of its validity.

It is in keeping with this objective that the statistical test selected should not measure gross "goodness of fit" but should instead be designed to examine those specific aspects of the model in which it seems to follow the target data and the points at which there are appreciable discrepancies. Visual inspection may be sufficient to determine relative agreement: if not, it would seem that some multivariate analysis technique could be devised that explicitly indicates the strengths and weaknesses of the simulation (Grant, 1962).

The tests that are relevant to this stage of testing include (1) the general functional parallelism of the computed output and the empirical data —whether the same variables tend to be related in both and whether they are related in the same direction, (2) whether the dependent data are descriptively similar to the available empirical data, and (3) whether there is fine structure reproduction; that is, whether the variability and other details of the simulated data incorporate or capture corresponding features in the empirical data.

The range of independent variables examined for this test stage should obviously match as closely as possible the corresponding independent variables in the empirical data. However this matching may not be automatic, particularly where there is an indirect measure of such variables as friendship. For this reason it often will be necessary to adjust the sampling range of the computer model in order to obtain order-of-magnitude alignment with empirical data; more detailed comparison would follow this gross adjustment. Finally the intensity of sampling should be such as to place the simulation data on at least as solid a basis as are the target data at corresponding points. If fine structure simulation is intended, it will also be necessary to compare the corresponding data not only for mean values but also for variability and other distributional features.

SECONDARY VALIDATION

As soon as the model provides a reasonable fit to a set of target data, the objective becomes one of showing that the model can be predictive for an essentially new situation. The problem of what is new is, however, a difficult one. Generalization to new data within the same domain of independent variation merely demonstrates the reliability of the empirical target data. On the other hand, it is too much to expect absolutely fresh flowers from a field as well trodden as that of organization theory, and the requirement that a model should generate surprising results may be over-stringent.

Thus it seems advisable to separate out several criteria for this secondary validation process. One criterion is the predictive scope of the model, and the other is its heuristic value. These are, in general, related but there is no strict logical dependence. It is quite possible for a model to be highly predictive over a wide range of phenomena but to give only humdrum predictions simply because the phenomena are familiar and well understood. On the other hand the model may give surprising and correct predictions within a narrow range yet still be quite wrong when used more broadly.

Although the surprise value of the model may carry more weight as far as its acceptability is concerned, scope is probably the more fundamental consideration. However if scope is to be elevated to primary importance as a criterion, it should be understood to include the degree to which the model articulates with other models and theories concerning related phenomena. Certainly the "environment" in which a model must prove its continued usefulness is characterized as distinctively by the presence of other theoretical postulations as it is by the body of established facts.

With these criteria in mind, it is clear that the sampling process should ideally be such that the model is interrogated for the whereabouts of its own "crucial" experiments. That is, it should be possible to program simulation runs in such a way as to test the limits over which the special dependent relationships characterizing the model will hold, and to suggest points of inflection or inversion of those relationships that can then be investigated in the laboratory.

PROCESS CORRESPONDENCE

If the computer simulation model is to be used as a conceptual or explanatory tool, process correspondence is absolutely essential; that is, the model will have explanatory value only to the extent that it reduces the overall operation of organizations to an articulated set of comprehensible and, presumable, testable mechanisms.

What is meant by "process correspondence" is roughly that the same things go on inside the black box, or the transfer function relating environmental inputs to subsequent outputs, in the simulation model and in its real-world counterpart. This is a highly ambiguous definition, however, and it is worth some space to try to develop a more useful picture of process correspondence. We begin by noting two tempting but, as we believe, narrow positions that may be taken in this matter.

One position is that process correspondence entails nothing more than the similarity of the interim output variables for the simulated and empirical systems. That is, does the simulated model, beginning with certain environmental conditions, transform them to a similar terminal set of environmental conditions through a set of steps similar to those of the observed empirical counterpart? Granting this test to be valid (in fact, trivially valid at the level of molecular disturbances), it is not directly helpful for several reasons. First, there may be real difficulties in measuring the interim products in many organizational processes (what, for example, is the instantaneous status of a certain piece of information?). Second, we are not, in general, interested in simulating just a single process but in studying the behavior of an organization over a variety of processes and of input conditions. Mere identity of interim products on each of these individually provides a criterion of correspondence but, in itself, gives little insight into the physiology of the organism.

A second position adopts the other extreme of descriptive verisimilitude: does the simulation model seem to engage in the same activities as are observed in the organization when faced with the same circumstances? To underscore the danger of this position it is not entirely unfair to cite the checkered history of television. There we used to see wrestlers displaying all the signs of rage and agony, and quiz contestants all the signs of deep cerebration; yet we now know that those life-like processes had little bearing on the final outcomes.

In order to examine the question more closely, a rather detailed notational scheme is required: Let X_i^0 denote the initial state of an environmental variable (perhaps multidimensional or vector-valued) of substantive type i, and X_i^T denote its terminal state after processing by the real or simulated organization over a period, T. Further, let G^T represent the total effect of the real group considered as an operator, and C^T represent the total effect of the simulation model considered as an operator. Then the minimal requirement for the validity of the model is established by the identity of the terminal products; symbolically:

$$G^T X_1^0 = X_1^T \qquad\qquad C^T X_1^0 = X_1^T$$
$$G^T X_2^0 = X_2^T \qquad\qquad C^T X_2^0 = X_2^T$$
$$\dots\dots\dots \qquad\qquad \dots\dots\dots$$
$$G^T X_n^0 = X_n^T \qquad\qquad C^T X_n^0 = X_n^T$$

(It is here assumed that a satisfactory way has been discovered for relating the X variables in the simulated environment to those in the real environment.) This result might be called *black box* correspondence, and it is the primary concern of the test phases described above. Although the parallelism of initial input, or abutting environmental states, and terminal outputs suggests strongly that there are similar mechanisms at work, it does not demonstrate it conclusively.

Proceeding from any specific instance of initial and terminal state agreement, it may be possible to discover interim coincidence, symbolically:

$$G X_i^0 = X_i^1 \qquad\qquad C X_i^0 = X_i^1$$
$$G X_i^1 = X_i^2 \qquad\qquad C X_i^1 = X_i^2$$
$$\dots\dots\dots \qquad\qquad \dots\dots\dots$$
$$G X_i^{T-1} = X_i^T \qquad\qquad C X_i^{T-1} = X_i^T$$

Each input variable or state X_i, for which this parallel holds, and each temporal point, $0\dots T$, for which there is coincidence, constitutes a case of *transfer correspondence*. Thus the overall degree of transfer correspondence may be partially ordered in terms of the range of input variables and of the density of interim values for which there is coincidence.

Left in this form, however, this is a rather tricky criterion. If the environmental variables, X_i, refer to complex, multidimensional conditions, then the incidence of strict agreement between processes may become vanishingly small, even if the systems are essentially identical. On the other hand, if the variables are compared one dimension at a time, then agreement is non-diagnostic; assuming a continuous monotonic progression in each dimension, there will be an infinity of coincidences between the two systems.

The measurement problem posed by this is the one of defining a "distance" between the paths followed by comparable environmental variables and intergrating this distance over the entire time of traversal. The most obvious measure of this kind, a Euclidean distance function, may entail assumptions—such as interval scaling of the separate variables and isometry between varibles—that cannot ordinarily be justified. An alternative is to compare the times at which the two systems pass through corresponding state values. An example will illustrate the two measures.

Figure 4 schematizes a process comparison between a real organization and a simulation model in which a certain two-dimensional variable is transformed from an initial state $X_i^0 = (0,0)$ to a terminal state $X_i^{10} = (5,5)$. It is supposed that the simulation program procedes by successive advances along the x and y axes whereas the live organization follows a more irregular path. Referring to an earlier remark, notice that exact coincidence of the two paths occurs at only five points. Presumably there would be even less coincidence in a problem of realistic dimensionality.

As a first step (already incorporated in Figure 4), intervals of measurement for both paths are made proportional to the total time of traversal. The suggested measures of path difference then are the discrepancy in the state values reached at particular times or in the intervals at which the two processes first touch each level of the component dimensions of X_i. Numerical values for this example are given in parallel columns at the bottom of the figure. Comparisons between state values or traversal times on each dimension might consist of correlations, mean-squared differences, or summed absolute differences.

This procedure is directly applicable only if there is terminal coincidence of environmental variables or "products." This condition has however already been assumed a necessary one for the further investigation of process correspondence. Given terminal coincidence, the spatial distance measure between paths depends on the metric properties of the environmental variables, but the temporal measure does not. Either comparison procedure may indicate not only the overall degree of transfer correspondence but also the particular aspects of the process in which the real and simulated systems are most at variance.

The other major aspect of the question of process correspondence concerns the similarity of activities by means of which the simulation model and the organization accomplish a given transformation. Determination of any such similarity depends on the availability of measures describing the real or simulated organization, but cannot, in the present view, be based directly on such measures. It requires a more conclusive test of homeomorphism which has to take into account both use and consequences of various operators.

FIGURE 4

A Schematic Comparison of Path Difference in the State and Temporal Domains

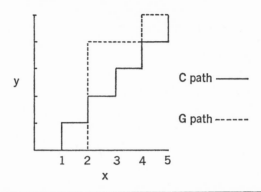

	Position					Traversal Time			
	x axis		y axis			x axis		y axis	
	C	G	C	G		C	G	C	G
0	0	0	0	0	0	0	0	0	0
1	1	1	0	0	1	1	1	2	3
2	1	2	1	0	2	3	2	4	4
Time 3	2	2	1	1	Scale 3	5	7	6	5
Units 4	2	2	2	2	Units 4	7	8	8	6
5	3	2	2	3	5	9	10	10	9
6	3	2	3	4					
7	4	3	3	4	Σd²	7		7	
8	4	4	4	4					
9	5	4	4	5					
10	5	5	5	5					
Σd²	5		5						

C path ———

G path ------

In order to illustrate the required test, consider the following paired sets of measured sequences:

$$G_aX_i^0 = X_i^1 \qquad C_uX_i^0 = X_i^1 \qquad G_aX_j^0 = X_j^1 \qquad C_uX_j^0 = X_j^1$$
$$G_bX_i^1 = X_i^2 \qquad C_vX_i^1 = X_i^2 \qquad G_bX_j^1 = X_j^2 \qquad C_zX_j^1 = X_j^2$$
$$G_cX_i^2 = X_i^3 \qquad C_wX_i^2 = X_i^3 \qquad G_cX_j^2 = X_j^3 \qquad C_wX_j^2 = X_j^4$$

Here it is assumed that certain transfer correspondences have been determined between G and C for the initial environmental state X_i^0 . It is also assumed that the important state variables describing G and C themselves have been recorded at the time these transformations are occurring. The question is, whether we are justified in equating the actions used in the respective systems, that is, whether G_a and C_u, G_b and C_v, G_c and C_w are equivalent by pairs? According to the present position, the necessary conditions for these operations to be equivalent are that they should be applied under comparable circumstances and should have similar operative effects at all points of application. This must be checked for a new initial state, X^0.

For these particular pairs, it will be noted, first, that C_u is used under the same conditions and has the same effect as G_a for a second state variable, X_j. Examining next the correspondence between G_b and C_v, it will be seen that C_v is not used at the point, X_j^1 , as G_b is, but is replaced by another operator, C_z, which happens to have the same effect as G_b. The correspondence between G_b and C_v fails because the two systems react in different ways to the same environmental state, X_j. The associated form of correspondence (in this case lacking) may be referred to as *activity* correspondence.

Finally, C_w cannot be equated with G_c because it has a different effect when both are applied at X_j^2 . This aspect of correspondence, present in the pair G_a and C_u but lacking in the pair G_c and C_w, will be referred to as *operator* correspondence. It might be noted that the distinction between activity and operator correspondence has somewhat the same implications as the distinction made in comparative physiology between "homology" and "analogy." In the former case, the emphasis is on the locus of involvement and, in the latter case, on functional effects.

In summary, the question of process correspondence has two major aspects; one relating to the results achieved by two systems under comparison and the other relating to direct measures on the organization system or its presumptive model. These two aspects are themselves compound, and any final measure of correspondence will likely be one of degree. In this discussion, we have been able only to hint at the necessary measurement procedures.

REVISION

Typically, necessary modifications and expansions of a model will be indicated by the nature of the diagnostic tests which the model has failed to satisfy. There are, however, certain general considerations on revision which will be the concern of this section. A principal objective is to present an ordered typology of revision procedures.

Computer simulation models permit, and indeed invite, more extensive tinkering than do analytical mathematical models. It is comparatively easy to add and make changes in a computer model and to investigate consequences. However, there are several reasons for introducing the changes both gradually and systematically. One reason is that this may be the best advised tactic for developing the model in question: that is, if small changes are unsuccessful, to introduce gradually greater changes until the model satisfies the criteria that are set for it. Second, the effects of a particular change may give useful insight into the working of the model only if the changes are introduced gradually enough so that their consequences can be traced. And, finally, any modification is likely to increase the complexity of the model; hence, generally speaking, the more gingerly modifications are introduced, the less complex will be the final product.

The proposed typology of revisions will be presented in an assumed order of increasing gravity. That is, the earlier presented revisions will be those which presumably have the least effect on the basic structure and substantive implications of the model; later revisions may entail more radical effects.

Calibrational revisions, first, are those which do not modify either the universe of discourse or the explicit form of assumed functional relations. Such revisions are aimed at increasing the descriptive correspondence between the model and empirical data. They do not necessarily imply any second thoughts about the basic mechanisms which are incorporated in the model or in the domain of relevance of the system being described.

Within this general category there is a secondary ordering, again becoming increasingly radical. The conservative extreme in this ordering consists of multiplying the variables in the model by a constant factor or adding a constant to algebraic variables. This will not at all affect linear functions hypothesized in the model, nor will it affect the general form of more complex relationships. A slightly more radical change is to impose a nonlinear transformation on a variable—for example, to transform it by a log or square-root function. Although this may have a more far-reaching effect on the mechanics of a model, it will not alter relations which depend only on ordinal properties; nor will it affect the general pattern of dependence between variables.[4] Lastly, the most profound changes of a calibrational nature are those in which the terms are reidentified in such a way as to alter their functional relationships.

To give these gradations concreteness, suppose one aspect of a com-

4. This statement requires some qualification since, for example, correlations between the mean and variance of a measure may be reduced to zero by transforming the measure. The statement then applies to "real" rather than artifactual relationships.

munication model is an assumed linear function relating social liking to the rate of communication between pairs of group members and that the model is to be compared with a set of data in which measured sociometric ratings are related to observed frequency of communication. A first revision might be made in order to equate the mean and variance of the liking and communication terms in the model with those in the target data. If this did not produce a satisfactory agreement of simulated and empirical results, it might then be attempted to relate the sociometric rating (still measured in the same fashion) to the probability of communication within a given time interval, thus setting an upper limit on the magnitude of the effect. Finally, it might be concluded that the sociometric measure as estimated was actually one of status equivalence, implying that the frequency of communication would be a function of the similarity of total sociometric scores obtained by two individuals rather than of their mutual sociometric ratings for each other. This third form of revision, without actually changing the universe of discourse, puts the terms in a new light and suggests new dynamics.

Functional revisions are those in which there is an explicit modification of the relationships among variables. The qualifier, "explicit," is emphasized because there may be equivalent changes induced by calibrational revision of the variables themselves (as illustrated above). Functional revision is not assumed to enlarge or essentially alter the universe of discourse of the model. The simplest form of functional revision entails only a change in the assumed relation between two variables— for example, a linear relation is changed to an exponential one. A more far-reaching sort of functional revision would be the decision that two independent variables originally assumed to have an additive effect are perhaps compensatory or facilitative.

Several special types of functional revision should be noted, as they are of wide applicability. The first is the gradual refinement of a relation in such a way as to take account of specific contingencies. To illustrate, a first approximation model might contain, as terms, the probabilities that any person, A, will communicate with any other person in the group. The refined model, then, might introduce the conditional probabilities that A communicates with anyone in the group given conditions X, Y, Z, . . . or, again, it might specify the probabilities that A will communicate with specific persons B, C, D, . . . given certain conditions. Such revision would typify the refinement of models which are initially aggregative in the hyletic and locative domains. Corresponding refinement is possible for the temporal domain, but it requires somewhat more discussion.

Suppose that two persons or other system components, A and B, jointly control some state variable, X. Using a terminology introduced earlier, this operative control may be represented by sequences of the type:

$$AX^0 = X^1$$
$$BX^1 = X^2$$
$$AX^2 = X^3$$
$$BX^3 = X^4$$

. . . .

That is, the output of either agent is treated as the input for the other agent in a continued alternation sequence.

The difficulty with this formulation is that most social interaction processes do not follow such a punctilious schedule. Typically the operators act simultaneously or else the several agents may act over varying time intervals. This is most troublesome if the operators, A and B, do not commute, that is, if the compound effect, A B, differs from the compound effect, B A.

This problem may be handled by requiring the operators A and B to take smaller bites–that is, by finding "roots" of the operators, say $A^{1/k}$, such that $A^{1/k}$ applied k times has the same effect as the original A. Then the simultaneous operation over an interval of length, l, by both operators may be represented by $(A^{1/k}B^{1/k})^l$ and successive operation over intervals of length l and m respectively may be represented by the term $(A^{1/k})^l (B^{1/k})^m$. The indicated revision then is to find an order of magnitude for the operator effect for which such representations give descriptive results.[5]

Substantive revision involves an enrichment of the system, an expansion of the universe of discourse. This raises two kinds of questions: first, of the intimacy of interaction between the original and supplementary systems; and, second, of the degree of comparability of the old and new variables. These are presented most readily by example. Suppose a first ap-

---

5. The following indication of proof is not intended to be rigorous:
Suppose there are two operators, A and B, which are noncommutative and for which, say:
$$AB - BA = D.$$
Next, suppose that, for both A and B, it is possible to find "roots", $A^{1/k}$, $B^{1/k}$, such that $(A^{1/k})^k = A$; $(B^{1/k})^k = B$.
Then consider the difference:
$$(A^{1/k}B^{1/k})^k - (B^{1/k}A^{1/k})^k = D_k.$$
It must be shown that D_k approaches O as k increases. Premultiplying through by $A^{1/k}$ one obtains:
$$A^{1/k}(A^{1/k}B^{1/k})^k - (A^{1/k}B^{1/k})^k A^{1/k} = A^{1/k}D_k.$$
As k increases, $A^{1/k}$ approaches the identity operator $A^0 = I$, hence the left-hand member of the equation goes to 0, and D_k must also vanish. Validity of the proof depends on the assumption that the roots do indeed exist and that the exponentiated products remain bounded.

proximation model of organizational communication is based entirely on normative considerations, that is, on how much communication is required by the task messages. It is almost certain that a model thus begun will require padding out in terms of social (non-task) communication. One question, then, is whether the latter can be treated as a separate system conforming to its own laws and not affecting or affected by task processes, or whether the non-task communications interact directly with task communications. A second question is whether the non-task communications have the same properties with respect to the other terms of the system as do the task communications, for example, whether liking is similarly increased by a given number of task of non-task communications.

The process of revision and the resulting modified model will tend to be simpler if new terms act in functional parallelism. It will also be simplified if there is a valid convertibility between the separate terms. If both conditions hold, a model may be augmented by simple superposition of the two processes. In the illustrative case the frequency of task and social communication, respectively, may be predicted from their separate functional rules and the total communication obtained by adding the two. Justification for these simplifying conditions must come from the correspondence between the model and the observed organizational behavior. It appears, though, that a more penetrating investigation could be made of theoretical aspects of the amalgamation of subsystem components. In particular, what is required is a "dimensional analysis" of organizational variables, that is, an investigation into what constitutes apples and oranges and the way in which apple systems and orange systems may interact (Langhaar, 1951; Ipsen, 1960).

Before leaving the topic of revision, it might be noted that, while many of the modifications discussed—and particularly the more complicated ones—must be based on fairly close auscultation of the model, it appears quite possible that certain revisions may be pre-programmed. As a first step in this direction, the computer might be programmed to compare simulation results with empirical results and to follow a systematic calibration process which minimizes the discrepancy. As has been noted, however, (see Minsky, 1963) this may be an extremely inefficient process unless some of the characteristics of the model are known in advance.

SUMMARY OF CRITERIA

Five general classes of criteria underly the foregoing discussion: coherence, validity (or predictiveness), scope (or generalizability), transparency, and parsimony. The ordering given is intended to convey a roughly defined priority in which the criteria should be met.

The coherence criterion concerns whether the assumptions on which the simulation model is based are sufficiently well defined to generate clear implications for some set of external data, whether the implications turn out to be right or wrong. The criterion includes the requirement that the terms of the model should retain the status that is intended for them; that is, parameters should remain constant, state variables should describe possible states, and independent variables should determine functionally the dependent variables in the system.

The second criterion is that of validity. The question is how well the computed outputs of the simulation model match the available empirical data under similar conditions. There are several facets of this matching: whether there is general duplication of phenomena—for example, whether a monotonic functional relationship is reflected in the simulation data; whether the same points of inflection occur; and whether there are comparable interaction effects between the independent variables. A second level of agreement concerns whether the simulation results are qualitatively and quantitatively similar to those of the empirical system. A third question concerns the variability of the system; ideally, both the between-organizations and within-organizations variability of behavior should compare with empirical results in the same task environment. It has been emphasized that the validity requirement entails both descriptive and functional fidelity. A successful model is one that continues to yield a descriptive picture of the organization under transformations by the assumed independent manipulations. It was suggested, moreover, that statistical tests should not be limited to gross "goodness-of-fit" but should indicate particular aspects of the simulated data which are most or least in agreement with empirical data.

The third criterion invoked was that of scope: over how wide a range of application does the model remain valid? To this consideration may be added the question of how well the model articulates with other hypotheses relating to the same domain of organizational processes.

The fourth criterion is that of transparency; that is, the degree to which a model is explanatory, the extent to which it reduces to meaningful and, presumably, testable components. A good model in this sense is one that suggests the points at which the predictions will be of an especially interesting or fruitful nature. It is also one which suggests its own limitations.[6]

6. Toulmin (1961, pp. 100 and 203) gives the example of finding a scientific explanation of the death on their birthdays of three children in one family.

The fifth criterion is that of parsimony. This is probably a secondary criterion but an extremely important one. It has at least three bases. The first basis is the well-known aesthetic appeal of an economic model. It is not a frivolous consideration; it has been identified time and again as a decisive factor in directing the thoughts of prominent theorists and in tipping the scales of general acceptance when competing theories could not otherwise be evaluated differentially.

The other two bases are perhaps more down to earth. One is the greater transparency of a parsimonious model (other things being equal) and the consequently greater suggestiveness and sharpness of implication. A final argument for parsimony is that it probably increases the viability of a model. In the present view, the special postulations tacked onto a model in disregard of parsimony have much the same long-run effect as the furbelows developed by trilobites and dinosaurs: immediate adaptability is obtained at the expense of total unsuitedness to new problems.

RECAPITULATION

A number of uses for computers in conjunction with organization research and theory were discussed and the simulation model was singled out as the special focus of interest. It was observed, however, that other applications are useful and not incompatible with the more puristic objective of this discussion.

Recognizing that the simulation model as here defined lies in the mainstream of the hypothetico-deductive scientific tradition, there are two strong implications for its further treatment; first, that it must be closely integrated with more conventional methods of scientific research —that is, analytical mathematical models and laboratory investigations— and, second, that there is no such thing as a "good enough" model. Testing and revision as here described is not a terminable process.

It was suggested that simulation models could be approached from several rather distinct initial assumptions labeled Organismic, Idealized, and Segmental. Each of these achieves a workable first approximation at the cost of certain explicit oversimplifications that are presumably repaired as the model is developed. The model may be aimed at an explanation of the development of organizations through time, of the asymptotic performance of organizations, or of the influence of the organization on the participant individuals. These processes interact very closely, but their separate investigation is warranted by differences in time scale and in the salience of certain functional relationships.

Because computer simulation affords complete control and a wide range of options, it is important to examine the status of terms in such a model as compared with more conventional scientific approaches. Three sets of classificatory distinctions were offered. The first set concerned the functional status of variables vis-à-vis the theorist and the hypothesized organization. A second set of distinctions concerned aggregation or extension along three axes: the locative (personal), the hyletic (substantive or referential), and the temporal. A final set of distinctions concerned the language in which the model is couched.

Although these distinctions represent a wide range of options, it was noted that there may be hidden constraints associated with terminological choices made by the experimenter and perhaps also resulting from the very structure of the simulation process. Methodological study is required to determine the severity of such constraints.

A four-part regimen was suggested for evaluating a model at a given level of development. The first part consists of internal testing and is aimed at both logical properties in the ordinary sense and also at the general conformity of the model to an intuitive or analytic picture of how it should behave in important respects. The second testing phase relates the computed output of the model to a set of target data that have been accessible during formulation. Here it was emphasized that the question is not just gross "goodness-of-fit," but a more detailed statement of where the model departs from observed data. Given such *prima facie* validity, the model may next be extended to "new" regions. It was emphasized that "surprisingness" or novelty of implications is a rather different criterion from scope and may be overstringent. The latter criterion is more fundamental, although it may not be as compelling. The concept of scope as here employed also includes compatibility with the existing body of theory concerning related aspects of the organization.

The last stage of testing covered process correspondence. It was shown that, in addition to "black box" correspondence, defined by comparable input-output relations over a wide range of inputs, at least three other forms of correspondence may be defined. Transfer correspondence refers to the similarity of interim outputs, or, more abstractly, to the temporal path of the process. Activity correspondence relates the internal state of the simulated organization to that of its real-life counterpart. Operator correspondence implies that equivalent internal states have equivalent transfer effects on the environment. It was stressed that the implied equivalence relations cannot be based on the literal similarity of variables, but must be analyzed through a bootstrap process.

Turning to the process of generalizing and revamping a model, the point was made that this should be as gradual and systematic as possible. Several broad types of revision were indicated. Calibrational revision changes the variables and the parameters explicitly. For convenience, one can think of these as successively modifying ratio and interval properties, ordinal properties, and nominal properties of the variables entering into the model. Functional revision involves an explicit alteration in the mechanics of the model or in the arguments of particular functional relations. Several special types of functional revisions were described which are aimed at refinement of the model. The third and generally most far-reaching form of revision entails an extension of the universe of discourse, bringing in new terms and new mechanisms. It was noted that the effects of this type of revision depend upon inter-convertibility of the effects and upon whether they are additive or interactional.

Finally, a set of five general classes of criteria were suggested by which a model may be evaluated. These are: coherence, validity, scope, transparency, and economy. The latter two criteria were given particular emphasis because of the suspicion that the relative ease of spawning computer simulation models may weaken extrinsic arguments for these criteria.

A GLANCE AHEAD

Having opened the discussion by noting computer applications that are current but fall short of the simulation model as here defined, it might be appropriate to close with some conceivable applications that seem to transcend current practices. These are suggested in full cognizance of the fact that they are not presently feasible. In compensation for this, there is the now trite observation that to state an apparent impossibility in the computer age is often a useful first step toward bringing it to realization.

The first suggested extension is the conduct of real experiments on the computer. By this, we mean building in the same error components as have been obtained in performance measures of the real organization and imposing experimental conditions as in a laboratory study. While few scientists would accept the findings of such an "experiment" without empirical verification, it might be possible to limit the latter to a spot check of sample results.

There are several types of investigation for which such experimentation seems especially suitable. One is to obtain a volume of parametric data for which the results would be essentially interpolative and not controversial. Here the use of the computer as opposed to live organizations is largely a matter of economy. However, computers might also be used to explore conditions precluded for humanitarian or ethical reasons from empirical investigation—for example, the behavior of an organization under disaster conditions. Such an application is not so much a search for new findings as an extrapolation of results obtained under more attainable conditions. Still, the computer study might pinpoint interactive effects which could then be more closely studied under infrequent natural conditions.

A second extension would be the use of the computer as a construct-generator. One of the great difficulties in theory in the biological and behavioral sciences has been to span levels of analysis, to apply results at one level to problems at another. As is well known, the communication between organic chemistry, biology, neurophysiology, psychology, and sociology has been extremely slow and uncertain. Even where the relevant principles are known at one level, it is extremely difficult to project them to a higher level and, conversely, to reduce the established phenomena at a higher level to those of the lower level. Perhaps the most striking example of this has been in evolutionary theory; the relevant factors here have been known for fifty to a hundred years, yet the task of translating them into a predictive ecology is still very far from complete.

What is suggested then is the possibility of a systematic programmed process akin to the forms of aggregation that the theorist has used in the past in order to make sense of extremely complicated systems, a procedure by means of which one learns not only what an immense number of infinitesimal processes will accomplish, but also obtains a conceptually manageable macrostructure. This becomes an especially important need if theory construction takes the segmental point of departure described earlier. Even supposing that it is possible to predict organizational behavior by entering a sufficiently detailed statement of individual actions and reactions, it is not clear that one can thereby obtain any idea of what is really going on. Granting the primacy of the predictive criterion, it is certain that scientists will not rest content until they can relate their predictions to a set of verbalizable mechanisms.

A kindred extension is the use of the computer as an instrument of genuine induction. In a way, it is odd that there has not been as concerted an attempt in this direction as there has been to develop programs for deductive theorizing. Certainly the special advantages of computers over humans seem as pronounced with respect to inductive as with respect to deductive reasoning. The drawback cannot be a dearth of raw material either; although there are, in the case of organization theory, many types of data for which no adequate measures exist, there are certainly enough solid statistical facts for a good beginning.

Of course the most probable explanation for the failure to develop computer programs for induction is the rather unsatisfactory philosophical and methodological state of the topic. Yet this difficulty itself may be a function of the fact that induction has never been systematically used. The major criticisms of Mills' system of canons, for example, is that they do not sound like what scientists do. It is at least possible that, if the computer were forced to this drudgery, it might lead to the development of an adequate and workable inductive theory. It was Darwin's regret in later years that he had to turn himself into a machine for digesting facts, but this is almost exactly what computers are designed for to begin with.

A final extended use of the computer would be in inter-theory translation. We mean by this more than just a comparative study of the performance of two models on similar data. Rather what is intended is an investigation into the equivalences of terms and syntax of two related theories and, of course, an analysis of their points of divergence. A typical, and familiar, problem to be examined would be whether the difference between two theories is substantive or "merely semantic."

REFERENCES

AFIPS Conference Proceedings, Vol. 25. Spring Joint Computer Conference. Baltimore: Spartan Books, 1964.

Bales, R. F. "Small Group Theory and Research." In R. K. Merton, L. Broom, and L. F. Cottrell, eds., Sociology Today. New York: Basic Books, 1959.

Borko, H., ed. Computer Applications in the Behavioral Sciences. Englewood Cliffs: Prentice Hall, 1962.

Cohen, B. P. "A Probability Model for Conformity." Sociometry, 1958, 21, 69–81.

Galanter, E. and Miller, G. A. "Some Comments on Stochastic Models and Psychological Theories." In K. Arrow, J. Karlin, P. Suppes, eds., Mathematical Methods in the Social Sciences. Stanford: Stanford U. Press, 1959.

Grant, D. A. "Testing the Null Hypothesis and the Strategy and Tactics of Investigating Theoretical Models. Psychological Rev., 1962, 69, 54–61.

Green, B. Digital Computers in Research: An Introduction for Behavioral and Social Scientists. New York: McGraw-Hill, 1963.

Guetzgow, H., ed., Simulation in Social Science: Readings. Englewood Cliffs: Prentice Hall, 1962.

Gullahorn, J. T. and Gullahorn, J. E. "Computer Simulation of Human Interaction in Small Groups." In AFIPS Conference Proceedings. Spring Joint Computer Conference. Baltimore: Spartan Books, 1964.

Homans, G. C. The Human Group. New York: Harper, 1950.

Ipsen, D. C. Units, Dimensions, and Dimensionless Numbers. New York: McGraw-Hill, 1960.

Langhaar, H. L. Dimension Analysis and Theory of Models. New York: J. Wiley, 1951.

Minsky, M. "Steps Toward Artificial Intelligence." In E. Feigenbaum and J. Feldman, eds., Computers and Thought. New York: McGraw-Hill, 1963.

Orcutt, G. H., Greenberger, M., Korbel, J., and Ruilin, A. M. *Micro-analysis of Socio-economic Systems: A Simulation Study.* New York: Harper, 1961.

Richardson, L. F. "War Moods." *Psychometrika,* 1948, *13,* 147–174 and 197–232.

Roby, T. B. and Lanzetta, J. T. "Work Group Structure, Communications, and Group Performance." *Sociometry,* 1956, *19,* 105–113.

Rome, S. C. and Rome, B. K. "Computer Simulation Toward a Theory of Large Organizations. In H. Borko, ed., *Computer Applications in the Behavioral Sciences.* Englewood Cliffs: Prentice Hall, 1962.

Siegel, A. I., Wolf, J. J., Borcik, J. D., and Mieble, W. *Digital Simulation of a Submarine Crew Performance, I, Logic of a Psychosocial "Model" for Digitally Simulating Crew Performance.* Report done under Contract NONR–4021(00), FBM, 1964.

Simon, H. A. *Models of Man: Social and Rational.* New York: Wiley, 1957.

Toulmin, S. E. *The Place of Reason in Ethics.* Cambridge: Cambridge U. Press, 1961.

Turing, A. M. "Computing Machinery and Intelligence." *Mind,* 1950, *59,* 433–460.

Whitrow, G. J. *The Natural Philosophy of Time.* London: Thomas Nelson, 1961.